JACKIE STEWART
A Restless Life

Timothy Collings and Stuart Sykes

WITHDRAWN

Virgin
BOOKS

This paperback edition published in Great Britain in 2004 by
Virgin Books Ltd
Thames Wharf Studios
Rainville Road
London
W6 9HA

First published in 2003 by Virgin Books Ltd

A catalogue record for this book is available from the British Library.

ISBN 0 7535 0945 8

Typeset by TW Typesetting, Plymouth, Devon
Printed and bound in Great Britain by Clays Ltd, St Ives PLC

CONTENTS

ACKNOWLEDGEMENTS

Many people have given valuable time to and cooperated generously with this book. Jackie Stewart himself made it clear he would not place any obstacles in our path. His family were courteous and helpful. The book would not have been possible without such assistance.

The following, in no fixed or particular order, contributed to the research and writing of *A Restless Life*, some by sparing time to talk, some through interviews, some by correcting facts and providing insights, and some by supplying valuable information in the public domain: Sir Jackie and Lady Helen Stewart, Paul Stewart, Mark Stewart, Jimmy Stewart, John and Nan Lindsay, Dumbarton library and staff, the Dumbuck Hotel and staff, Jonathan Taylor, Vanessa Daubney, Daniel Balado, Jacques Deschenaux, Maurice Hamilton, William Court, David Tremayne, Nigel Roebuck, Louis T. Stanley, Derick Allsop, Tony Rudd, Christopher Hilton, John Blunsden, Steve Small, Ian Summers, Sean Connery, Hunter Davies, Eric Dymock, Graham Gauld, Alistair MacLean, Hugh McIlvanney, Stuart Turner, Eric Dymock, Lyle Kenyon Engel and the editors of *Auto Racing* magazine, Peter Manso, Joe Saward, Graham Gauld, Karl Ludvigsen, Bernie Ecclestone, Max Mosley, Craig Pollock, David Coulthard, Peter Phillips, Jackie Oliver, Herbie Blash, Sid Watkins, Ian Gordon, Martin Brundle, Jonathan Legard, Kevin Eason, Will Gray, Gary Emmerson, Lorraine Varney, Henry Brown, Carl McKellar, Josh Collings, Kitty Collings, Andy Miller, Andy Foster, Dave Stubbs, Allan McNish, François Guiter, Tim Schenken, Niki Lauda, Rubens Barrichello, David McKay and William Parry. We would also like to thank the many local and national newspapers and magazines, as listed in the Bibliography, and acknowledge the work of the photographers who have recorded so many of the key moments in a remarkable life.

Finally, a very special thank you to our wives, Ruth Collings and Claire Sykes, and families for putting up with deadlines and grumpy moods during a summer of record heat in Britain. Some, too, will have been forgotten or overlooked, and to those we apologise.

INTRODUCTION: CASTING SHADOWS

London, 25 January 2000. 'I cast a big shadow.' Even on Burns Night, it was a strange thing for a diminutive Scot to say. But Jackie Stewart knew it was the truth. He had been casting that same shadow for over 26 years, ever since the November day in 1973 when he announced his retirement as a driver at the end of a 99-race Formula One career.

Retirement? Who did John Young Stewart think he was kidding? His had been a restless life, almost from the cradle, but never so full of sound and fury as in the aftermath of his title-winning years. Now, though, the three-times world champion was retiring for the second time. Stewart Grand Prix, the Formula One team he founded for his son Paul, had been sold at the end of the previous year to Ford and rebadged as Jaguar Racing. Stewart, chairman and CEO, had decided it was time to take a big backward step and move into the shadows himself. On the day he mentioned his desire to lift that long shadow from the new-look team, Stewart was also able to say that the last four years had been the hardest of his working life.

It was the turn of the century, Jackie Stewart was 60, and he was ducking out of the limelight.

London, 23 July 2003. Jackie Stewart was tense, but prepared. Perhaps, he was a little angry. But he was not showing it. It was a warm morning and he was hosting, with Martin Brundle, a key news conference with the British media, just three days after the British Grand Prix at Silverstone. The meeting, on a Wednesday morning, was held at the Institute of Directors in Pall Mall, a place on the edge of 'club land' and close to the entertainments and theatres of the West End. Stewart must have wondered if the aggravation, pressure and criticism he had faced in the previous few months, leading up to and running through and beyond the British race, made it worth his while to keep his position as president of the British Racing Drivers' Club (BRDC), one of the most august institutions in motor sport. His brother, Jimmy Stewart, saved from alcoholism by Jackie's attentions and chequebook, and his old friend John Lindsay certainly believed it was a responsibility and a 'hassle' he no longer needed in his life. But Jackie knew, or at least he believed, that the BRDC, and he personally, were being lambasted by a concerted media campaign, orchestrated by Bernie Ecclestone and Max Mosley, in order to force major changes at Silverstone, the circuit owned by the BRDC, and to safeguard the future of the British race on terms that suited the sport's ruling bodies and the promoter rather than the landlords or the British establishment. Jackie, like Brundle, felt a sense of duty to stand and fight.

The story, in which both sides had criticised the other, had raged on the sports pages of the British national daily newspapers for weeks. Ecclestone had ridiculed Stewart and the BRDC for failing to borrow money against a rental income from the race promoters Brands Hatch Circuits (previously known as Octagon Motorsports), and for failing to build a circuit with facilities that put the British event on a par with other leading races around the world. The Formula One calendar was under pressure. Supply and demand demonstrated that there were more venues wanting to host a race than there were dates on the calendar, and therefore Silverstone, with its traditional facilities, inaccessible location and ponderous image, was being threatened with removal. It was, as Mosley put it during one briefing session, time to push 'the blazers' out and to bring the whole place up to date. But Stewart and Brundle, himself a former chairman of the BRDC and an equally vociferous defender of the British Grand Prix and British motor sport industry, were adamant that it was a fight worth fighting. Indeed, Brundle had flown back to London from his holiday home in Spain to attend. Together, they decided to give the media an honest, open and accurate account of their position and that of the BRDC, and to explain also the BRDC's relationships with Ecclestone and his Formula One Management (FOM) companies; with Mosley and his rulemaking organisation, the Fédération Internationale de l'Automobile (FIA); with Brands Hatch Circuits; and with any other bodies or organisations involved in the complexities behind the running of the race.

Stewart had celebrated his sixty-fourth birthday only a few weeks earlier. This remarkable 'wee Scot' had through sheer determination, a dogged refusal ever to give in to anything, and a comprehensive exploitation of all his talents enjoyed a remarkable life in motor sport, television, business and public work. He was a champion clay pigeon shot, a marksman worthy of a place in the British Olympics team. He was a fast and remarkable driver at a very young age, a workaholic and perfectionist who left school early believing he was stupid – not knowing that he was, in fact, dyslexic – who became a champion motor racing driver, mixed with celebrity and royalty, and who built a portfolio of lucrative business contracts, businesses of his own, a Grand Prix team, a shooting school and, above all, a reputation for integrity and industry. His life, from Dumbuck to London, from Glasgow to Geneva, from Dumbarton to Milton Keynes, had taken him around the globe further, faster and more frequently than most other people, and he had supposedly retired on two occasions, yet now, at an age when many men were stretching out in the sunshine, he was in the midst of another drawn-out campaign. At the time, too, his wife Helen was recovering from breast cancer, his son Paul was in remission from a major cancer threat of his own, and Stewart – who had been knighted by Prince Charles fewer than two years before – was also on the recovery trail after a minor operation to remove a cancerous mole from his left cheek. But that morning in Pall Mall, Jackie Stewart faced up to his inquisitors knowing that the many and varied facets of his life experiences and reputation would count for little, that he and the British Grand Prix were on the line together, that his career and his success would earn him a hearing and some sympathy but his prospects for the future were to hang by his own words on the strategy for the years to come at Silverstone.

To see him, sitting in the arc lights set up for the television cameras, facing up to the pressures that come with media activity, fame, duties and responsibilities, it was difficult not to join Jimmy Stewart and John Lindsay in thinking, 'Why go on?' What had driven him into this difficult corner of the sporting world as the representative of an organisation under attack from others in the glare of a ravenous and often Machiavellian publicity machine? Why was he not retired, long gone to the beach, or playing golf?

1. AND THEY ALL THOUGHT I WAS STUPID . . .

'The happiest time of my school life was every day at four o'clock when the bell went.'

Jackie Stewart

Even in these advanced days of the twenty-first century, with smoother and quieter asphalt, better maintenance and fewer potholes, the roads north from Dumbarton into the Scottish Highlands are treacherous, sinuous affairs. They are a challenge for any driver. A wheel off the road here, or a lapse of concentration there, and a motorist's car can soon be slithering and bucking for grip, for traction and direction. Sometimes, the hedges bear down on the driver as he charts a safety-first route down the middle of a particularly uneven and difficult sequence of corners, with alternate cambers and little clear view of the road ahead. The weather, of course, is seldom helpful. It often leaves a glistening sheen on the surface, or covers it in leaves and debris; or, worse still, a sheet of ice or packed white snow. Such roads are common north of Glasgow, in the western sweep from the Firth of Clyde away north towards Oban and Fort William, around or alongside Loch Lomond and through the atmospheric and moody passages of Glencoe, dripping with history.

Most tourists, appreciating the mountainous scenery in summer, or even the wintry wonderland, would hardly think of such routes as useful for any aspiring driver. Too challenging for a learner, they might think, although the twin-track road cut through the hills above the Clyde, bypassing the old village of Bowling near Dumbarton, did encourage a greater feeling of space and safety. But they would be wrong. For it was here, where the Firth of Clyde oozes between the Kilpatrick Hills and the flatter lands of Abbotsinch, close to the oil storage tanks and docks at Bowling and the Ballantines distillery on the Glasgow road, that Jackie Stewart, three-times Formula One drivers' world champion and a world-famous sports personality who succeeded in business and built his own Grand Prix team, learnt his trade.

By delivering, fetching and returning cars for his father Robert Stewart's garage business at Dumbuck – a village now known as Milton, close to the outskirts of Dumbarton in Dunbartonshire – Jackie Stewart learnt about speed and control. He also learnt how differently one car handled compared to another, how valuable each vehicle was to its owner and to his family's business at the Dumbuck Garage, and how easily such a valuable cargo could slip away from his control. He learnt, therefore, to drive smoothly and quickly, to avoid dramas and to preserve his and his family's reputation. It was a meticulous, elegant and restless process of survival for car and driver that he underwent through those formative years. And, since Dumbuck Garage enjoyed its status as an appointed dealer for Jaguar and Austin in the 1950s and the 1960s, not to mention a reputation as the best workshop within miles for the preparation of any other high-performance or racing car owned by keen motorists and amateur competitors, this meant also that Stewart was often driving cars of pedigree and power. He had a good teacher, too. His older brother Jimmy, the senior sibling by eight years, was a highly respected Ecurie Ecosse team driver with a good racing history and a generous nature towards his younger brother. But that was not the end of Jackie's lucky blessings. He also had exceptionally good eyesight. As a clay pigeon shot, he was considered to be one of the finest marksmen of his generation; as a footballer, a flying Scottish winger, he was always deemed to be determined, industrious and highly competitive, a never-say-die sportsman. Little wonder that he became such an outstanding record-breaker in his chosen career in motor sport.

Jackie Stewart grew up around little Dumbuck, his local towns Dumbarton and elegant Helensburgh, an eighteenth-century 'watering place' some eight miles north-west along the Clyde estuary. The city life of Glasgow lay some fifteen miles away, so Jackie developed as a young man amid the rural peace of the rolling hills, mountains and lochs of his part of Scotland. The family garage business, known then as the Dumbuck Garage, was close to the wooded Dumbuck itself, a place that derived its name from the old Scots meaning 'the hill of the deer'. The hill is extraordinary, a spectacular and unusual landmark, a stark and bold abutment from the south-western range of the Kilpatrick Hills that stoops precipitously towards the Dumbarton plains. According to the locals, it commands 'a magnificent prospect from Tinto to Arran and from the Grampians to Ayrshire, and out-tops Dumbarton Castle'. For its impressive stature, the Dumbuck was a significant military capture in much earlier days as it gave its controllers a wide view of the campaigns below. A stunning landmark, it was the place beneath which Stewart was born and learnt to drive, to shoot, to run, to earn his tips, to calculate his savings, to become shrewd with his money and silvery with his tongue, and to stay loyal to his family and friends.

More than anything else, however, it was at Dumbuck that he learnt to overcome setbacks and to go about making magnificent recoveries, from dyslexia, disappointment, physical disadvantage, the deaths of close friends, obdurate officials in dangerous sports, and cancer in the family. 'Some people believe that they've got to think of themselves as the best in order to succeed,' he said in a voice-over for a splendid film, *Jackie Stewart: The Flying Scot*, made by his son Mark Stewart. 'I never thought that. I was always thinking I wasn't going to win. I thought that everybody else was better than me . . .' The voice is sincere. The man has felt the pain of failure, the pressure of disappointment, the frustration of being unable to demonstrate his true potential and worth. At school, in Dumbarton, he was dismissed as stupid and unworthy of a place in the academic fast lanes. Some of his friends left him behind; none of them knew he was dyslexic. Instead, Jackie channelled his energies into sport, the outdoor life he understood, the garage's forecourt, the cleaning of the workshops and the driving of the cars. As surely as the majestic mountains, lochs and winding roads north of Dumbarton moulded his character, those disciplines forged his career.

John Young Stewart, always to be known as 'Jackie', was born on an oak table in the front room at Rockview, a modest dwelling in Dumbuck and the first house to the north-west of Dumbuck Garage, on 11 June 1939. His brother Jimmy had been born in the same bungalow some eight years before. In the *Lennox Herald*, the event was recorded thus: 'STEWART – at Rockview, Dumbuck, Bowling, on 11th June, 1939, to Mr and Mrs R. P. Stewart, a son. Both well.' His father was Robert Paul Stewart, formerly a keen motorcyclist who raced as an amateur in TT events – he finished sixth in the senior TT races on the Isle of Man in 1928/29 – his mother Jeannie, a lady also known as a formidable driver on the local roads around Dumbarton. She was the stronger of the two in terms of commanding character; Robert was generous and had a softer, perhaps kinder, nature. Born as Jean Clark Young, Jeannie came from a substantial Scottish farming family in Eaglesham, Renfrewshire (her farming parents reportedly bought the bungalow, Rockview, for the couple as a wedding present following their marriage in 1930), while Robert's father was a gamekeeper on the Eaglesham estate of Lord Weir – a connection that almost certainly played a part in his working in the drawing office of G. & J. Weir of Cathcart, Glasgow, where he was chief draughtsman, before settling in Dumbuck in 1926.

Outside work, Robert Stewart, better known by the locals as 'Bob Stewart of Dumbuck', was keenly interested in fishing and shooting and was regarded as one of the most knowledgeable anglers in the country. He often fished with Lord Weir, who suggested the idea of a petrol station at Dumbuck. He enjoyed golf, too, and was a president of the Big Green in Dumbarton and an honorary life member of Cardross Golf Club. He was also a fine bass baritone singer with a deep interest in music, and a stalwart of the Dumbarton Burns Club, where he enjoyed a spell as president. He was a regular member of the trio of singers who sang Burns songs on social occasions. He played the violin, too. Jimmy, the elder son, inherited much of his father's affection for singing, and his vocal ability.

It should have been a blissful childhood for the younger Stewart boy. His family was secure, his bespectacled, kindly and humorous father, who befriended everyone, was establishing a garage at the fork of two busy roads (one to Dumbarton and the other into the Highlands) where he sold a lot of petrol to passing motorists, and little more than five miles away was John Brown's shipyard, one of the centres of Scottish employment and industry. Growing up surrounded by much natural splendour in one of the most beautiful parts of Britain, given the love and security of two hard-working, diligent parents, and sheltered in the world by his kind, generous older brother Jimmy, it should have been delightful. But it wasn't. And not because the Luftwaffe made the Clyde a major target for its bombing raids, nor because Jackie would lie awake at night as a small boy listening to the sirens, an experience he has often said he will never forget. No. Wee Jackie, who was relatively frail as an infant and always had a 'heavy' right eyelid, suffered from dyslexia, though he was not to know this until many years later when, as a 42-year-old man, he was diagnosed as a sufferer and finally understood why he could not easily read, write or remember people's names. The pain, however, was dished out during his childhood.

'When I think back to my childhood,' he recalled in *A Scottish Childhood*, 'I think of school. Which, sadly, was the unhappiest period of my life. I hear parents constantly saying to their children and to young people in general, "You'll never have it so good. You'll look back with fond memories. You'll realise in later years how lucky you were to have the camaraderie school provides." For me, none of those things is true.

'When I was young, almost from the beginning, as I remember it, school hung over me like a thunder cloud. I simply was not a good student. In fact, I was very poor in the learning process. In the end, I was considered dumb, stupid and thick because I could not keep up with the rest of the children in whatever class I was in. It was therefore with great relief to all concerned when, at fifteen, I was able to part with my formal education and go to work in a garage.

'When I think back now, I am only frustrated. Because I know a little more about what learning disabilities are and what dyslexia is, it perhaps annoys me a little more that people did not realise that maybe there was something in Jackie Stewart which would allow him to learn, if they used a different method of teaching. But in those days, it seems, people did not realise there was such a thing as a "learning disability". I was lucky. I was able to overcome my academic inabilities to work well with my hands, to get on with people, and in later life God blessed me by affording me the talent to drive racing cars.

'The happiest time of my school life was every day at four o'clock when the bell went. I made my merry way by bicycle back to the village of Dumbuck and more often than not worked on the farm next door to my father's garage, or in the garage itself. In both of those activities, I was able to use my energy and my non-scholastic talents, and was rewarded with praise and appreciation for the effort I put into my small duties. I can assure you, it was most rewarding to be praised for something.'

Jackie was often a sick as well as a recalcitrant student. 'I was ill a lot as a child,' he said. 'I would have more blood tests and check-ups than they do in a week at the Mayo Clinic. I'd run a temperature at the drop of a hat. We know now it was psychosomatic. I'd find any way to avoid going to school. I was being eaten up inside. If I'd been told it was something called dyslexia, I would have tried to deal with it. I'm bright enough to believe there is a way around things, to agree with Lenin that there are no problems, only solutions. Sometimes you can't put a fire out, you have to go around it.'

His brother Jimmy remembered one night when 'the headmaster saw my parents and said, "We're really worried about Jackie. His reading is terribly behind, his spelling is absolutely deplorable, and yet he is not a stupid boy." My father and mother pulled Jackie aside and said, "Look, you're going to have to work harder at school. This is ridiculous." ' But to this day, as Jackie admitted in an interview with Gavin Bell for the *Glasgow Herald* in the mid-1990s, 'I still cannot read properly. I have no speech tonight [he was about to address a black-tie dinner at the Gleneagles Hotel]. I have headings, because it would be a waste of my time to try to read a speech. If you paid me ten million now, I could not recite the alphabet. I have never known it, and I cannot for the life of me even today learn it. I can't even sing my own national anthem. I have stood beside Her Majesty when it was being played and I couldn't sing it, because I didn't know the words.' Typically, Stewart had granted this interview not only to explain himself, but also to help draw attention, and funds, to the Scottish Dyslexia Trust, of which he was president. His efforts helped raise £10,000 towards placing a teacher qualified to help dyslexics in every school in Scotland.

The key to Jackie's personal discovery of his own dyslexia came from his son Mark's own problems. After only a few months at his boarding school in Switzerland, it became clear that Mark could not keep up with the class. The headmaster suggested a trip to London to consult a dyslexia expert, and this resulted in a diagnosis that confirmed he had the disability. 'I still had no idea what it was,' said Stewart. 'I told the professor he must be wrong. Mark, I said, was no different from what I was, and he would come out of it as I had. Then the professor tested me, and guess what? The truth came out. It was wonderful finally to have an explanation for all the misery and confusion I had endured over the years. It was like somebody had saved me from drowning.' The Stewarts learnt quickly that they were in good company. Winston Churchill, John Wayne, Michael Heseltine, King Olav of Norway, Susan Hampshire and Albert Einstein are all on the list of those who have been affected by dyslexia. Luckily for Mark, he found he had a father who understood the problems and had the purse to deal with them. Mark was sent to an American school dedicated to helping students with learning problems, and later he tackled his problem head-on by training as an actor at the Repertory Theatre at Perth, in Scotland.

But Jackie Stewart was not satisfied with just helping his son. 'For every one who is properly diagnosed and helped,' he said, 'how many are left cowering in corners? How many try to live in a rainbow of alcohol or ride a magic carpet of drugs and end up in a life of crime because society isn't giving them a hand? Our aim is to put somebody to help them in every school in Scotland, no matter how small. If we can do that, we will give young people the possibility to reach their true potential, and there is nothing worse in the world than robbing someone of their potential. There are stars out there, there is brilliance out there, being suffocated by ignorance and lack of resources.' He knew. He'd been one of the sufferers.

Still, the misunderstandings and disappointments of his schooldays gave Jackie a sharper appetite for other areas in his life and a deeper understanding of the value of real achievement. Remarkably, too, they also probably enhanced his other talents; certainly they made them seem remarkable. For example, even a quarter of a century after he collected his third drivers' world championship and completed his career with a then unprecedented total of 27 Grand Prix wins, he could still recall in detail the corners and the gear-changes required at the famous old Nürburgring circuit in the Eifel mountains in Germany. Indeed, it was there, on the swooping, long, spinning, awkward and often wet track known as the Nordschleife, where any driver knew he was endangered as soon as he made the commitment that separates the racers from the also-rans, that Jackie won magnificently by more than four minutes on 4 August 1968. It was only his second race there, but he was able to commit to memory every one of the 174 corners on the 14.189-mile circuit, including precise recollections of braking points and distances and the best gears and gear-change points. (He came home, in his Tyrrell-entered Matra Ford, that soaking afternoon among the mountains, forests and clouds, four minutes and 3.2 seconds ahead of Graham Hill in his Lotus Ford after fourteen laps of the vast and amazing circuit, despite driving with his right arm in a plastic splint after suffering a hairline fracture of his wrist during a Formula Two race meeting at Jarama in Spain.)

'Nothing gave me more satisfaction than to win at the Nürburgring,' Jackie mused many years later, 'yet I was always afraid. When I left home before the German Grand Prix, I always used to pause at the end of the driveway and take a long look back. I was never sure I'd come home again.' Such fear, such anxiety; they remained with him from schooldays to stardom, from racing to boardroom. It is clear that his ability to memorise what was required, while sitting in a Formula One car on the grid of arguably the greatest circuit, certainly the most daunting, ever built to challenge man and machine at speed, was complete; yet this same man, who knew the undulations, curves, bumps and dangers of this German giant so well, would struggle to say the Lord's Prayer and could not recite the alphabet at a time when boys at school could shout it forwards and backwards at speed. That he was unaware of his own learning disability and overcame it to such effect has earned Jackie Stewart plaudits and honours that he has accepted and, in turn, used to help draw attention to others' problems in a spirit of generosity that enhanced his own standing as a man.

This part of his life, his schooling, his misery and disappointment, was the creative moulding of the man. Stewart knows this now. His brother Jimmy, physically accomplished, powerfully built, considerate and avuncular in his father's mould, looks back now and understands that, thanks to Jackie's care and attention, a life of alcoholism, and all that goes with it, was avoided. Their good friend John Lindsay, the bluff, loyal, lifelong rock of humanity who played with Jackie at school and at home, who was in his football team, who followed his racing career, and who now owns and runs the Dumbuck Garage, was also witness to the failures of the examination room, the pain in Jackie's disappointment, and the unquenchable spirit that rose to overcome these setbacks. 'I remember when we were ten or eleven years old,' said Lindsay. 'We had to sit an exam, a qualifying thing. You sat the exam and it put you in A, B, C or D. I was B and Jackie was C. Both times. We ended up in the same classroom. We knew each other before that, of course, but this threw us together even more. The garage was our playground then. We messed about there so much of the time. Jimmy was eight years older than us and he was something else. He had a Healey Silverstone and he drove for Ecurie Ecosse and Jaguar and, well, I just thought he was mega in those days.'

Jimmy had a different recollection of those early days. 'As children,' he recalled, 'we didn't get to know one another terribly well. It was only when I got into my teens that I realised my younger brother was becoming a bit of a nuisance to me.' Some say the Stewart brothers are similar, others that they are as different as chalk and cheese. The truth is somewhere between the two. Bob Stewart was kind and generous, astute and determined. His sons inherited these traits, but as Eric Dymock, the Scottish journalist who followed Jackie's early career, commented in *Jackie Stewart, World Champion*, 'the proportions varied . . . Jimmy got most of the first two (kindness and generosity), Jackie predominantly the second two (astuteness and determination). Which is the main reason why Jimmy gave up racing and Jackie did not.' As we shall see, it was in fact pressure from Jeannie that was the chief reason why Jimmy, a gifted but unlucky racing driver, abandoned a life in pursuit of motor sport glory. Jackie, as Dymock observed, resisted the pressure. 'Our father,' Jimmy recalled, 'was a disciplinarian, but he was such a good man that, for me certainly, he was more like my best friend than my father.' His mother, however, was another story, and her anxiety over his racing was ultimately overwhelming. 'I found my mother consumed by nervous exhaustion. That was what made me finally stop my career. I had to decide that the family came first.' By then, of course, Jackie was used to travelling to race meetings with his father and brother. 'At an early age,' said Jimmy, 'he'd been all over the place. To Silverstone, to Goodwood, to Snetterton, even to Le Mans. Because of the age difference, and because he was such a little lad wearing wee shorts, it was as if I had my son with me. I was a fully grown man and a racing driver. I was naturally protective towards him.'

As soon as he left school, Jackie began to enjoy life. He worked on the forecourt, serving petrol, checking the oil and the batteries, topping up fluid and often checking the tyres too. Jeannie made sure all the jobs were done properly. At Rockview, on the wall facing the garage, there was a 'port hole' window that enabled her to keep an eye on the forecourt. 'Mother used to look out to see if there was anyone not being served petrol,' said Jackie. 'So you would get a call saying, "There's four cars waiting – and nobody serving!"' 'It's amazing,' said Lindsay, 'looking back now. The sons of all those different parents who all had cars at that time. I think about it now, and they've all gone backwards; it's only Jackie who went forward. Of course, like people say, it is only when you pass your driving test that you start to learn, and that's what Jackie did all right! People say you don't learn about life till you leave school. Well, Jackie is a good example of that. You should just see him! And that work ethic!'

To illustrate that work ethic, or the guilt complex as some would have it, Lindsay described part of a weekend in March 2003 when he shared time with Stewart during a short visit to Scotland, taking in two talks he gave – one in Aberdeen, another in Edinburgh – and a flying visit, literally, to the west coast. 'We [Lindsay and his wife Nan] were in Aberdeen with him, on a charity thing. There were maybe 300 people there. And his performance was just astonishing, for this kids' hospital or something. And then in Edinburgh we were there for this BRDC [British Racing Drivers' Club] dinner. On the Saturday, we came down to Edinburgh and it was just a beautiful day with not a single cloud in the sky. Jackie took us out in a rented helicopter for a couple of hours away up the west coast beyond Oban and back down through Glencoe, down past Loch Lomond. We did three circuits of the loch and it was absolutely fantastic, so beautiful, and we finished up back at the Balmoral Hotel, in Edinburgh. Jackie was there to speak to the BRDC members, and to keep them up to speed with all the goings-on at Silverstone. And it was just so marvellous. At lunch on the Sunday, I went to him and said thank you for such a marvellous trip around the Highlands and islands. He had enjoyed it as much as we had. And you know, at the Balmoral, he asked for questions from the floor and there were only about twenty members there, and there was just one wee question and that was it. I was amazed they didn't ask more! But he still gave it everything, as usual.'

Lindsay has known Stewart well for a lifetime. 'I first met Jackie when I was about five years old,' he said. 'I got to know him later, when I was about seven or eight. That was at the Dumbarton Academy, as it was then. A few people about now will remember him from those days. I should say they will know him, but he probably doesn't know them any more. He just won't remember them all. I remember they did that programme with Sarah Kennedy on television, *Classmates*, but there were very few people in that class of ours really. The chairman of Dumbarton Football Club, just taken over, he was one of our classmates, but I'm sure Jackie won't know him. He meets so many people.

'We used to come out here to the garage and we played a lot. His mother had a Triumph TR2, a really nice soft-top sportscar. Quite a trendy car in its day. And I remember you could drive in the far end of the workshop, round the back past a kind of centrepost in the workshop, and out the side again. We did that in a kind of circuit. We had to go out past the petrol pumps on the forecourt, and we would do this maybe a dozen times or something. We would give it some acceleration and go up and down the gears, that sort of thing. And we would be watching out to see if Father or Mother Stewart came out of the house. More likely they were away at the time!'

The laughter that accompanied Lindsay's recollection was infectious. These were the early days of Jackie Stewart in his first racing school, the days when he could enjoy a carefree approach – so long as his parents didn't know about it. And he was careful. He kept his car away from danger and away from accidents. He was proud of his driving, proud also of the shiny condition in which he kept his areas of the family garage. He excelled in the menial tasks of keeping the forecourt immaculate and serving customers with a smile. When he took charge of the lubrication bay, he transformed it, in his own words, into 'the best lube bay in the county, and possibly in Scotland'.

'We left school at the same time, together,' Lindsay continued. 'Jackie was a year ahead of me, and in those days an apprenticeship lasted for six years, and he was doing his "lubritorium", as he used to call it. He had it immaculate. And it was brand new of course. The red ramp, the white surrounding the ramp, the dark blue around that, the cabinets and so on. He "Simonized" [wax polished] the cabinets, too, and the cars were serviced every thousand miles or so. It was Jaguar and Austin in those days, and they were all looked after, serviced, lubricated, greased up and so on. I suppose the icing on the cake came with the Jaguar customers. They were fairly widespread. I mean, they came from up north, or from Ayrshire, for example, and we used to go and collect these cars. It was good fun. Jackie had a Healey at the time, a 56. We would go out in this Healey, get these cars, and then we'd drive them back. They were good to drive, and remember, these were the pre-70mph days. I think that driving then was more or less his training ground. Jimmy was his guiding light too, and Jackie was then, as he still is to this day, an exceptional driver. He really made an art form out of something like changing gear.'

Jimmy also had vivid memories of the early days of his younger brother's life, and his own early racing days with the famous Edinburgh team created by David Murray, Ecurie Ecosse, and Aston Martin, owned by the sportscar and racing enthusiast David Brown from 1948 to 1972. 'I was just 22, or thereabouts, in 1953, and at that time Jackie was with me at quite a number of the events I participated in, not only with Ecurie Ecosse, but also for Jaguar and Aston Martin in 1954, and at Le Mans. In those days, Jackie was just pleased to be there. He went to so many places, and we saw so many of the great drivers of the time. My father was interested in this, but not my mother. Jackie, of course, shared my interest in motor racing, perhaps with even more passion than me. I had big problems with my mother. I was doing my National Service, and they let me off to go racing at weekends. I did two years, but I doubt if I did half the time! I went with David Murray to Argentina for the 1,000 Kilometres, participated in the sportscar world championship and drove C-types with Ecurie Ecosse. By the time I was out of the army, I was ready to do more racing, and I went to do the 1,000 Kilometres at the Nürburgring with the first of the D-types. The first one was for me and the second one was for Desmond Titterington. Both had brake failures. Desmond was hurt, but not me. On the first lap they found my old friend in a state of nervous exhaustion, so I phoned Lofty [England, who ran Jaguar's racing operation] and I had to explain I couldn't go on. And so I quit and went back to the garage at Dumbuck.'

Understandably, Mrs Stewart was happy at this. She had preserved her son for the future after a short career during which Jimmy had survived several big accidents. But little did she know then that her younger boy would prove to be even more determined to drive racing cars, and would do so with greater success. His family, after all, had encouraged this interest in motor racing. His mother drove fast and notable cars, his father had raced motorcycles, they had gone as passionate followers of motor racing to see the action at Silverstone, Goodwood and Le Mans, *en famille.* 'I suppose I was bound to become interested in motor racing,' Jackie said. 'My brother was keen, my father had the garage, and we were surrounded by cars and motoring magazines. By the age of ten, I'd started a scrapbook. I went to the race tracks with my brother and I collected autographs. I still have that book, with names like Stirling Moss, Peter Collins, Mike Hawthorn, Duncan Hamilton and Tony Rolt.'

At that time he was still content to follow the likes of Alberto Ascari and Juan Manuel Fangio around, to study Harry Schell, whom he considered to be the ultimate playboy character of the time, and to watch Peter Collins working at close quarters, even though he'd been driving since the age of nine, as he confessed to James Leasor for a feature in *Road and Car* in the autumn of 1985. 'I first learnt to drive in the parking area of the garage my father owned at Dumbuck. My father had built the garage with his own hands. The car was a pre-war Austin 16, and the memory of that first drive is still clear in my mind. I was so small that I had to sit on an empty two-gallon petrol can to reach the pedals. Even so, I couldn't see over the steering wheel, but I could just see between it and the dashboard, and I remember skidding around that parking area on a wintry day. My parents had a taxi service contract with Denholm and Company, handling agents for tankers that would come in to what is now the big Esso terminal at Bowling, and for this they used two post-war Austin 16s, one dark blue and the other dark green.'

According to Jackie, despite her aversion to her sons' efforts on the race track, his mother actually played a prominent part in his early love affair with speed and fast cars. Not, of course, averse to a rapid spin around the local lanes herself, she inspired her second child with her accomplished driving and her chosen series of interesting high-performance cars. 'My mother was the one who really started me driving enthusiastically,' Jackie recalled. 'She was a very talented driver. In those days, you did not often hear of a lady driving fast cars, but she had a variety of interesting cars over the years. While I was still at school, at Dumbarton Academy, before my eleven-plus exam, she ran an Austin Atlantic. This was a great cruiser-looking thing with electric windows and a radio – both rare in those days – and lots of chrome. It was made for the American market. Then she ran a 2.5-litre Riley saloon with a vinyl roof, which again was a great, fast car, and later on she drove a Jaguar XK120.' Jackie's recollections of his mother were accurate, and supported with real feeling by both Jimmy Stewart and John Lindsay. Both remembered Mrs Stewart as a quick and capable woman behind the wheel with a string of fast cars in which she used to demonstrate her flair for speed.

In those early days, of course, as Stewart grew up, as his brother found his way into racing and his mother tore around in vehicles that caught the eye, the family garage business was selling first Austin cars and, later, Jaguars. This was a more than useful connection for the Stewart boys, particularly instrumental in helping Jimmy into Ecurie Ecosse when David Murray made room for him in 1953, Dumbuck Garage having been asked to supply the new C-type he drove after ordering it from Jaguar's Edinburgh distributors. Similarly, if any car of a particular level of performance caught Jeannie Stewart's eye, it was often held in stock far longer than usual and was frequently subjected to extensive testing. It was helpful that the Dumbuck Garage was known for its decent stock of used cars. In this atmosphere of post-war freedom and with such a family business on his doorstep, therefore, Jackie had plenty of opportunities to gain experience of sitting behind the wheel in a range of vehicles. 'The first car I drove on the road, quite illegally, for I was only about twelve or thirteen years old, was a Triumph TR2,' Jackie told James Leasor. 'Mother sat beside me. This car was originally dark green, but my mother had it resprayed powder blue. I did not like that colour. It was not a definite enough blue, I thought, but it was her car and her choice.'

After his fifteenth birthday, Jackie went to night school in Glasgow three times a week, but it was on the forecourt in Dumbuck that he was assembling the armoury of charm, the good business sense and the deep love for and understanding of cars that were to stand him in such exceptional stead for the future. 'I liked to hustle and to bustle in the forecourt and in the lubrication bay,' Jackie recalled. 'I made more in tips than I did in wages and saved up enough to buy my first new car a month before I was legally old enough to drive it.' In the book *Jackie Stewart: World Driving Champion*, Lyle Kenyon Engel quoted Stewart as saying that 'I used to get £3.12.6 a week, plus about £3.15 in tips at the pumps', but according to others around at the time this version of affairs at Dumbuck Garage cannot be entirely accurate. For John Lindsay, it is virtually certain that Jackie's memory is playing small tricks, and that in fact he required some financial assistance to buy his first car. 'He was determined, and he liked to get tips off the petrol pumps. He said he used them to save up for his first car, but if it was possible, I think I'd have done it too. I saved up for a motorbike, and I went on the forecourt as well – at nights! I think obviously there was some financial assistance for Jackie there. I'm pretty sure about that.'

Lindsay recalled that the young Stewart's first car was a spruce-green Austin A30. Jackie had Hunting Stewart tartan covers made for the seats and he fitted an enamel lion rampant, to denote Scotland, above each front wheel arch. He paid £375 for it, he said. It was cleaned and cleaned and cleaned – 'I must have put ten coats of Simoniz on it' – and he had it undersealed. 'That brand-new A30 sat in the showroom for about a month before he got his licence,' Lindsay added, 'and it was Simonized and Simonized. Then he got an A35, which was pretty powerful in its day. Then he wanted to go for an MGA, and he must have been eighteen at the time, but his old man introduced this Austin Healey, a six-cylinder thing, and that was that. Jimmy was going around in Jaguar Mark IIs at the time, I think, purchasing three suits at a time and doing things my family couldn't even think about. Looking back, that, obviously, was the family norm!'

Lindsay's happy laughter at these recollections summed up the atmosphere of the age. Jackie clearly enjoyed his freedom too. When in 1957 he decided to take part in the clay pigeon shooting West of England Championship, he saw the trip from Scotland to Bournemouth in Dorset as a motoring odyssey and tackled it in his new A30. 'I think that this little car probably gave me the most pleasure of all the cars I have owned,' he told James Leasor, 'maybe because it was the first.' His next car, as Lindsay said, was an A35, powder-blue, a little faster. 'John Lindsay was my passenger on some nightmare trips connected with shooting,' Jackie admitted. 'There was no speed limit then. He would time me with a stopwatch, sitting in the passenger seat. I could reach Stirling from our garage – that's about 39 miles – in 39 minutes.' It does not take an expert mathematician to calculate that Jackie was therefore *averaging* 60mph on those ancient Scottish roads in a car that was probably being driven relatively close to its limits. Once this news is digested, it is easier to understand how much he learnt on Scotland's road system before he fled south and east to earn his fortune, and how, too, he managed to perform so magnificently in the fog and rain of the Nürburgring on that famous summer's afternoon in 1968.

After the A35, in Jackie's chronology of cars, came a red and black Farina-designed Austin A40. It was a hatchback, probably the first, and was regarded as very fashionable and stylish. Jackie ordered his with black upholstery with red piping, and added red wheels and a chrome trim. He followed this with a white Austin Healey Sprite that he cited, rather amusingly, as being 'not very good for courting' when he described it to Leasor. 'With much ingenious thinking, you could get a young lady into a suitably amorous position without any great trouble, but you needed a lot of help and cooperation from her, with the gear lever in third out of the way and the driver's seat leaning forward against the steering wheel.' Interestingly, at this time, when the boy Stewart was growing rapidly into a man, he chose to fit Speedwell tuning modifications to the engine of this particular car. He telephoned Speedwell to place his order for two new SU carburettors and a special cylinder head and camshaft, and found that the call was taken by Graham Hill, later to be his first Formula One team-mate at BRM. 'It was a big deal speaking personally to Graham Hill,' he admitted, 'even then. This was in his early days, in the late 1950s, before he became big-time and long before I had even started.'

With the Healey; he was on the road to racing professionally with a spell during which he entered his races as A.N. Other. For Jackie, it was a matter of course, a route that carried him forwards relentlessly, leaving John Lindsay, Dumbuck and, eventually, Scotland and the terrible days at Dumbarton Academy behind him. He was fulfilling a destiny, as Lindsay recalled. 'At school,' he said, 'he was always practising his signature. Always. You can tell a lot from someone's signature. His is theatrical, really, with an "o" with a circle and a dot. He practised it all the time from ten to fifteen. I always say how different we are. I have never been asked for my autograph in all my life! I sometimes thought I could be as quick as he is, or as he was. But I tell you what, I never could do what he does with the television, or standing up to speak. I just wouldn't want to know. I'd be put in there just to make the others look good.

'I always say that if you want to make it and be a big success you need to be theatrical, to be insecure and have a lot of talent. He was insecure, financially, when he started out racing, so he worked all the hours. He knew early on that the place here [Dumbuck Garage] was going in the wrong direction, financially. It was difficult for him to stop it going belly-up, he had trouble with that. But he did what he was good at better than anybody else.' Eventually, having bought the ailing family business himself, Jackie sold it to Lindsay. It has remained in his hands.

Before the cars and the racing and the money, however, came the shooting and the fishing. When Jackie was struggling so pitiably at school, with people all around him thinking he was stupid, it was shooting, not driving, that saved him.

2. THE GREATEST DISAPPOINTMENTS, THE MOST VALUABLE LESSONS

'To be in the Olympics was something bigger than being a Formula One driver.'

Jackie Stewart

In the summer of 1954, Juan Manuel Fangio won his second drivers' world title driving for Maserati and Mercedes Benz, the first of his wonderful run of four championships in succession. It was a feat that made him the envy of many men, but it wasn't enough to secure the imagination of a new generation of teenagers. A new world of popular imagery and culture began to flow across the Atlantic that year, and it brought widespread change. A chubby chortler with a curled slick of oiled hair across his forehead who wore an extraordinary range of checked jackets and baggy trousers was strutting his stuff in front of a band that haw-hawed and scuffled behind him, and he was the coolest thing around. Fangio, a heavy-armed Argentinian with sublime driving talents, belonged to an older and different Latin generation; it didn't seem at home in a changing social landscape where tinny twanging sent adolescents' pulses racing. As food rationing finally came to an end, as Sir Winston Churchill headed towards his eightieth birthday and celebrated his recent Nobel Prize for Literature, as Roger Bannister became the first human being to run a mile in less than four minutes, as West Bromwich Albion beat Preston North End 3–2 to win the FA Cup, as J.R.R. Tolkien published *Lord of the Rings*, and as the contraceptive pill was invented, America was rocking, Britain was rolling, and traditions were being shaken upside down.

When Bill Haley and his Comets thumped out the first true rock 'n' roll hit single to excite widespread masses of screaming teenagers across America and beyond, Eminem wasn't even born yet; Andy Warhol was still growing up; John Osborne's *Look Back in Anger* was two years from its first production, as was 'the angry young man' as a popular hero from his debut; the Beat Generation was still waiting for Jack Kerouac to finish writing *On the Road*, the older generation to be shocked by Vladimir Nabokov's *Lolita*; the Beatles were eight years away from 'Love Me Do'; and Marilyn Monroe's star was burning towards its zenith from *Niagara* and *Gentlemen Prefer Blondes* to *How to Marry a Millionaire* and a famous nine-month marriage to the baseball superstar Joe DiMaggio. 'Rock around the Clock' signalled the age of jukebox music, slot machines, *Waiting for Godot*, the end of the Korean War, the start of the Cold War, France's withdrawal from Indochina, the creation of extraordinary new religions such as the Church of Scientology and the Unification Church (as founded by the South Korean religious leader Sun Myung Moon), and a shift from the last shadows of abstinence, parental control, discipline and automatic deference into a new era of intellectual rebellion, freedom and youthful escapism. Haley's music was as much a signal of these seismic shifts in social culture as Monroe's impact on celluloid had been of the arrival of female sexual imagery in the addled minds of filmgoers, and adolescents, all over the world. It was the end of monochrome life; it was goodbye to the old picture houses and, in a hint at the far more violently reactionary 1960s, welcome to America, Coke, cowboys, movies, pop and sex.

Even in Dunbartonshire. As a fifteen-year-old, Jackie Stewart, fresh from his miseries at Dumbarton Academy, was stepping out into a changing world. Pleasure and self-fulfilment were in fashion. Jimmy had just retired from participation in competitive motor racing after one accident, and one warning, too many. Jeannie was happy and relieved, but by then, of course, even in his rural pocket of Scotland, the smell of change was apparent and Jackie Stewart, like everyone of his generation, had flared his nostrils and taken in a lungful of the intoxicating oxygen of freedom blowing in from the west.

Having just escaped from school, however, Jackie knew he had difficulties. He was miserable. He was dyslexic, but did not know it. He much preferred life at the garage. Only on the football field, it seemed, could he find an outlet and engage in a freedom that saw him display a talent that was rewarded. Once upon a time, as even an Englishman knows, Scotland was the source of some of the world's greatest footballers, in particular that breed of player known as a winger. Usually they were small, nimble, quick of wit and feet, fast, unpredictable, tricky to understand and spectacular to watch. Often they were also fiery, competitive and driven by a never-say-die spirit that made them crowd-pleasers long before they could show off their skills. They were like buzzing insects, incessantly attacking, never flying away; and they were the players that captured the young Jackie Stewart's heart for a few fleeting seasons in his teenage years when he was a regular in the Dumbarton Academy's forward line. For a time, he thought he might be one too, joining a line of great names that had thrilled the spectators at Glasgow's Hampden Park, home of the famous 'roar' of approval for those men who scuttled and fell, rose again and, shrugging off the mud caked to their legs and shirts, would beat defender after defender before passing or shooting on goal. 'I enjoyed sports,' Stewart said. 'I used to play football for the school, then the county. Yes, I was a bit competitive in school sports. As long as I can remember, I've always wanted to have a go.' He always listened to the Scotland matches on the radio, and loved the Hampden Roar. 'You never hear of the Wembley Roar, do you?' he once asked.

'He was a good outside-right in the football team at school,' John Lindsay recalled. 'I played in goal, because I didn't like running about! But we were in the same football team and we won two very memorable matches that we can both still remember. We couldn't play rugby because we didn't have a grass pitch. We had an ash pitch, and it was a very wet day for one of these matches and there were a lot of puddles everywhere. The whole place was flooded. We were playing against a local school. Everyone was so determined to win, especially Jackie. He just kept kicking the ball away up the park. That is the one match I remember when I look back for his determination to get a result. He can remember every Grand Prix he won, but he can hardly remember any in which he was second. He only remembers winning. But then Jackie kind of invented the idea of being focused on the job, you know, professionally.'

But his skills with a ball at his feet weren't the only gifts that could draw out praise and success. Jackie always loved the outdoors life; his brother Jimmy did too. 'Farming was on one side of the family, gamekeeping on the other side,' Jackie explained. His grandfather's connections with Lord Weir's estate at Eaglesham – much of which stretched over steep hills above the loch, usually heavily stocked with deer – had imbued his son, Robert Stewart, with the same love of deerstalking as that which bound the lord and his head gamekeeper together for so long. The same sort of network of country folk, around Inverbeg and Loch Lomond, assisted in Jackie's education. It was through Jimmy's friend Alastair Kerr of Inverbeg that, it was said, as a teenager Jackie befriended Sir Iain Colquhoun's head gillie Duncan Macbeth. Together, they spent five summers stalking, Jackie learning the stealth, silence and cunning that were to translate into a valuable part of his racecraft later in his career. 'Duncan was responsible for my breakthrough,' said Jackie in an interview with the *Scotsman*. 'He turned me from a boy into a man, and a particular sort of man at that. He taught me endless patience, how to pick out what others might miss, and why it is vital to keep going to the end, however weary and disheartened you are. On a Scottish hillside, under huge skies, I learnt the skills that finally turned me into a racing driver.'

Jackie's father would drive him to Inverbeg 'almost every morning in the season', and Duncan, a tall, lanky, rosy-cheeked young man, would lead him into the high beyond, loping off at a pace like a mountain goat traversing the side of a steep valley. 'The stags had to be culled after the rutting season in September and October,' Jackie explained, 'otherwise no one's roses were safe.' On Ben Dhu, he stalked one magnificent animal, a royal stag, 'time and time again, just for the fun of it. We never dreamt of pulling the trigger on him. He was truly the Monarch of the Glen.' Jackie was fifteen when he got his first stag. 'The actual moment I broke through was the split second it took for a bullet to leave the barrel of my father's rifle and find its target,' he said. 'It was an eight-pointer, and I managed a clean kill at the base of the neck. Duncan solemnly blooded me on the forehead, a strange ritual for two among the waving bracken fronds that had turned russet and gold in the full flush of autumn. It was weeks before the last traces wore away because I refused to wash them off.'

After this initiation, Jackie enjoyed four years' tramping the hills and valleys he regarded as the most beautiful in the world, knowing that if he wanted to master something that was generally thought of as challenging or difficult, then he could do it. It mattered little, later on, that when he shot his first hind, as a nineteen-year-old, he shot her badly – so badly, according to the *Scotsman*, that 'she was dead when we reached her, but still upright on her straddled legs . . . Her eyes were fixed and open. I'll never forget the expression. After that I could never kill another animal.' By then, Jackie Stewart had 'broken through' in life, found some confidence and learnt how to understand his world. Duncan Macbeth had introduced him to tea laced with a shot of whisky from his flask, to keep out the cold; and to the joy of his mother's cheese and chutney sandwiches when eaten overlooking the loch, in its still and reflective pomp, the boats appearing to him as if 'an artist had stippled them on canvas', his back protected from the wind by a thick tree trunk as Macbeth talked the philosophy of a simple life, of imperishable values and unquestioned truths and loyalties. 'Thanks to the quiet man's careful tuition, either on the misty hills or on the way back to the Land Rover, dragging our kill behind us, I was primed and ready to go,' said Jackie.

Fishing, too, featured heavily in his life. The Stewarts spent many happy holidays by a stretch of the River Spey over which Bob Stewart had fishing rights. 'I used to go to the same stretch of river that I have now, in syndicate,' Jackie revealed in 1970 for Lyle Kenyon Engel. 'I don't get there very often these days, but I love it when I can. My father has been going there for 35 years, and as children my brother and I were taken to that place more than to any other.' Through example and encouragement, Bob patiently taught his sons to be competent anglers, just as he'd shown Jackie how to handle a gun and use it correctly. 'He was a disciple of the etiquette of shooting,' Jackie said. 'It had to be done exactly the right way. I started shooting very early on, mostly rabbits, up behind our house. I was trained the right way. But, apart from the rabbits, there was nothing to shoot, so I started on clay pigeons.' Luckily for Stewart, his grandfather had a clay pigeon trap, normally used at the start of each grouse season to help the Weirs, or their guests, prepare their eyes and arms. Jackie borrowed the trap, bought some clay targets and practised each day after school, up on the hill at Dumbuck. He could only afford ten shots at a time, and this restriction no doubt contributed towards both his accuracy and his economy. When he had developed and improved so that he was hitting eight or more out of ten in each session, he knew he was good enough to enter competitions. He won his first contest against other Scots at the age of fourteen. 'It was New Year's Day,' he recalled. 'I probably won because all the other Scotsmen were stoned! But that started the competition bug off – I wanted to enter every one there was.'

It was around this time, too, that Jackie began to appreciate the scale of the world and its opportunities, particularly in North America. He might have been slow at school, but he wasn't slow to realise that life wasn't restricted to Dumbarton Academy. The realisation came when Jeannie took him on holiday with her to the United States and Canada, a vacation that came about thanks to invitations from the tanker captains and others who had used the Clyde dockyards and the Dumbuck Garage taxi services. 'I can remember it very clearly – New York, the Empire State Building, Niagara Falls, Canada . . .' Jackie reminisced. 'We went over on a stratocruiser, which was a big double-decked plane that took fourteen hours to cross. I was very impressed by the whole thing.'

His shooting career, his ambitions no doubt fired by such travelling experiences, not only with his mother but also with his father and brother throughout the United Kingdom and in Europe, took off as soon as he left school. His eye for distance, speed and trajectory, and his extraordinary reflexes, earned him a place in the Scottish team in 1955. The following year, at the age of seventeen, he won the West of England Championship after that hugely satisfying drive to Bournemouth in his spruce-green Austin A30. 'The win was just a terrific pleasure for me, far more intense than the pleasure I had later in motor racing,' Jackie said. 'But I was so intense then. Too much so for success, really.' By 1956, it was clear that his grandfather's friendship with Lord Weir, and the weekends he had enjoyed out shooting and fishing on his estate, had left their mark. The wee Stewart, the boy without a hope in the classroom, had grown into a world-class shot, and he had an older brother who had made his name as a racing driver all over Europe before retiring when the risks began to outweigh the thrills.

His self-esteem had first begun to rise thanks to brother Jimmy's exploits. 'Jackie came along with me to most of the early hillclimb events that I was participating in and seemed to really enjoy it,' said Jimmy. 'He had a great appreciation of motor sport, all sport really.' The progression seemed natural: football, the garage, the cars, the outdoor life, the guns and the shooting, the sport, the success in competition. He was Jack the lad, and he began to enjoy his life, particularly when love struck when it was least expected.

'I remember you coming back from Jaguar saying that you had seen Bill Haley and his Comets, and he had a sort of curl on his forehead,' Jackie recalled with a laugh as he and his brother shared a wander down memory lane for the film *The Flying Scot*. 'I think that was when the Twist started, and the Radio Café in Helensburgh was the centre of all the action. It was all young people. It was all night, too. You went in there and there was a jukebox. It was a great place! I was going to be on a blind date, and this girl was at the table, but she didn't fancy me at all and decided I wasn't the one she was going to be going out with that night. And Helen happened to be there . . .'

That night, Helen made up a foursome with Jackie and two others, a girlfriend of Helen's and a boy Jackie knew. She remembered them having dinner together, and that the dashing young Stewart was well mannered and attentive. 'He was very correct in all he did and in the way he treated me,' she said. 'I thought, "Well, this is nice." And I think that's why I fell in love with him – because of the way he was with me.' In many ways, this was one of the earliest, probably most successful and almost certainly the most important example of Stewart's powers of diplomacy, tact and personal attention, mind- and emotions-management working in harmony to enable him to achieve an objective. Few men can out-talk him. He possesses charm and intelligence. And he has an uncanny ability to make sure that the people he is with, or speaking to, feel they are receiving a singular and special level of attention.

At that time, Helen McNeil McGregor, from nearby Helensburgh, where her mother ran a smart bakery, was only sixteen, a year younger than Jackie, who was old enough to drive and keen to take his girl with him to Glasgow and beyond as their relationship blossomed. 'We would go occasionally to the movies, whether it be in Glasgow or in Helensburgh. It was a big deal to go to Glasgow then. It wasn't that far, but the seats in the cinema were more expensive than they were at

Helensburgh. The picture houses, that's what they were called then . . .'

Outings with Helen to the latest films, work at the family garage, excursions with Jimmy (and sometimes father Bob) as spectators to motor races around the country, and a rapidly growing interest in clay pigeon shooting gave Jackie a carefree and happy life. He enjoyed his days as a young Scot, as summed up neatly by Hunter Davies in *The Exciting World of Jackie Stewart*, penned in aid of the Scottish Educational Trust. 'They took their holidays,' he wrote of the Stewart family of the 1950s and 1960s, 'like all good Scottish families, at Rothesay, staying in a rather posh hydro, the Glenburn, as the garage was usually doing rather well. For day trips, like everyone else, they went down the water from the Broomielaw, on the *Waverley* or the *Jeanie Deans*. For a special night out, Jackie was taken into Glasgow to see Harry Gordon at the Alhambra.' This very traditional Scot in Stewart was always celebrated, and it remained an integral part of the success of his marriage to Helen as time passed by.

At the time, however, 'Shooting was really the single most important thing in my life. It was the first thing I found that I was really good at, and the first thing I was given any credit for, in the fullest sense.' After being picked to represent his country, and Great Britain, in 1955, Stewart won the Scottish, the English, the Irish, the Welsh and the British Championships, and the Coupe des Nations, 'which is the European and Mediterranean Championship. Of course, it was an amateur business, and in fact it cost me a lot of money. Everything I had was put into it. But I knew I wasn't going to get anything out of it financially. It was just pleasure.' His successes in competition meant amusing adventures and long journeys that gave him valuable experience at the wheel, especially in terms of concentrating for lengthy spells, as well as a sense of personal esteem he had never experienced before. In *A Scottish Childhood*, Jackie described national clay pigeon shooting honours as 'my first experience in life where I could stand up and be counted with pride'.

This first happy break in his life, however, came to a disappointing conclusion in 1960. By then Stewart was regarded as one of the outstanding shots in Britain, a near certainty to be a member of the two-man British shooting team for the Olympic Games in Rome. Most observers believed just prior to the final trials in June that it was only a formality for Stewart to join the 4,738 bright young people of the world making their way to Italy for a memorable season in the sun. He had been in scintillating form, especially during the Coupe des Nations weekend in North Wales. 'Of all the things that I have ever won,' he said, 'that gave me most pleasure because I was young, much more impressed by success, and I won it fair and square against the best shots in the world.' Photographs taken at the time of a trophy-laden young Stewart grinning broadly from ear to ear support his recollections. In one, for which he had combed his neatly trimmed and short hair across his head, he is seen wearing a traditional blazer and a sports shirt, the blazer buttons done up, his eyes squinting into a camera and his expression nothing short of utter satisfaction.

But on his twenty-first birthday, 11 June 1960, the smile disappeared, wiped off his face by what he later described as the biggest disappointment of his life – worse for him than missing out on victory at Indianapolis in 1966; worse than running out of fuel at Spa Francorchamps and missing the world championship in 1968. Instead of receiving the present he most wanted, a competitor's ticket to the ancient capital of Italy, Jackie was left to digest how a near certainty had turned to failure. Losing his timing, his form and his unerring eye, he literally missed his target. 'I suddenly dropped eight targets out of 25, and I found myself losing my place in the Olympics by one point,' he said nearly a decade later after celebrating his first drivers' championship. 'I was relegated to reserve, but I didn't even get to travel. I still feel annoyed about it. Here was something I desperately wanted to do, to be a member of the Olympic team. To be in the Olympics was something bigger than being a Formula One driver. It was big! And I was shooting very well that year, but I got thrashed. I had beaten the other guns consistently, but on one run of 25 clays I missed eight. It was unheard of, but there it was. It was a terrible blow to my ego, but it was the first time I had really learnt to face disappointment. It taught me to be philosophical about it.' Helen had given him a beautiful pair of cufflinks for his birthday, more expensive than her moderate means at that time could afford. She knew they were ideal for Jackie and he was delighted to receive them, but it was not enough to dissipate his deep unhappiness. 'He was absolutely miserable,' Helen recalled.

Two years later, the disappointment stored away for motivational use, Jackie married Helen in a traditional white wedding, the well-scrubbed groom kitted out in a full morning suit including top hat and gloves, and the bride resplendent in a full ivory dress with veil. In contemporary photographs, taken in black and white, they look assured and happy as they gaze steadily at the camera. Helen believed she was marrying a local boy from a decent family that owned the garage on Glasgow Road, a boy with a decent eye who was an excellent shot. By 1962 Jackie had, after all, taken part in only a handful of motor races, and all of them anonymously under the entry name of A.N. Other. It was all done more for fun than anything else. Helen knew Jackie was a car enthusiast who raced a little at weekends, but she believed it was no more than a hobby, a passing phase. However, while they were on honeymoon, Stewart drove his Jaguar saloon round the Nürburgring. He had been before, in 1960, with his Welsh shooting friend Allan Jones (now a partner in Jackie's famous shooting school at Gleneagles). 'I took the firm's 3.4-litre Jaguar demonstrator to Oslo and then down to Berne,' Jackie recalled. 'I went round the Nürburgring in it. You could pay so many Deutschmarks and drive your own car round. We saw Wolfgang von Trips and Phil Hill preparing for the German Grand Prix. Of course, I was not racing then, but by the time 1962 came around, I was determined to become a professional racing driver.'

As she said, Helen had been drawn to Jackie because of his manners and the attention he paid her, but also by his vitality. In an interview with Elizabeth Hayward in 1970, she recalled, 'It wasn't love at first sight on either part, nothing like that. We went out together occasionally. I think Jackie was fonder of me than I was of him at that time. Fortunately, I realised that liking him was one thing, but I didn't know what it was like to be in love with anyone, never having experienced it. So I suggested we split up for a while, which was a good thing, because he went out with other girls and I went out with other boys. I think it's a thing you have to do. I don't think you can go steady with one person at that age. Although Jackie had mentioned marriage, I never thought I would marry him. I'd always reckoned to marry someone tall, dark and handsome . . . the usual girl's idea, but it never works out that way. I can remember exactly when I felt I was in love with him. I was nineteen at the time, and he came walking into the same coffee shop.' This encounter revived their romance, and a game involving a ring that Jackie pretended to refuse to give back to Helen, who promptly decided to walk home, which resulted in him finally giving her a lift home in his red Austin Healey. Eighteen months later, they got engaged. 'When we were first married,' Helen continued, 'he was only racing about twice a year and there was no prospect of him becoming a professional racing driver. It is amazing how your life changes!' She recalled, amusingly, that she was never interested in the racing Jackie enjoyed in those early days and would sit in the car and read the Sunday newspapers. He was, after all, only A.N. Other.

His married life was a success from the start. He and Helen shared similar views on many things, and agreed on the need for sensible economy. They lived at first in a modest, small flat in Rhu near Helensburgh, a pretty little town facing south across the water. After Rhu, Jackie and Helen moved to a bungalow in Dumbuck, two doors along from the dwelling in which Jackie was born and where his parents were then still living and running the garage. Not until later, when his income began to rise, did Jackie invest in a more substantial home by buying a beautiful turn-of-the-century house standing in its own grounds on top of the hill at Helensburgh. It was called Clayton House, a name he and Helen used again and again for the homes that followed (some say the name came from a combination of 'clay', for his shooting days, and 'ton', for 100mph). Jackie and Helen loved that first Clayton House. 'It was a super house, very old, with terrific character, beautiful inside with a lot of wood panels and so on,' Helen remembered. 'We completely gutted it, except for the woodwork, put in central heating and a completely new kitchen.' It was at Clayton House, Dunbartonshire, that Paul Stewart was born, but it was not ideal as it was too remote from London and Europe and the circuits that became Stewart's workplaces.

Marriage to Helen, long after his sobering defeat in the trials for the British Olympic clay pigeon shooting team, provided Jackie with an anchor and a stimulus. He drew from her support and her love, but at the same time he felt driven to provide for his family. He admitted, in an article he contributed to an illustrated book put together by the Scottish Educational Trust in 1974, that he had given serious and reflective thought to his decision to marry right up to the final seconds. 'I remember being driven to the church for my marriage in 1962,' he recalled. 'I turned to my best man and said, "God, I hope I'm doing the right thing!" Even at that late hour, I wasn't certain. I had only known Helen for six years. What if she changed? What if I changed? What if we wanted to get out of it? Happily, all my fears, at least at the time of writing, have proved unfounded!'

If only he had listened to his friends more carefully, and had more instinctive trust in them, wary wee Jackie might have walked down the aisle without a fear or concern in the world. John Lindsay, the Dumbuck 'rock' in human form, a man who is palpably comfortable in his own Scottish world at Dumbarton, remembered it all well. As a close friend of the Stewarts, of course, Lindsay was at close quarters during Jackie's courtship with Helen. 'Helen was special,' he said. 'She was upmarket. She was from Helensburgh! Her parents had a very good business. They were in demand as bakers, and they made cherry cakes and wedding cakes and stuff like that. Helen worked in the bank in Helensburgh, and she was certainly very lovely then, as she still is. Really fantastic. Beautiful. I remember one time at, I think, the Queen's Hotel. A very nice, quiet place, upmarket really, no guitars or noise, nothing like that. Helen was trying to unload his nibs and he was a little concerned, so I was requested by Jackie to go and have a dance with Helen to find out what the problem was! Well, it wasn't too serious. It all worked out.

'When he got married, well, she was "Lady Helen"! And these days, she really is, of course!' He roared with Dumbuck laughter as he reminisced in 2003. 'I would always put her alongside Grace Kelly, for style especially. At one point, though, I think she wanted rid of him – before they married. At just one point . . . But I think it was his charm and the fact that he was doing his clay pigeon shooting then – and nobody else I knew did that, and they were only about seventeen or eighteen anyway – that rescued him. And, you know, one cartridge in those days was about two shillings. Nobody could think of that! So that made a difference.'

The suggestion that the Stewarts had enough money and sufficiently good prospects to persuade Helen McGregor and her successful cake-making mother to think again about a lifelong liaison with Jackie Stewart might have played on Lindsay's lips, but he never quite articulated the thought. He was certainly not afraid to talk of money, though, or the bloodlines that produced his friends Jimmy and Jackie Stewart. 'The money came from the farm on [Jeannie's] side of the family,' he said. 'They had a huge farm at Eaglesham, and still do to this day. Young's Farm. That's where his name is from, John Young Stewart. Young was his mother's maiden name. It is still a very healthy-looking farm. His grandfather on his father's side, those grandparents, they were from just further along from the farm, in a wee kind of wood. He was the gamekeeper for Lord Weir. That's where the shooting came into it, of course. But I wasn't into it. I couldn't even think of affording it. They had a shoot here [at Dumbuck] once, up the back somewhere, and they were looking for some help. I just said, "No way, not me. I'm not going beating for this lot." But I remember one or two of the guys from the garage went out and did the beating for them. And we used to go down to Wales to see the Joneses, of Jones Bailers, who are now Massey-Ferguson. Well, they were a pretty well-off family, obviously, and they went shooting and so on. Allan Jones himself, he had a 190SL. It was a beautiful motor car, white with a blue interior. A drop-head. Jackie had the Healey, and it made so much noise! So Allan, well, he went and changed his 190SL for a Healey. It was noisy too, and it made tunes with the exhaust, as it were. They were quite extravagant!'

Marriage and moneymaking might have been in Jackie's and Helen's minds when they set off to church in Helensburgh that day, but motor racing was certainly not a shared ambition. By 1962, Jimmy's successes were no longer fresh in the local memories either. Instead, he was busy on the sales side of the Dumbuck Garage business, still handling demonstration vehicles with an aplomb that was admired by his mother. The Stewart parents, Bob and Jeannie, were also hard at work, building the business that Helen doubtless believed would remain successful enough to keep everyone comfortable. But, as Lindsay revealed, it was not to work out that way. As Jackie's driving talents soared, so his family's business fortunes fell.

'Jimmy today?' said Lindsay, repeating a question. 'Oh, he's now just down the road [in Rhu, where Jackie and Helen had first lived together, in a flat organised and paid for by his younger sibling]. He's retired now, and Jackie looks after him very well. Very well indeed. He's had 40 years in the wilderness, really. The parents? They were the characters. His old boy was a right old – well, a you-know-what, as far as business goes. He had a saying: "A wee fire can heat you, but a big one can roast you." And it's true! There's another one that someone came out with: "Expansion is vanity, the bottom line is sanity." Well, the Stewarts were old-fashioned, very hard working, and they made a good living at it in the old days. His mother did a lot. To this day this [Rockview] is still a reasonable little place. These three houses were each built by different builders, and this is the best one.

'Eventually, they [the Stewart family] made money. But in the 1950s and 1960s I would say there were three families involved in the dealership here for Jaguar and Austin, and the garage could support only one, really. And so, eventually, it went in the wrong direction. In 1966, Jackie had to buy his brother and his father out to keep the place going, to stop it going belly up. He put a manager in. He had the same lawyer and accountant that Jim Clark had at the time, and to put it politely, they didn't have a tight rein on the way the numbers were going. To cut a long story short, Jackie tried to flog it in 1969, but nobody would touch it. Not even with a bargepole. Not with the liabilities then, which had become ginormous, and the assets weren't a lot. We had looked at so many places, and obviously the [Stewarts'] place had been let go a bit, but we eventually bought the company for a pound, took on the liabilities, the whole lot. In Grand Prix terms, it probably put us 50 laps behind before we started! And, yes, Jackie lost a bit!' Lindsay roared with laughter. 'Jackie was living in Helensburgh, in that beautiful big house, but he was more worried than happy. It was Harold Wilson then, and the more you earned, the more tax you paid. Jackie was doing well, but I think he paid nineteen-and-six in the pound in tax. There was no way he could stay. He had to move out of the country for that reason alone. He didn't want this millstone [the garage at Dumbuck] around his neck as well. He was losing money everywhere, to the taxman and down a black hole here, too. The place wasn't going forward at all. It was crazy, absolutely crazy, and it was terrible for him.'

In fewer than ten years, then, to his dismay, in different times and in different ways, Jackie had suffered two precious losses: his longed-for place in the Olympic team and his father's family garage business. The first stimulated a sporting response in motor racing, the second an undying passion to establish his family name over the door of a business that would provide enormous security, support and wealth to him and his family in the years that followed. Both resulted in the creation of Jackie Stewart, world champion, business consultant, team owner and knight, a man whose reputation became a brand name and image that have rarely been equalled by any other sportsman. He owes a debt of gratitude to Duncan Macbeth, John and Nan Lindsay, his brother Jimmy, his father Robert, his mother Jeannie, his wife Helen and several others for cultivating the character that enabled him to mould his talents into a successful package. But, almost as much, his successes were forged in the fires of his failures, by those missed targets at the Olympic trials and by his inability to save Dumbuck Garage from a sale that at the time had become as inevitable as his rise to stardom and global glory.

3. EARLY DAYS, ECURIE ECOSSE AND THE MOMENT OF TRUTH

'There are few more impressive sights in the world than a Scotsman on the make.'

J.M. Barrie

After his failure, in 1960, to claim a place in the Olympic team, Jackie's attitude to shooting and competition changed. The experience left him disillusioned, but it opened his mind. He realised that there was more to life than firing a gun at clay pigeons. He realised, too, that more was required of him if he was to succeed in competition and in life. But it was not an overnight realisation; it dawned gently over the years that followed his twenty-first birthday, years that saw his interest in motor racing grow until it became an all-consuming fascination that pulled him irresistibly into the professional arena. Two major factors were decisive in this: his brother's career, and the encouragement of customers at Dumbuck Garage, whose own amateur racing days, with their own cars, had often required the skilled assistance of the young Jackie as a mechanic at race meetings.

Jimmy and Jackie, Jackie and Jimmy. It is difficult to disentangle the two, at times, when looking for early clues as to why one of them became a three-times world champion. Was it Jimmy's role to be the ice-breaker? Was it Jackie's fate that he had a brother who was established and respected, who had raced in a British Grand Prix at Silverstone, in 1953, spinning off after running sixth in the Ecurie Ecosse Cooper Bristol, a brother whose connections and experience helped pave the way for his own success? It is hard to imagine the one without the other, or either of them without their father Robert, the enthusiast, providing the bedrock of financial, emotional and automotive support from Dumbuck Garage. No wonder, indeed, that Jackie, with his heavy-lidded right eye, his extraordinary sight, his gift for speed and his appetite for competition, efficiency and profit chose to succeed in the career that was made for such talents. Apart from Jimmy, his early heroes were the other bold men in dirty goggles, men who braved oil, dust and heat to race for glory. Jackie grew up among them all, chasing some for autographs, studying others to acquire tips for stardom, all the time believing that as he practised his signature and cleaned the forecourt, he was improving and moving closer to the indefinable early goals of his life, the ambitions that came into focus when he first began to experience that unique sensation of control, in a racing car, at high speed.

He was a late starter in racing. He was 21 before he drove his first racing car. By comparison with the Grand Prix striplings of the early twenty-first century, the likes of Kimi Raikkonen and Fernando Alonso who leapfrogged the junior formulae to become key members of Formula One teams, he was ancient before he began. In modern racing, a driver has to be competitive and successful in karting long before his voice breaks if he wants to be taken seriously as a driver of potential. In Jackie Stewart's case, it was the disappointment of his clay pigeon shooting career that prepared him for motor racing, hardening him for the heat of competition and instilling in him the resolution to disengage from emotional and personal considerations whenever he was preparing to slide into a cockpit. But some emotional support was required, and it came, when most needed, from Jimmy. His own disappointment, from abandoning a racing career to calm and soothe his mother's fraught nerves, fuelled his attitude to Jackie's dream and enabled him, in a spirit of pure generosity and without a trace of envy, to help him when help was needed. As Robert Stewart had backed his first son, so Jimmy supported his brother. Even when Jeannie made it plain she would have none of it by closing her mind completely to the thought that Jackie might go racing,

Jimmy stood firm. 'I think that Jackie was right to go racing, despite this attitude taken by our mother,' he said. 'He had his own life to live. No matter that I had made a different decision. The point is that he was an absolute natural from the start. He opened people's eyes to what he could do very, very quickly.' By the time Jackie was established, of course, Jimmy was being forgotten, but his own career was considerable and very worthy of being recalled, not only because of the part he played in his brother's life, but because he was a fine racing driver in his own right. He set the example. A little history is called for.

Out of the box, as motor racing people say, the Jaguar was a disappointment. The D-type should have been sleek, race-ready and rigged out superbly in the Flag Metallic Blue of Scotland; instead, it came in pieces, it needed a complete rebuild, and it was green. All right, it was only a 1/24th scale plastic model, but to its young owner, an Ecurie Ecosse Jaguar in the 1950s was the pinnacle of the motor racing world. Why couldn't it at least look like the real thing, damn it?

The real thing is what Ecurie Ecosse most certainly was in those halcyon days. How could a bunch of (mainly) Scottish drivers based in Edinburgh, of all places, take on and beat the world in the race then regarded, quite rightly, as the toughest in the world? Le Mans was the province of the greatest names in motor racing history, of Bentley and Bugatti, Aston Martin and Alfa Romeo, Delage and Delahaye. The Circuit de la Sarthe was also destined to become the field on which the battle royal between Ford and Ferrari would be fought out. But not in the 1950s. In that far-off decade, Le Mans belonged to one marque. That marque was British, and its name was Jaguar. In 1951, victory went to the Walker/Whitehead Jaguar XK120. In 1953, C-types finished first, second and fourth, the winning car piloted by Rolt/Hamilton, the runner-up by Walker/Moss, the sister car by Whitehead and a man called Stewart (no, not that Stewart . . .). The winning Jaguar, disc brakes and all, was the first to do so at an average speed over the 2,540 miles of more than 100mph. In 1954, the Rolt/Hamilton car was a gallant second to José Froilán González and Maurice Trintignant in their five-litre Ferrari. The tragic 1955 race went to the Hawthorn/Bueb D-type, and then along came 'Team Scotland'.

Ecurie Ecosse was the brainchild of Edinburgh enthusiast and sometime racing driver David Murray. Or was it? As Peter Ustinov said, the great thing about history is that it is so adaptable, and the history of Ecurie Ecosse varies markedly from version to version. (Anyone wishing to acquaint himself fully with the story of Ecurie Ecosse, incidentally, could do no better than read the book of that name by the admirable Graham Gauld. By his own admission a 'callow youth' of twenty in Edinburgh when the team was still a twinkle in its owners' eyes, Gauld matched his passion for motor sport with the presence of mind to see what was coming and has remained a faithful friend of Ecurie Ecosse throughout his long and distinguished journalistic career.) Whoever you read, however, it is a matter of historical fact that Murray, an accountant and the owner of several public houses in Scotland's capital city, also had a business called Merchiston Motors. To this establishment in the early 1950s he lured a mechanical wizard by the name of W.E. Wilkinson, better known throughout the racing world as 'Wilkie'. Their paths might well have crossed when Murray took on racing engagements for Reg Parnell, Wilkinson's previous employer. Wilkie claimed in his own autobiography that the 'Ecurie Ecosse' label was his idea, chiming in nicely with the flavour of the times when 'Ecurie' and 'Scuderia' added an exotically European touch to plain-Jane British names.

Murray himself had started competitive driving in Scottish hillclimbs with an ERA, and in a Maserati 4CL at the south-east Scotland circuit known as Winfield. The original idea on Wilkinson's arrival in Edinburgh was to go Grand Prix racing with Murray himself at the wheel, as he was at Monza in 1950, when his Maserati's gearbox disgraced itself, and again in 1951 at Silverstone's British Grand Prix, where he qualified fifteenth and retired with a broken valve spring after 45 laps. Unnerved, perhaps, by a practice crash at the Nürburgring that kept him out of the German Grand Prix that year, Murray had his final crack at one of these Grandes Epreuves the following year, his Cooper Bristol's engine crying 'Enough!' after just 25 laps of the British Grand Prix, for which he had qualified in twenty-second spot.

Wilkinson insists that Ecurie Ecosse was not originally conceived as a Scottish national motor racing team, but in the public eye that is unquestionably what it would become. It also became synonymous with Jaguar, and if we dwell at some length on Ecurie Ecosse it is because the team and its Jaguars carved a niche for themselves in motor racing history that only grows more remarkable with the passage of time. David Murray was the first client to take a new XK120 north of the border; the second was a young Scot who would end up racing for Ecurie Ecosse and would bring to the team the famous name of Stewart – but once again, it wasn't Jimmy or Jackie.

Ian Stewart was the scion of a Scots whisky-distilling family that had sold up and focused on cattle-breeding instead, keeping a few pubs up the collective sleeve, one of which belonged to Ian himself. Though never able to explain what attracted him to motor sport, he was out of the army, footloose and fancy-free, as motor racing began to emerge from its post-war slumbers. Falling in with Wilkie as one of his tune-up customers was the happy accident that brought Ian's brand-new XK120 into the Ecurie Ecosse fold. While Ron Flockhart, later to earn undying fame at the wheel of the Ecurie Ecosse Jaguars, was in on the original meetings that brought the 'stable' into being, he was not one of its founder members. With Stewart, a young man called Bill Dobson was briefly involved until he eventually heeded stern warnings from his father that the family transport business was more important than his son's racing career.

Whisky and transport – good, sound, traditional Scottish business activities. What was needed now was a touch of the aristocratic, something solidly based on the land. Enter Sir James Scott-Douglas, a club-racing 21-year-old from a Borders land-owning family, himself resident in London. It was there, at a British Motor Racing Mechanics' Club dinner, that Wilkie and Scott-Douglas crossed paths; this is the occasion on which Wilkie claims to have had the inspired idea of the three-car Jaguar-based team. The fact that the young aristocrat had his own XK120 parked right outside did nothing to discourage that line of thinking. Within weeks, the first sound backing had come from Reg Tanner at Esso's competitions department, and the birth of Ecurie Ecosse was formally announced on 11 January 1952.

Three months later came the racing debut of Ecurie Ecosse at the Borders airfield circuit of Charterhall. The tone was set when Dobson and Stewart scored their first one-two finish. Stewart went on to consolidate with a fine victory in the Jersey Road Race, then beat Stirling Moss himself in another event at Charterhall. For 1953, a Cooper Bristol and a Connaught were added to the three-car Jaguar stable, along with Jimmy Stewart, elder brother of the man who was to claim his third world championship exactly two decades later.

Bob Stewart, by no means hostile to motor sport himself, had been in contact with Murray and agreed to acquire a new C-type Jaguar for his elder son so that he might join the ranks of Ecurie Ecosse. A sportscar driver before those heady days, Jimmy also had to circumvent the problem of his National Service to go racing in exotic spots such as Ireland and the Isle of Man. This new Stewart won first time out for the team in the Cooper Bristol at Goodwood, but of more interest was the overall performance in their first overseas ventures. The ringing names of Reims, with its 12-Hour race, Spa Francorchamps and the awesome Nürburgring were now added to the list of Ecurie Ecosse destinations, as was Buenos Aires and its 1,000 Kilo-

metres event the following year, when Ecurie Ecosse took over
the ex-works C-types. But it was at places like Castle Coombe,
Oulton Park and Goodwood that the team continued to do their
bread-and-butter racing.

The close, if occasionally spiky, alliance with Jaguar developed further when Ecurie Ecosse 'inherited' the 1954 works
D-types for 1955, including the legendary XKC051 – 'legendary'
because the following year David Murray at last had his heart's
desire. When Ecurie Francorchamps could not accept its
invitation to the 24 Hours of Le Mans, those 1956 places went
instead to Ecurie Ecosse. So, too, did the most important place
of all: the winner's, Ninian Sanderson and Ron Flockhart
pulling off one of the most famous victories in Scottish sporting
history. 'Just a pleasant drive down a fast stretch of French
highway' was how the easy-going Sanderson described it, but
even the absence of marques such as Mercedes Benz and Lancia
could do little to detract from their achievement. Once the
works D-types had succumbed to accidents and inadequate
mechanicals, the Flockhart/Sanderson Jaguar was left in hot
pursuit of the Aston Martin driven by two of the brightest stars
of the day. It must have added an extra degree or two of warmth
to the glow surrounding the victorious D-type when they
remembered that those two great drivers, Stirling Moss and
Peter Collins, were English. The 'Scottish amateurs', as the
writer Ian Bamsey later described them, came home a lap to the
good at an average speed of 105mph. As well as undying fame,
Ecurie Ecosse also won the right to fly the Jaguar flag at Le Mans
the following year.

In 1957, the team's Le Mans opposition included a welter of
Ferraris in the hands of formidable driver pairings such as
Moss/Phil Hill, Hawthorn/Musso and Gendebien/Trintignant, as
well as a Moss/Schell Maserati. Flockhart, now partnered by
Ivor Bueb, drove a fuel-injected 3.8-litre D-type, with Sander-
son and John Lawrence in a 3.4-litre standard version. As the
Ferraris and Maseratis fell by the wayside, the world's greatest

race again came down to a Jaguar–Aston Martin duel, but only until the wee small hours of the Le Mans morning. As five out of five D-types finished, Ecurie Ecosse claimed a glorious one-two result, Flockhart coming in first for the second year in a row. With hindsight, as ever, we can now see that this was the absolute high watermark for the Edinburgh team. There was only one way to go, and Ecurie Ecosse duly took that downward path, but not before a certain Scottish prodigy had honed his considerable talents at the wheel of David Murray's cars.

Jimmy's example had already introduced Jackie to the wider world of motor racing and the talents of other men, notably Jim Clark, who had once pulled into Dumbuck Garage for petrol on his way to a Rest and Be Thankful hillclimb. Jackie recalled the episode clearly because people used to point to Clark, in his trademark dark-blue round-necked pullover, and say, 'See that fellow over there? He is the big hope for the future. He's going to be a great racing driver.' Clark was young and meek, but polite. He had a quality that inspired the young Stewart boy, and a style of driving, with finesse, that later influenced his own efforts on the track. Something sparked inside Jackie Stewart that day. The spark grew brighter when he followed in his brother's racing footsteps.

Jackie Stewart joined the growing list of Ecurie Ecosse drivers in 1963. By this time, he'd established a local reputation as a driver interested in cars, and had already graduated from cleaning the garage forecourt to helping friends and customers with some race-car preparation and a little, very successful, racing. One of them, Barry Filer, encouraged Jackie to try his hand in some of his own cars, with notable results. Filer was glad to have found a young driver he could trust not to add to his repair and maintenance bills, so often run up with gay abandon by his own friends and associates who had enjoyed racing for him in the past, though Jackie had already had his first road accident. As he confessed, to James Leasor, he was lucky to escape uninjured when he left the road in his red

Healey. 'I was still serving my apprenticeship, and aged about eighteen or nineteen, when I went into the big time with my acquisition of a Healey 100/6,' he said. 'I wanted one with chrome wire wheels, but apparently this would have taken three months to provide, so I took the car with disc wheels and an overdrive. It was red and beautiful, with a Pye radio, a tonneau cover and sliding windows instead of the old celluloid side-screens. At £1,250, it was also an expensive car. It was really much too flashy for me, and I couldn't afford it, but it was run as the company demonstrator. The thing I remember most about the car was its appetite for tyres. With hard cornering, it could wear through tyres as though they were going out of fashion. I had an accident in this Healey. I hit a telegraph pole at the bottom of the Lea Brae on my way to Cardross to play golf. A float with sheep in it suddenly turned right without signalling at the bottom of the Brae, while I was in the process of overtaking it. I had to go parallel with it and ran into the guy wire of a telegraph pole, which nearly wrote off the car. Fortunately, I wasn't hurt. I was wearing a great big sheepskin coat at the time and that cushioned me. There were no seat belts, of course, because they did not exist in those days.'

Jackie also ran a second-hand Mark I Jaguar 2.4 fitted with a Derrington steering wheel with aluminium rivets. 'We fitted platinum-pointed plugs and platinum points in the distributor and we removed all the air cleaners. Big deal!' he said. 'The cam covers were polished aluminium. I must say, all my cars were always immaculate. I always had the engine blocks and the exhaust pipes black.' It was the attention to detail, this fastidiousness, that partly explained why Filer took note, as well as Jackie's normal level of care behind the wheel. 'When I married, I had a Mini,' he told Leasor, 'and that was when I started to race. I was preparing cars for Barry Filer, quite a wealthy young man in Glasgow. His parents would not permit him to race, but he owned two cars: a battleship-grey Porsche Super 90 and a magnificent AC Bristol in what I call Scottish blue, my favourite colour and that of Ecurie Ecosse.' Jackie prepared these cars for others to drive, notably Jimmy McInnes, and with some pride said, 'You could have eaten your breakfast off any part of each car. They were so clean. We used to do sprints and hillclimbs and races, and I was his [McInnes'] mechanic. The AC Bristol was the one he mainly raced. It was a gem to work on, like a new pin all the time. I did all the usual things, warming it up, taking it to the line and all that sort of thing, and then Jimmy used to drive it.' According to Stewart, McInnes was 'a very nice bloke – and it was a part of my education to work with someone like that, in that capacity'. McInnes, he said, did decently well, but made mistakes, like 'running over the odd five-gallon drum', and this led to Filer inviting Jackie to drive.

John Lindsay recalled the period well, and the hurdles the younger Stewart faced. 'His mother was a strong character and she liked to rule the roost a bit,' Lindsay said. 'She didn't like him going racing. That's why he entered as A.N. Other and all that.' Indeed, to Lyle Kenyon Engel, Jackie admitted, 'I was scared stiff and refused, the first time he [Barry Filer] asked me. My mother had made it very clear that if I raced, either she left home or I left.' Lindsay continued: 'Barry Filer had a DB4GT Aston Martin, a Porsche Super 90, an AC Bristol and a financial interest in Marcos, and he used to do sprints and hillclimbs in these cars. Jim McInnes used to drive Barry's cars all the time. One day it was a disaster for Barry: there was a chicane marked out by five-gallon drums and Barry came down the main runway into the chicane, fast, and in the Porsche, the old 911, the old shape, at full speed. He thought he went from fourth to third, but no, he went into first and let the clutch out. The valves dropped, and that was it: choog-a-choog-a-choot, and he nearly knackered the thing. At the same time Jimmy appeared to be too quick in his AC Bristol – metallic dark blue, a beautiful car, spoked wheels – and he spun the car and hit every drum in sight. So that was it, that was how Jackie moved in.

'Jackie was driving the DB4GT around Charterhall, and he was only about eighteen at the time, and he was taking care while the rich boys with their toys, nice people, had no real idea. Jackie drove it beautifully and did not put a wheel out, and that spoke volumes, obviously. And he kept it on the island, because he knew what he was doing. That was how he got spotted. Amazing. Ecurie Ecosse just couldn't get past him. Then, in the Cooper Monaco that other previously well-known drivers had driven, he got lap times at different circuits where he was really significantly quicker. I remember one occasion at some place, I think it was a club meeting at Oulton Park, I was at Lodge Corner, which is the last corner before Deer's Leap, and I could hear the commentary. All the cars were on their way, and there was one car coming round and into Deer's Leap, powersliding into it, and it was just amazing.'

A chance opportunity to travel south, in 1960, to Oulton Park, with his friend the great Scottish motorcyclist Bob McIntyre, in Filer's Bristol (which he let them take for the trip), gave Jackie his first taste of track speed. McIntyre wanted to drive the Bristol around the circuit to see if he had the talent and desire to switch from two wheels to four. In less than a morning, he decided he had. Jackie said he was heartbroken when they stopped and headed home. So, when Filer asked him, again, if he would like to try his hand as a racing driver in one of his cars, he said, 'Yes.' Thus Jackie Stewart's competitive career began in Filer's Porsche, as a reward, Jackie said, for his hard work.

He entered, as A.N. Other, a little sprint at Heathfield, near Prestwick in Ayrshire, and finished second, according to *Road and Car*, to a Geordie called Charlie Harrison, who was driving a TVR. The bug bit. It was fun. It was satisfying. And Jackie knew he had the talent and understanding to succeed at it. Filer invited him back. He raced again. He built up his stripling's confidence. 'And then,' said Jackie. 'He bought me a Marcos to race. I didn't go into racing very quickly because I had recently married and I simply did not have the money to pay the insurance premium in case anything nasty happened. Helen and I were living in a rented flat and, even if we really bent over backwards, all we could save was about three pounds a week, and the premium then was fifty for a day's insurance.' Jackie's first outing in the Marcos, powered with a one-litre Ford engine, was at Charterhall, as A.N. Other again, an identity that avoided attracting his mother's eye and, presumably, did little to detract from Filer's pleasure at seeing one of his well-prepared cars driven well. Stewart, therefore, owed his career, in this respect, to Filer. Without his backing, he might not have raced at all. At Charterhall, he finished third, but won his class in the second race. He had started his winning habit. The economies thrust upon him by married life had already persuaded him to give up shooting due to the high cost of taking part, but now another life was beckoning.

The Marcos, now infamous thanks to Jackie's later successes, was an early and ugly model with a wooden chassis. It was followed by an Aston Martin DB4GT, an AC Ace and then an E-type Jaguar that was really a demonstrator at the Dumbuck Garage, but became part of the Filer racing team at weekends. But if the cars were reasonably impressive, they were put into the shade by their driver. Jackie Stewart shone from the start. Never one to dally later in his career at the start of a Formula One Grand Prix ('Flag would drop and he would just open up a gap, straight out of the box, extremely quick,' his GP contemporary Jackie Oliver later recalled), he was certainly not slow off the mark early on either. His first few races proved it. In 1961, he was placed in all the four meetings he took part in at Charterhall. The following year, he did four again and won three, retiring in the other. In April 1962, he led from start to finish to win the Sports Cars up to 1600cc race, and earned a mention in *Autosport* magazine (not his first, as he had gained an entry in print in October the previous year), a fact that both pleased him and filled him with fear that his mother, the only person in the house who did not know what he was doing at weekends, would find out. She did not, not then, but before long it became impossible to dissemble, with every motor racing follower in Scotland taking careful note of the exploits of their latest rising star. In effect, the path to future glories in three world championship seasons was mapped out in the spring of 1962, a few months before his wedding. It was when Jeannie read the notices and reports of the marriage in the newspapers that she found out that Jackie was known already to be an up-and-coming racing driver.

It was also around this time, spring 1962, that Jackie went to Oulton Park in Cheshire for a private test day with Filer in the Jaguar, the Aston Martin and the Marcos. The trip was seen 'as a bit of a lark', according to Eric Dymock, then one of Scotland's youngest new motoring journalists, later the *Guardian*'s correspondent. Dymock was one of the three friends who travelled down with Jackie; the others were Jimmy Pirie, a farmer and local golf champion from Bearsden, and Gordon Hunter, a Glasgow motor trade executive and raconteur. Jimmy Stewart went down too, in order to provide times for comparison in the same cars on the same circuit. Jackie, said Dymock, might have been light-hearted on the surface, but he was deadly serious deep down. 'This was Jackie's moment of truth,' he said.

As always, he made it look easy. On a circuit still carrying traces of the winter, Jackie lapped at impressive speeds. In the E-type Jaguar, he clocked times that were as good as those of a world-class driver who had raced at Oulton the previous autumn in a fully tuned lightweight E-type. The gang from Scotland knew what this meant: Jackie had to give motor racing a serious go. His mother, poor Jeannie, now faced years of self-inflicted anxiety. Jimmy, of course, was all for it and backed him fully. Jackie's father was clearly supportive, if less obviously so. His friends were with him. Helen, soon to be his bride, knew little of the scale of his ambitions following this test, but was hardly set against him doing what he wanted. Bob

McIntyre, the first man to lap the Isle of Man TT course at 100mph in 1957, one of Jackie's great heroes and something of a mentor to him, was also very encouraging. He seemed to recognise true talent when he saw it. A shame, therefore, indeed a tragedy, that he died after crashing on his Norton in August 1962, just as Jackie began his own career on the track in earnest.

McIntyre's death played on Jackie's mind, but it did not stop him from going racing. His autograph book, filled with the signatures of sportscar drivers, some Formula One stars, and singers and musicians (his father was keen on music and often went to events in Glasgow, taking the family with him), was, like his memories of McIntyre and his exploits, a reminder of the past and an inspiration for the future. He went into 1963 with his mind set on racing and success, and he kept his hand in at the wheel by demonstrating cars to prospective customers of Dumbuck Garage with thrilling – or terrifying, depending on your point of view – drives along the Dunbartonshire roads.

On a bleak and wet Easter Saturday, he raced at Rufforth airfield, near York, in the E-type, and won twice in a meeting organised by the British Racing and Sports Car Club, the car 'bog standard, except for a set of racing tyres'. He continued his impressive and winning form at Charterhall, displaying growing natural ability, rising confidence and much style, and then went to Ouston, near Newcastle-upon-Tyne, and won again in the E-type, despite pitting to have a coil lead put back. It was enough to impress all serious and knowledgeable observers, and soon afterwards David Murray of Ecurie Ecosse, who knew Jackie well from childhood and beyond, asked him if he would race for the team for the rest of that year. 'It was a great moment for me,' said Jackie, stepping into his brother's shoes ten years after Jimmy had shown the way. 'I knew all the people: David Murray, Wilkie, [mechanics] Stan [Sproat] and Sandy [Arthur] . . . For me, it was the big time.'

By the time Jackie came into close contact with David Murray, the glory days of the Le Mans Jaguars were part of history, the

Jaguar alliance having formally ended at the close of 1961. Their successors included GT cars designed by John Tojeiro, one of them powered by a Coventry Climax engine, which soon gave way to an American Buick V8. Ten years after his big brother had been recruited, it was in this car and in the team's Cooper Monaco that Jackie Stewart took his first steps with Ecurie Ecosse. His first race took place at Charterhall on 30 June 1963, after three 'almost sleepless nights'. When the team said they wanted to adjust the pedals of the Tojeiro car for him and put a footrest in, Jackie was almost nonplussed, but not quite. Pleased, excited and inspired, he won his first race, and, after spinning, finished third in his second. In 23 events that year, he won fourteen times, earned *Autosport* headlines aplenty, cracked lap records and established himself. He was on his way to becoming a successful full-time professional racing driver with a contract, with Ecurie Ecosse, for 1964 worth £500, plus expenses, an annual premium for a life assurance policy and half of the prize money he won. The offer was made on 24 January 1964 and signed by Jackie on 4 March. Race wins in the Cooper Monaco at Oulton Park and Goodwood followed, in what was the second and last year of his liaison with Murray's team.

As Graham Gauld recounted, Stewart has always been full-hearted in his assessment of his Ecurie Ecosse years and Murray's tutelage. 'He taught me how to look at things professionally,' Stewart said, 'and tried to wipe out the excitement and spontaneous reaction young racing drivers have.' Anyone who has ever seen Jackie in avuncular action with the young drivers trying to climb the Paul Stewart Racing 'Staircase of Talent' must have been struck by the similarities between what Stewart senior had learnt from Murray and what he was trying to do with the precocious youths now in his care, not only in terms of professionalism, but also when it came to that meticulous eye for preparation that was the Stewart trademark. Even in those early days he would be on the telephone to

Murray checking tyres used, pressures, and times recorded to add to his 'wee black book', which charted his performances in exhaustive detail.

Once Jackie Stewart had shot across the Ecurie Ecosse horizons, it was really only a matter of time before failing finances and, perhaps, Murray's own flagging enthusiasm signalled the end. Murray's eventual decampment to the Canary Islands was the saddest of ways to close such a glorious chapter in the history of Scottish motor sport. But Ecurie Ecosse had undeniably set the standards by which Jackie Stewart became accustomed to being judged, and enhanced his ability to look at things professionally, to approach the big time as if he belonged there, and to appreciate and understand the efforts a team makes on behalf of its drivers.

4. THE KEEN APPRENTICE FINDS HIS FEET

'But I haven't gone fast yet, Mr Coombs!'

Jackie Stewart at Silverstone in 1964

'My first commercial break came with Formula Three, when I could still divide my time between the garage and my racing,' said Jackie Stewart in one of many interviews he gave during which his remuneration came to the fore. 'There wasn't much money in it, of course, until I got an offer from BRM to go into Formula One. In 1965, they paid me £4,000 to sign a contract. It seemed a lot at the time, and I bought a 4.2 Jaguar 420 on the strength of it. The family garage could not have afforded to have me "swanning around" in expensive cars like that! The previous year, I had gone through Formula Three with Ken Tyrrell, but I had also been with Ecurie Ecosse and had driven for several other private owners, like John Coombs of Guildford, a great Jaguar enthusiast and entrant. But it was in 1964 that I felt I came of age as a racing driver because I was asked to drive by most of the Formula One teams.'

In 1964, the aforesaid John Coombs held a private test session with Jack Brabham and Dan Gurney during which they tried out his lightweight E-type Jaguar. 'They both thought the E-type was a terrible car and not very quick,' Coombs reported. A few days later, Coombs was sitting in his office in Guildford when the telephone rang. It was Jaguar's racing manager, Lofty England. 'He suggested I use Jimmy Stewart's younger brother Jackie, which I was not very keen about. I told Lofty, "He's an amateur, he has just started. Come on!"' But once Coombs extracted an agreement from England that if Jackie damaged the car during a planned test session at Silverstone, Jaguar would repair it, Coombs agreed to let Jackie try out his E-type.

On the appointed day, Coombs, rather than running the car from the normal pit area, set himself up on Hangar Straight where he could look across and see Jackie through Club Corner and the notorious Abbey Curve. The man in question arrived in his Mini from Glasgow and was clearly impressed. Coombs takes up the story again. 'I sat Jackie in the car and told him to remember that he was only here to test the car so please go out and do one lap and then come in. Which he did. We made a few adjustments, and then I told him to go out and do three laps and just take it easy and work himself in. Well, he came past at the end of the first lap and was flying. He went through Abbey Curve without lifting, because the engine noise didn't change, so I told the mechanics to bring him in. He was really quick, so when he stopped I opened the door of the car and said, "You were asked to go out in the car and test it, slowly. Please will you do that, or forget it." Whereupon Stewart replied, "But I haven't gone fast yet, Mr Coombs!"

'Now, both Jack Brabham and Dan Gurney had complained about the brakes, so I asked Jackie about them next. "They're fantastic. It's a fantastic wee car." So I let him out again, and by the third lap he was as quick as Gurney and Brabham had been. By the seventh lap he had broken the outright GT lap record for Silverstone. It was all over in seven laps! That was the start of Stewart; absolutely brilliant. He was the best driver I ever had for setting up a car. Some drivers go round and round all day, but Jackie would go out, stop, go out again, stop, and sometimes never complete an entire lap until he wanted to. He would then go out and do five quick laps and come back and say, "No, I think you've overdone that. You should drop it back a wee bit." The other thing about him was he would allow you to do things that *you* thought might help out.'

Coombs signed Stewart up to race the lightweight E-type Jaguar for 1964, a deal that included one of the support races at Brands Hatch for the British Grand Prix. However, Jackie was also driving at that meeting for David Murray of Ecurie Ecosse in the Tojeiro-Buick coupé, for Ken Tyrrell in the Formula Junior Cooper, and for Lotus in a Lotus Cortina. When Jackie had signed for John Coombs, he had explained it was a long way from Scotland to races in England, and could John see his way clear to giving him a wee bit towards his travelling expenses? It was therefore agreed that Jackie would get £15 travelling expenses for racing with John. But when John saw that Jackie was racing in four different cars at that Brands Hatch meeting, he casually asked Ken Tyrrell if he was giving Jackie any travelling expenses. Ken replied that he was giving him £15. Coombs then challenged Jackie about this, and the wee Scot replied, 'Well, you have to try, don't you?' 'Actually,' said the forgiving Coombs, 'I had a very good relationship with Jackie Stewart: a brilliant, brilliant driver. I was very lucky to have the experience of him driving for me. He later drove the Matra, March and Brabham Formula Two cars for me. I took Jackie in the Brabham to Japan for the Japanese Grand Prix – which was a non-championship Formula Two race – and he won it by a mile.'

The story is important for two reasons. It highlights not only the self-confident streak in the cocky Scottish stripling, but the go-anywhere-drive-anything mentality that was prevalent during his years of apprenticeship. In 1963 and 1964, Jackie Stewart did indeed go just about everywhere in his bid to learn, to win and to make the name better known, putting down markers for his greatest years. In 1963, he won more club races than anyone, but he had to put in some mileage to achieve that feat. His first race win of note, on 19 April 1963 when he steered an E-type to success at Rufforth, not far from York, in a meeting organised by the British Racing and Sports Car Club's Northern Centre, was typical. 'This one introduced a newcomer from Scotland in the shape of Jackie Stewart with an E-type Jaguar,' said one report. 'Driving in the style of another of that name, he won just as he liked.' Stewart won both the ten-lapper for GT cars and a sixteen-lap event for Sports and GT cars, but to his 26 laps should be added a 530-mile round trip: he left home at five in the morning, drove down, did his racing, netted around £25 for his trouble, then drove straight back home in a bid to keep his expenses down. 'In my case,' he said, 'it was much easier in that we have a garage business, and our costs of preparation, even when I used my own E-type Jaguar, were negligible.' No wonder, though, that Jackie started asking for his £15.

Stewart and money; love and marriage; horse and carriage – a pairing, indeed, that the young apprentice was keen to enjoy. By the end of 1963, Stewart was scorching to track records, gaining fame and speed, and establishing his reputation as a man to watch. By the end of 1964, he was obviously going to places other than Ecurie Ecosse for the following year, despite their having shown the foresight to include a 'first option' clause on his services for 1965. He was hot property, and, as so often, money management was a dominant factor in the architecture of Jackie Stewart's career, even in these early stages. He knew his own talent. He knew his own value. He had not arrived at this threshold in his racing life after sailing into Scotland, as they used to say, on a banana boat up the Clyde. Indeed, according to Engel, even by early 1964 a survey of club racing had shown that Stewart's name 'appeared with monotonous regularity on the top of the results sheets'. This was praise indeed for the rising Scot, though, as Engel added, it came at a time when there were some dubious fellow competitors around in British club racing. In the same survey, it was revealed that another competitor had earned almost as much praise, one Roy James. He had 'actually won more club races than anyone else up until his disappearance in August'. No wonder. He had found another risky job with profitable potential, as the getaway driver for the Great Train Robbery.

This amusing tale not only helps to illustrate the social landscape of club racing in Britain at that time, but also the fact that there was a truly vigorous racing scene, one in which drivers like Jackie could become deeply involved by racing in many different cars and in different categories throughout a single day or weekend. In 1963 and 1964, Jackie learnt to make his pennies count for him. During his period of anonymity on the race track, according to Graham Gauld, Jim Clark had approached Stewart to test a Lotus Formula Three car for Colin Chapman, but Jackie had turned him down due to fear of his then-unknown identity emerging. Now, having had his disguise as A.N. Other rumbled just before his wedding, he determined to make the most of his opportunities.

According to Jimmy Stewart, his mother's attitude towards Jackie's decision to go racing, and the 'anonymous' manner in which he had hitherto done it to hide it from her, hardened into a form of hatred and created a difficult situation, one that Jackie showed great strength of character, and a personal sense of resolution, in determining to see through so successfully on the track. 'She never read the paper,' said Jackie, 'and at home my driving career was never discussed. My mother never accepted that I was a racing driver. She never recognised it because I cheated her.' Motor racing was anathema to Jeannie. She had seen one son, Jimmy, injured on the track and had pressurised him into abandoning a highly promising career by opposing it so forcefully. Her nervous disposition and, sometimes, desperate behaviour won out in that battle, but it did not work a second time. Stewart's decision was irrevocable. Helen, on the other hand, though somewhat nonplussed by the turn of events (she, of course, had never expected to be married to a racing driver) decided that, after all, life might be more exciting.

In the meantime, Jackie ploughed on. He learnt trackcraft from any number of experiences with some wild and wayward rivals. 'It is not simply knowing that you can drive 50mph faster than the next chap,' he warned, 'you have also got to anticipate his movements.' In 1963, during his first serious season in a motor racing classroom, Jackie had learnt his lessons well. He'd won at least one race at every circuit where he took part. His contemporaries, to appear again at a later date, also began to earn notice here and there: Jochen Rindt, Piers Courage, Jackie Oliver. What a dreadful shame, and a condemnation of the safety arrangements of that era, that only Oliver of that trio survived his racing career to enjoy a life beyond the cockpit.

Early in March 1964, Jackie's career moved through the gears with the élan for which his older brother Jimmy was famous in his own racing days. Ecurie Ecosse had retained him for the year, and Charles Bridges, a racing enthusiast from northern England, gave him a 3.8-litre Jaguar saloon for a club relay race at Oulton Park. They won. Bridges, encouraged, then offered to buy a Lotus Cortina for him – and all this before Stewart had even considered racing in single-seater 'formula' cars. His ambitions were to succeed in saloon and GT cars, to impress people like the Jaguar dealer John Coombs. Little did he know it, but his exploits had spread his name far and wide.

On the first weekend of that March, a racing driver lost his life while practising for an event at Longford in Tasmania. That distant event had an enormous bearing, not only on the life of Jackie Stewart, but on the history of motor racing at the highest level. Longford formed part of the Tasman Series, with which Jackie himself would become intimately acquainted soon enough. It was a daunting test in itself, a sprint over public roads and through the streets of the northern Tasmanian township. The driver who died there was American Timmy Mayer. The connection with the wee Scot was a tall, angular Englishman who went by the name of Ken Tyrrell.

Those were also transitional years for the man who would come to be known as 'Uncle Ken'. Setting aside his own racing ambitions when he discovered his bent for team management, Tyrrell had impressed when called in to assist the Coopers after John's own serious road accident in a Mini. The Tyrrell Racing Organisation was set up in 1963, with Ken running entries in Formula Two and Formula Junior, then in its final year. One of those entries was a Cooper BMC for Timmy Mayer. When the luckless Mayer perished at Longford, Tyrrell immediately thought of Jackie Stewart. Stewart, in his Ecurie Ecosse Cooper Monaco, had equalled the Goodwood lap record on his last visit, proceeding, as Tyrrell later described it, like 'a dose of salts'. Though Jackie had spun in the race, mainly due to a burst of over-enthusiasm, he had started from pole position and had finished second. Tyrrell, clearly impressed by what he had learnt of the wee Scot, decided to ring the Stewart home in Scotland.

'I had this phone call from Goodwood, from Robin McKay, the track manager,' explained Tyrrell. 'He called me up about this young Scotsman who had been driving this out-of-date Ecurie Ecosse sportscar around Goodwood – and driving it with some verve. He said he looked very good. I knew that Robin was a decent judge of this sort of thing so I rang Scotland and spoke to Jackie's brother. I asked him if he knew what Jackie really wanted to do. Did he want to stay in club racing or go on and try to do a lot better? Jimmy told me he thought Jackie was capable of going a lot further, and that that was what he wanted to do. That's when I told him there was a test drive on offer.' Jimmy, speaking in 2003, concurred. 'He asked me, in fact, how serious this younger brother of mine was about going motor racing, so I told him he was bloody serious and he was bloody good!' Tyrrell had a reputation as a talent-spotter and used to receive many telephone calls like that one from McKay. He was keen to make sure he signed only the best, and he was thorough in his testing of potential drivers. 'A lot of people had told me, "You must see this brilliant youngster," ' he recalled. 'But I had to be careful. I wasn't running a nursery for racing drivers.' Indeed, he was not. He was running a successful and professional team, and for 1964 he had two Coopers to run. His call to Scotland, therefore, was part of his routine in order to make sure he maintained his reputation and his team's success.

Jimmy, however, knew what the consequences were likely to be as soon as he replaced the receiver. 'I knew they would kick up all holy bloody hell again at home when they found out. Jackie said he had to go and sort things out with my mother, but, as I said, I don't think Mother ever forgave him. Never. Even when he won all those Grands Prix, it made no difference. You know, he would win a Grand Prix, at somewhere like Monaco, for example, a famous victory, and she was not interested. She did not want to know! Not at all. It was such a shame. If it was mentioned, she might say something like, "And what was the weather like outside today?" It was such a selfish outlook to have on life. I looked back on those times years later and, when I thought of it, I just asked myself, "Why did I give up?" But I never had any sense of jealousy. It was like a reward *to me* to see Jackie so successful. I felt very proud. I felt it was a success that was partly a product of me, too. A reward. He was doing something beyond me. I knew that. So I never felt any envy, or anything like that. My brother was a very great racing driver.'

Almost predictably, of course, when Tyrrell made his call to Dumbuck, Jackie was absent. He had gone shooting. That was why Jimmy took the call. He soon informed Jackie that he had been invited, by Ken Tyrrell, to Goodwood to test the new Cooper Formula Three car. When Jackie heard the news, on his return, he was flabbergasted. He did not know what to do. He had little idea who Ken Tyrrell was, if he was a good man or a rogue, if he was a competent team manager or not. So, as he has done throughout his life, Jackie did his homework. He rang his friends. He called David Murray and Jim Clark. By then, Clark was a good friend, and Jackie and Helen quite frequently travelled down to the Borders and stayed on his farm where they often went out together to motor club dances. According to most good sources, Clark was keen for Stewart to join Tyrrell and said so. He told his young compatriot that if he was serious about going racing, then he had to move into single-seaters, and that there was no one better to begin with than Ken Tyrrell. He was likely to be given good experience, sound advice and not to be pushed too hard. Little did any of them know that the meeting of this Englishman, the son of a gamekeeper, and this Scot, the grandson of a gamekeeper, would produce such a fabulous motor racing union and so much future success.

Both men probably had no idea of this, nor did they realise that they had met before, very briefly, when Jackie had accompanied his friend and idol Bob McIntyre (who owned a 3.8 Jaguar bought from Dumbuck Garage) to Goodwood for a test session of his own, with Tyrrell, earlier in the 1960s. Like John Surtees, who made such a successful switch from two wheels to four, McIntyre wanted to move from motorcycle racing to car racing. 'It was the same Ken I was to get to know so well – the same flat cap, the same walk, the same jacket . . . everything,' Stewart told Maurice Hamilton for his authorised biography of Tyrrell, recalling that day. 'He was totally in charge and typically to the point. He gave Bob a test, but Bob didn't meet up with what Ken thought was acceptable. And that was it. Bobby didn't get the drive. He was an artist on a bike, the first man to lap the Isle of Man at 100mph, but Surtees had more experience on four wheels and could make the switch. Bobby couldn't. End of story. We went back to Scotland.'

The Stewart test at Goodwood is one of the most famous episodes in the folklore of the sport. Jackie not only turned up and impressed all and sundry, he outpaced Bruce McLaren, the Cooper team's works Formula One driver at the time – after he had driven all the way from his home in Scotland, a journey of more than 400 miles. 'I had never driven a car that was specially made to go motor racing,' he said. 'This was it. I was not only getting into a fast car, but it was a super car, and new, a Cooper T72.' The car was set up and prepared for Stewart by McLaren, who had been brought in by Tyrrell to set a time. This was the normal arrangement for such tests. Before they began, Tyrrell lectured the young Scot on taking his time and not trying to rush anything. 'We've got all day,' Tyrrell told Stewart. Very soon, the young Scot was faster than the experienced Kiwi, one of the most established men in the Grand Prix world. 'I was very surprised because, I admit, I must have been doing it very blindly,' said Stewart. Tyrrell, horrified at seeing Stewart deliver such immediate speed, called him in and asked him, in typically blunt style, 'what the hell he thought he was doing!' McLaren, motivated to improve his own time in response, said, 'Let me get back in that car.' He went out again and improved his time, overhauling the young Stewart's in the process. But when Jackie went out again, the same thing happened. 'This is ridiculous,' said McLaren. He went out again. Again Stewart responded with a faster time. A slow and broad grin spread across the faces of Tyrrell and John Cooper.

Cooper, a man who had vast experience of motor racing and whose cars had won many Grands Prix and two world championships, wanted Tyrrell to sign the outrageous young Scot on the spot that very afternoon. He had been out to take a look at his driving through one of Goodwood's fastest corners and was impressed and excited. According to Tyrrell, he ran back to the pits and told him to get his signature quick. Tyrrell was impressed, too. 'If you couldn't see that Jackie was something really special on that day, probably a future champion, then you were a complete bloody idiot!' he declared. And Tyrrell was no fool. They agreed to meet and discuss a drive, and after a preliminary chat at the team headquarters – which was, in fact, a wooden hut – they went back to Tyrrell's home, Hook House, a mile or so from the famous timber yard at Ockham, where they met again the following day.

This meeting, their first to negotiate a Stewart contract, saw Tyrrell offer Jackie a five-year deal. He promised a very substantial payment to sign (the reported figures for this offer vary from £3,000 to a full retainer of £10,000) and, in return, said he would take 10 per cent of Stewart's earnings for the full period of five years. The sum of £3,000, as referred to in Stewart's quoted comments in Engel's 1970 book, itself represented more money than Stewart had ever dreamt about; it was a figure that dwarfed the earnings he collected at Dumbuck Garage and the balance in his bank account. The £10,000 Jackie talks about in Hamilton's book (2002), and elsewhere, clearly dwarfed even that fortune. Yet, he turned it down. 'I recognised it as a pretty shrewd deal on Ken's part,' he told Engel. 'I felt that if he, having seen me drive only once, was going to offer me £3,000, then there must be more in this racing business than I could see. It was a big, big gamble, but I turned it down. Looking back, I'm amazed at myself. I mean, a Grand Prix driver wasn't getting that much to sign on with Cooper!' In Hamilton's biography, Stewart said, 'Ten thousand pounds! That was a huge amount of money. But I was thinking, "There's something I don't know here!" I was trying to work out Ken's agenda.'

Whatever the precise figure (and £10,000 seems more likely) and terms Jackie turned down, it was not the end of the affair. Instead of a five-year agreement, Tyrrell and Stewart settled on a one-year deal (which, according to Hamilton, was for a retainer worth just £5 but which gave Jackie 50 per cent of all the prize and bonus money he earned through his racing). Little more than a week later, on 15 March 1964, Stewart, partnered by Warwick Banks in the Tyrrell BMC Cooper Formula Three team, lined up on the grid at Snetterton, in a Norfolk downpour. It was his first professional race and the start of his real apprenticeship for stardom. 'That was the start of it,' said Stewart, who had calculated that he could 'get by' on the combined income from his expenses-paid drives in sportscars and touring cars, plus his garage wages of around £20 a week. Single-seater Formula Three racing was seen as a chance to add some icing on the cake, but he recognised it was a risky strategy having turned down an offer that would have transformed his life.

On his Formula Three debut at Snetterton, that open, bleak and so often wet and windy former airfield circuit in Norfolk, just eight days after his test drive at Goodwood, Jackie was utterly sensational. It was the first international race meeting of the year and it featured a Formula One race (in which Graham Hill was lucky to escape uninjured after an accident at Coram Curve as a result of which his BRM flew off the circuit and lost a wheel) won by Innes Ireland in a Lotus Climax, and a touring car race won by Jack Brabham in a Ford Galaxy. Jackie won the Formula Three race. After only three laps, he led by 48 seconds, having made light of the puddles and standing water, the danger of aquaplaning, and the dreadful conditions. He told Gauld, 'Even to this day, I don't know where the hell the rest of them got to. I don't know why they were so slow. It wasn't as impossible as all that. There were loads of puddles, but as long as you were careful, you could drive reasonably quickly.' The skills, and experience, acquired from those wet and windswept drives in Dunbartonshire came in handy that day, not to mention the dexterity he had developed through handling bigger and more powerful cars in his early racing career. (It is worth noting here that Michael Schumacher, who won his fifth drivers' world championship in 2002, spent much of his early career sampling the massive power and weight of the Mercedes Benz vehicles in the Sportscar World Championship before he settled into Formula One. The experience did him no harm either.) At Snetterton, said Tyrrell, 'Jackie just vanished in a cloud of spray.' He won £186, his first professional prize money, out of which he was required to pay his own expenses. As he admitted, 'It was still damn good . . . it was all my money. I had arrived! I had riches.'

But if 1964 was to be a decisive, progressive, spectacular and successful year for Stewart's career (he reeled off seven straight wins, including the blue riband event at Monaco and eleven of the thirteen events he entered), it was also a learning season, too, and the one in which he had his first major accident. On 11 April, at Oulton Park, he crashed heavily and wrote off the famous Ecurie Ecosse Cooper Monaco (registration 174 PPE, according to Gauld) that had been in service since 1960, carrying such men as Tommy Dickson, Roy Salvadori, Bruce Halford and Jackie himself to victories. 'I don't know what the hell I did,' he said, 'but I remember where I went. I climbed down a branch of the tree to get out of the car and it was a sorry sight ... [car owner] Major Thomson's Monaco met its Waterloo with me, and I was very sorry as it was a wonderful car and I won a lot of races with it, even though at the time it was somewhat antiquated. David's [Murray] reaction to the accident was typical. There was no wobbly, no tantrum and no anger. But it was my mistake.' On the same day, however, when Jim Clark won all three races he entered, Jackie won the Formula Three contest in remarkable circumstances.

Triumphs, varied and satisfying, in many different cars on many different circuits, followed. So, too, did more and more offers and opportunities as Jackie decided to take advantage of the chance to stretch and test himself in as many vehicles as he could. He ran a Lotus Elan for Ian Walker Racing, he joined Jim Clark and Peter Arundell in the Team Lotus Lotus Cortina, after being approached by Colin Chapman in Monaco (having been released from his contract with Charles Bridges). Then he raced in it at Watkins Glen, in the United States. He accepted drives from John Coombs, in a lightweight E-type Jaguar, and from Eric Brown, an old friend, in a beautiful Jaguar XK120. He drove a Lotus Formula One car in practice at Brands Hatch before the British Grand Prix, and later in the year, during a race heat in South Africa in December, he had his first official (non-championship) Formula One race when he deputised for the injured Jim Clark for Lotus. Clark had injured his back (he'd suffered a slipped disc while throwing snowballs) and could not take part in the Rand Grand Prix. Stewart stood in, driving Clark's Formula One car and a Lotus Cortina at the event, breaking both driveshafts at the start of the first heat but winning the second.

Graham Hill won the event, but Stewart had established his versatility, and he attracted offers like a magnet draws iron filings. For 1965, he was, metaphorically and literally, in the driving seat when it came to the choice. By travelling, too, he had broadened his mind. He knew, for example, that he did not approve of much he had seen in American motor racing, particularly sportscar racing. His style was also now developed and honed. He became known for his smooth and relaxed approach in all cars in all competitions. In 1964, he drove 53 races in 26 different cars, winning 24 of them at circuits such as Snetterton, Oulton Park, Goodwood, Aintree, Brands Hatch, Silverstone, Monte Carlo, Mallory Park and Crystal Palace. He also won at Rouen, in France; at Zolder, in Belgium; at Zandvoort, in Holland; and at Kyalami, in South Africa. At La Chatre in central France, the team's chief mechanic was in an anxious stew when the clutch broke on Jackie's car before the start, and he began without it. Jackie made light of the problem, as he told Eric Dymock: 'There was one hairpin which was particularly difficult, and I had to get round in a big old slide. During the race, I came up behind one particularly slow car and, unable to slip the clutch, rode up on his wheels and completely over him. The car came back to earth with a tremendous wallop just beside the pits, and I found myself looking straight at Ken. He gazed for a moment in sheer astonishment, but his appraisal of the situation was instantaneous. He made a lightning count of the wheels, found they added up to four, and, in reply to my quizzical shrug, waved his arms and yelled across the road, "*Go on!*" ' At Oulton Park, in another spectacular demonstration of his ability, he started from pole position in his Cooper but lost his clutch on the grid again. He switched off, engaged first gear, and then, coolly, pressed the starter when the flag fell. Cars scattered in all directions. Jackie was sixth at the end of the first lap, led after eight, and won handsomely, setting another record along the way. If confirmation of his consummate talent was required, this was it. The talent scouts and the Formula One team managers were enthralled. But the 'boy wonder' himself, as unaware of his outstanding talent as his mother preferred to be, could barely understand what all the fuss was about. He knew what he could do, he believed in himself, but he never thought of himself as the best. It was a trait that had stayed with him from the classroom in Dumbarton Academy, and it would stay with him for the rest of his life.

That year, 1964, saw the introduction of two categories of formula racing: Formula Three and Formula Two. Both were for cars powered by engines with a maximum capacity of 1000cc, but the Formula Two cars were unrestricted in engine design, apart from having to be limited to four cylinders, while the Formula Three cars had to derive from production touring cars with a single carburettor. Other restrictions, intended to make Formula Three cheaper, moved it apart from Formula Two, the series that was seen as the junior version of Formula One. In many ways, Formula Three was seen as the club racing preserve of amateur racers – until Messrs Tyrrell and Stewart entered the fray.

Ken Tyrrell was a robust and straightforward man, not given to unnecessary subtleties. He wanted to see Formula Three supported by manufacturers and suppliers, not cast aside as a frivolous distraction, and he also wanted to see much-improved prize money paid. He was keen to see the formula developed professionally as a feeder series for the teams and their drivers towards the higher echelons of motor racing. His thinking was precisely in line with much of Stewart's. Tyrrell wrote to magazines, notably the British motor sport weekly *Autosport*, and his views were published. He pushed for progress, knowing, of course, that his driver was likely to be the main beneficiary of any, and all, steps taken to add professionalism and polish to the junior formulae. Years later, reflecting on Tyrrell's enormous contribution to his racing career, Stewart acknowledged that he had been hugely influenced by this man of great stature but modest ego, on and off the race tracks of the world. 'It was quite a small operation in the early days,' said

Stewart, 'but he was the best team manager I was ever exposed to, and I had some pretty good people. He told you exactly how things were, you told him the same. We were totally honest and frank, and had complete and total confidence in each other. I trusted him implicitly. We had quite a few arguments, or disagreements, of course, and I got the famous "froth job". But when you got it, you got it; ten seconds later it was gone. He was never a man who harboured a grudge. Nothing was protracted. We didn't have a contract, and I would never have needed a contract with Ken Tyrrell. The first one was the only written one we had.'

Stewart, who contributed a touching foreword to Hamilton's authorised biography of Tyrrell, added that his fondest recollections of their fabulous association were not the glory years of Formula One that came later, but those early Formula Three days. 'It was all so fresh and so new,' he said. 'And he was like a father to me. I was so lacking in knowledge and experience, which meant I relied on him even more.' Many times during his career, Jackie would say that Tyrrell had probably been the single most important influence on him in his racing career. In the early days, he was not to realise the importance of the relationship; nor, indeed, could he have known that it was to become as famous and successful, or more so, as the partnership of Jim Clark and Colin Chapman. Of Tyrrell, he said, 'His strength lies mostly in having been entirely his own boss for so long. He has an independent nature which gives him a great ability for taking decisions, and in racing it is important to have someone who can take decisions without reference to a committee.' This strength of character in Tyrrell, mirrored by many of the authority figures who had an influence on Jackie's life, was a source of energy for Stewart. He relied on him, and learnt from him. 'Ken's forcefulness, especially in moments of crisis, often took people aback,' he added, conceding that it was only when he had won his first world drivers' championship that he felt sufficiently self-confident to question Tyrrell's authority in a manner he felt was complementary to his experience. 'We worked together by having a conversation, or a debate, not to argue out a compromise, just to see who is right. For example, Ken taught me all about gear ratios when I drove for him in Formula Three. I came to his team as a raw boy from the Highlands, unused to a professional approach in motor racing. He had the car set up for me and educated me in the selection of a high gear for slipstreaming circuits, or the most suitable intermediate gear for pulling away from an important corner. It was only when I returned to him in Formula One and demonstrated that I could analyse a car's behaviour to the satisfaction of experts such as Iain Mills of Dunlop and Bruno Morin of Matra in our tyre testing and development sessions that he really believed I knew enough about it to discuss his decisions with him.'

Jackie, from the start, was never short of confidence in his ability or his concentration. This was demonstrated, perhaps more clearly than ever, in 1964 at the Monaco Grand Prix. By tradition, a junior event was always run on the afternoon before the Formula One race, and on 9 May 1964 it was a Formula Three contest. It was Jackie's first race outside Britain. As usual, a great deal of prestige was attached to it, and it began with practice on Thursday, another at dawn on Friday and then two heats on Saturday, each of sixteen laps, before timed practice for the Formula One cars, followed by the much-anticipated and keenly watched Formula Three final just when the shadows began to grow long across the famous Mediterranean harbour. Stewart, who was staying outside Monte Carlo in a modest hotel in a village in the hills (a typical result of being a part of the Tyrrell team because, when it came to hotels, they frequently booked the least glamorous and most economic rooms available within reach of the circuit), won the first heat by leading from start to finish; Silvio Moser of Switzerland won the second heat, but took eight seconds longer to do so. At the start of the final, Moser led through Ste Devote and stayed in front for two laps.

Stewart was sitting back and waiting. He passed him on lap three and then drew clear, eating up time as if it did not exist, his smooth driving style making the job look easy. He won by seventeen seconds and was cheered by many of the top Grand Prix drivers who were watching the race unfold from their hotel balconies. It was a famous victory. Little did he know then that he would be dicing with those Formula One stars on the same circuit just a year later.

'Anyone in those days who won the Monaco Formula Three race was really on a rocket ship for the future,' said Tyrrell. 'Jackie won, I think, every race he'd taken part in, more or less, before the Monaco Formula Three event, so I think the only thing we discussed before the race was me telling him to take it slow enough to make sure he won it! I knew it was going to be important for his future career.' For Stewart, as Tyrrell predicted, it was a victory with many benefits. It was a famous win, one that underlined his potential and stimulated the Formula One teams to pursue him, and an occasion that ushered in his first experience of contact with royalty and high society. 'I sat next to Princess Grace and Helen sat next to Prince Rainier the night after that Formula Three race, at the Grand Prix Ball. I'd never dreamt that I would be doing anything like that. Princess Grace was very special.'

That Monaco race was also the first major international exposure for the new F3. It was an opportunity not to be missed. Stewart didn't. It was time for the telephone to start ringing.

5. A FOOTHOLD IN FORMULA ONE

'Just because he gets to Formula One, it doesn't mean a guy is home and dry.'

Jackie Stewart in 1996

As the triumphs piled up, the plaudits followed, Stewart's reputation grew, and the overtures from Formula One teams began to materialise. Colin Chapman was certainly keen. Cooper and BRM were very interested, too. BRM's team principal Tony Rudd had been one of the fascinated spectators in Monte Carlo. 'I watched that Formula Three race,' he said, 'and I noticed that there was either somebody a long way last, or a hell of a long way in front. As I watched, he got further in front, and I realised it was Jackie.' Rudd, a guest in the flat of his old friend Eddie Hall, a pre-war MG and Bentley driver, where there was a good supply of marvellous food and 'fearsome gin and tonics', borrowed his host's binoculars to witness the Stewart demonstration. 'He was very smooth and obviously in a class of his own,' he wrote in his autobiography.

For some time, though, Lotus looked like the leading contenders. In July 1964, at Clermont-Ferrand, Stewart drove a Ron Harris Lotus 32 Cosworth in a Formula Two event and finished second, seven seconds behind the victorious Denny Hulme. Jackie later revealed that this was a very significant race for him because it was at Clermont that he took the step up to Formula Two for the first time, learning a great deal in the process; it was also the event at which he met for the first time a brilliant young Austrian driver, later to become a great friend of Jackie's and Helen's, Jochen Rindt. In accepting Ron Harris's drive, however, Jackie had had to turn down an offer from Colin Chapman to drive a third Lotus, behind Jim Clark and Peter Arundell, in a Formula One event on the same day at Solitude, a closed-roads circuit near Stuttgart in West Germany.

His replacement ended up involved in a multiple collision while Jackie was following Hulme home in France. 'As it was, I learnt a great deal, although my starting fee of £75 barely covered my air fare!' said Stewart.

In spite of that, as the summer unfolded the odds appeared, in public at least, to favour an all-Scottish Clark–Stewart pairing at Team Lotus in 1965, though this thought was never seriously harboured by either of them. They were friends, but rivals, and Jackie did not know Clark as well then as he would later on. They were also two very different kinds of men: one from the east of Scotland, dry and shy; the other from the west, talkative and extrovert. Furthermore, to race against Clark in a team where Chapman and Clark had such a special and close relationship was a situation that did not appeal to Stewart. When it came to a choice, then, it was between BRM and Cooper, and, as usual, circumstances played a role in helping Jackie with his final decision. Cooper had lost the services of Bruce McLaren, who departed to form his own team, while John Cooper himself had had a serious road accident. His championship-winning outfit went into decline. BRM, on the other hand, were consistent, successful and also had a highly rated 1.5-litre V8 engine. They had won the championship in 1962 with Graham Hill and had finished runners-up twice in succession. Since the regulations for Formula One were to permit 1.5-litre engines as the limit until the end of 1965 (after which they were allowed to use three litres), the BRM offer was a good one, albeit that, at times, their hierarchy and organisation were imperfect. 'I spent the Friday evening aboard a boat on the Seine trying to talk Jackie Stewart into joining BRM,' explained Tony Rudd, referring to the weekend of the 1964 French Grand Prix at Rouen. 'Colin Chapman was also on his track. But BRM's cause, as far as Jackie was concerned, was not helped when I introduced him to RM [director of racing Raymond Mays] next day, as drivers' contracts were his responsibility. He did not even know who Jackie was! Fortunately, Mrs Stanley [wife of BRM chairman Louis Stanley] did.'

During this season, his first successful one as a professional, Jackie had decided to stop drawing any money from the family garage business in Dumbuck. He was earning from his winnings, and he recognised, too, that the old place was unable to support the three families that were now, to different degrees, dependent upon it for a living. 'I went on working there when I was at home,' he said, 'but I was, to all intents and purposes, a real professional racing driver.' His successes had already assisted him in a move out of his first flat in Rhu and into the bungalow at Dumbuck, close to his family. It was his and Helen's first real home, and it was a signal, too, that he was ready for the next big move in his career: the leap to Formula One. Finally, he elected to join BRM as team-mate to Graham Hill. The decision was made and announced by the Owen Organisation in September. In an official statement, Raymond Mays said, 'I am delighted that we have been able to sign such a young and promising driver. I do know that Sir Alfred Owen wants to encourage such a relatively new driver rather than drawing on the existing Formula One drivers for next year.' In one report, Stewart was quoted as saying he was 'excited and grateful' for this 'very big opportunity'. Even then, he spoke like a veteran of motor sport's slick public relations machinery. 'BRM had offered me no more money than Lotus,' he told Dymock. 'It was £4,000, but the difference was that Lotus had doubled and redoubled their figure to match BRM's. I felt dubious about accepting something which they had had such difficulty in arriving at. I joined BRM to gain first-class experience. It was a team where I could learn at my own pace, and also learn very much from someone as experienced as Graham. I knew I would be looked after well and not rushed too much.'

His meteoric passage through Formula Three was almost over as soon as it had begun. He had finished his first apprenticeship, with Ken Tyrrell; now came a second, with Graham Hill. It was time to find his feet at the highest level of all. But, typically, and valuably, given the successes of their association, Stewart remained with Tyrrell in Formula Two, driving his ageing space-frame Cooper chassis with a BRM engine. He was learning from two of the sport's greatest characters in different formulae at the same time, and he was moving up in the world, as his news cuttings proved. Indeed, in a feature published in the *Weekly Scotsman* on 14 January 1965, author Wendy Jones pointed out that only ten years previously, in 1955, Jackie, as a fifteen-year-old youngster, had been one of a mob of boys who had fought at Silverstone to collect the autograph of Stirling Moss.

On New Year's Day 1965, Stewart lined up on the fifth row of the grid for his maiden world championship event, the South African Grand Prix at Kyalami. Stewart had taken over the seat vacated by American Richie Ginther, who had left to join compatriot Ronnie Bucknum at Honda, as the Japanese company set about building on its debut late in the 1964 season. With only a year to go until the 'Return to Power', the 1965 season was not an innovator's dream: there were just six major teams involved in that year's series, no fewer than four of them based in Britain, and the majority of those running the tried and tested Coventry Climax engine. This would be that company's final Grand Prix year. Among the privateers, pride of place went to the admirable Rob Walker with Brabhams driven by the two Jo's, Siffert and Bonnier.

Three world champions occupied the front row of a twenty-car Kyalami grid: the incumbent, John Surtees, in his V8 Ferrari; 1963 winner Jim Clark in a Lotus 33; and double title-winner Jack Brabham in one of his own cars. Stewart's best practice lap of 1m 30.5s was 2.3 seconds slower than the pace his illustrious compatriot had set in taking pole position, and 1.9 seconds behind his own BRM team-mate Graham Hill. By the end of lap one, of 85, Stewart had made up two places to ninth as Clark and his Lotus sidekick Mike Spence disappeared into the distance. As drivers like Bonnier, Bandini and Gurney fell victim to gremlins of one kind or another, a rather processional race finished with the Dumbarton driver in sixth place, and therefore with his first world championship point on debut. That feat should not be underestimated: Stewart was only the thirty-fourth driver to achieve it. Even by 2002, when Mark Webber finished fifth for Minardi at Melbourne's Albert Park, the young Australian's name was only the fifty-first addition to the list. Another, grimmer, statistic should also be noted. Of the nineteen drivers who lined up around Stewart in South Africa in January 1965, nine – almost 50 per cent – failed to make it to the end of their racing careers. Some of them, like Clark, McLaren and Rindt, were ranked among the finest drivers ever to grace motor sport; others – Siffert, Bonnier, Bandini – had their brief moments in the sunshine; two more – Bob Anderson and Mike Spence – were unfulfilled talents; and Graham Hill, the tutor to Stewart in his maiden Formula One year, would die at the controls of his own light plane *en route* home from testing in the south of France ten years later.

If there was one man to whom such epithets as 'experienced' and 'popular' applied in British motor racing in the mid-1960s, it was Graham Hill. He was, like Ken Tyrrell, a quintessentially British character with a quintessentially British personality. They shared many qualities, among them experiences with the armed services, but were very different, too. Like Jackie Stewart, however, they emerged from relatively humble origins to set their world alight, carrying with them their individual reputations for independence of mind, strength of character, sheer dogged determination to overcome all obstacles set in front of them, and a willingness to bear pain, exhaustion, occasional humiliation or ridicule and any number of severe, sometimes grievous, disappointments in order to achieve their ambitions. All three were winners and champions, and all three were loyal to their families, homes and countries. Few patriotic trios could command such overwhelming respect as Messrs Hill, Stewart and Tyrrell if motor sport was to select them at the head of any representative team. Only Jackie Stewart knows how valuable the other two were to him in his development from a wee Scot with bags of talent and a heart full of hope into one of Formula One's most consummate drivers and ambassadors. We know that Tyrrell, who ushered him into single-seater racing, was regarded as a father figure, and it is plain that from 1965 Jackie took to treating Hill like an older relative, often referring to him as 'Grandpa'. This habit was a mixture of showing respect, seizing a subtle psychological advantage and exercising the sense of humour he knew the larger-than-life Hill possessed.

Like Stewart, Hill, who was born in Hampstead in February 1929, came relatively late to motor racing, and in fact did not even drive a car until he was 24. His early years were marked by a profound shortage of money. One of his first cars, for example, was a 1929 Austin for which he paid, allegedly, less than £50. It was widely regarded as a wreck, and soon after he purchased it he found the brakes were useless. To stop it, he had to drive the car against kerbs. Later in his career, he paid a warm tribute to the vehicle for helping make him into a world champion driver. 'The chief qualities of a racing driver are concentration, determination and anticipation,' he explained. 'A 1929 Austin, without brakes, develops all three, but anticipation rather more than the first two, perhaps!' At sixteen, Hill joined Smiths, the instrument makers, where he served a five-year apprenticeship before joining the Royal Navy. It is worth remembering here, too, that not only did Jackie's brother Jimmy serve his National Service (albeit with a lenient commander who permitted him time off to go motor racing), but also that Ken Tyrrell had flown with Bomber Command in the Second World War, his release papers showing that he flew a total of 268 hours in daylight and 216 at night, mostly in Halifax and Lancaster bombers. These experiences provided bonds between these men and permeated their relationships. For modern readers, this was another age. Hill served two years in the navy and then returned to Smiths, having, during that period, taken up rowing as a competitive sport and become familiar with the vertical striped helmets of the London Rowing Club that were to become synonymous with him during his motor racing career. Through his rowing, he also met his wife, Betty.

In another experience that mirrored Tyrrell's career, Hill's life changed the day he experienced motor racing for the first time, though in his case it was at Brands Hatch, not Silverstone. One day, glancing through a magazine, he saw an advertisement for a new racing school, the Universal Motor Racing Club, which stated that anyone interested could drive a racing car at Brands Hatch for five shillings a lap. Hill went to Kent and raced four laps. Inspired by his experience, Hill volunteered to work as a mechanic in exchange for a chance to drive a racing car, an arrangement that did not work out at the first attempt, but at the second, with a different man who owned another racing school. This time, it is said, he raced the cars and soon found himself installed as the school's senior, and most experienced, instructor. Further experience brought him promising results and, at one event, a meeting with Colin Chapman, who invited him to work at Lotus for a pound a day. This in turn, after many arguments, led to Hill being given a chance to race for Team Lotus, with whom he made his Formula One breakthrough in 1958 at the Monaco Grand Prix, where he retired when a wheel fell off. Typically, Hill stuck at the task with Lotus for two seasons and nothing to speak of in the way of encouraging results before joining BRM in 1960. There, he rose to the challenge after two disappointing years, and in 1962 he took the world drivers' title with four victories including his maiden triumph in the Dutch Grand Prix at Zandvoort. He had been frustrated when from seemingly invincible positions in the Monaco and French races he had failed to win, though in due course he was to enjoy himself enormously at Monte Carlo with a total of five wins that earned him the sobriquet 'Master of Monaco'.

That particular coronation lay ahead of him, however, when he greeted Jackie Stewart and proceeded to help him settle into Formula One for the 1965 season. Hill, after all, had seven seasons of Grand Prix racing behind him when the bouncy and innocent young Scot came into the BRM team. He could not have dreamt of a better teacher. 'From my point of view, he was the perfect team-mate,' said Stewart. 'A man who, above all, was one of the fairest men I have ever raced with. I came in as a real greenhorn, and I was going quite quickly. He could have made life difficult for me, but he never did.' Hill, of course, enjoyed the choice of engines and equipment when it was appropriate, but he had earned that privilege through his five years' service, and Stewart never complained. 'Graham's assistance was very valuable,' Stewart remarked to Engel, 'and he gave it in such a way that I shall always respect him for it. I don't think I'd have been able to learn so much on any other team.' He also appreciated Hill's polished professionalism. 'When 1965 came around, suddenly I was a Formula One driver. I was a Grand Prix driver! I was driving for BRM, with a really slick transporter and Graham Hill as my team-mate. Everybody was very professional. And you had to go testing! It was very intoxicating. The people I raced against were my heroes. Graham Hill was larger than life really in so many ways. There is nobody even close now to what Graham was as a character. He was very polished. Having somebody like me arrive in his team couldn't have been an easy thing to face because there were quite a few race tracks where I was quicker than Graham straight away.'

If a point on his debut in South Africa was a good start, Stewart was clearly not content. His second championship outing came at the end of May on the famous streets of Monte Carlo, a circuit with which Stewart would become almost as closely associated as Hill himself. He had already won that inaugural F3 event there the previous year, of course, and the experience could only stand him in good stead as he faced the challenge of guiding a Formula One car through that unforgiv-

ing cityscape. This time, Messrs Hill and Brabham comman-
deered the front row, but Stewart was right behind his
pole-sitting team-mate and just four-tenths of a second slower.
The Scot ran second to Hill in the opening stages, and led when
Graham took to an escape road to avoid a slow-moving Bob
Anderson in the Brabham. An uncharacteristic Stewart spin at
Ste Devote then ended his brief flirtation with first place. Hill's
superb comeback drive earned him his third consecutive
Monaco win, Stewart claiming his first top-three finish at a place
where the podium is an affair of a rather higher class than at
most circuits.

There is a footnote to that first Monaco F1 appearance. While
the unique venue produced its usual crop of incidents for Hill,
Dickie Attwood and others, it also gave Stewart his first taste of
the unforgiving nature of F1 racing at the limit. With 80 of the
100 laps gone, Monaco's tragic history almost repeated itself. A
decade earlier, Alberto Ascari had escaped relatively unharmed
after his Lancia plunged into the harbour; in 1965, it was the
turn of Australian Paul Hawkins, whose Lotus Climax clipped
the barrier at the chicane on exit from the tunnel, found the
then-standard straw bales useless, bypassed them and followed
Ascari's route into the waters of the Mediterranean. Hawkins,
too, escaped unhurt. Others, in years to come, would pay a far
greater price for their Monaco gamble.

The next stop on Stewart's first F1 world tour was a place that
would come back to haunt him. In mid-June, Clark was back
from Indianapolis duty and ready to resume normal Grand Prix
service at Spa Francorchamps where, like Hill in Monaco, he
had been victorious for the last three seasons. Stewart's heady
progress was underlined by the fact that there were two Scots
on that Belgian front row. Jackie, who had been driven around
the circuit in a Volkswagen Beetle, might have been 3.4 seconds
behind Hill's pole position, but that gap comes into focus when
we remember that a lap of Spa was then a journey of some 14.1
kilometres. It was to Stewart's considerable credit that he was

the only driver to remain in touch with Clark on the same lap when the two Scots reached the end of the race, giving their country her first one-two finish in a world championship race.

Sixth, third, and now second. Phrases like 'a duck to water' spring to mind, and given the heavy rain that fell on the Ardennes that year, they seem even more appropriate. To continue a watery metaphor, round four found everyone in the same boat. The French Grand Prix was staged, for the first time, in the beautiful countryside of the Auvergne, at Clermont-Ferrand. Perhaps reminded of his native heath, Stewart now moved up from third quickest in qualifying to second, behind the inevitable Clark, by half a second, as Scotland's speed twins started to take over. So it would remain: 40 laps of the eight-kilometre, undulating circuit where open-faced helmets were *de rigueur* saw Clark and Stewart come home in that order once again, the two of them more than two minutes clear of a pursuing field headed by Surtees in a Ferrari.

As Silverstone could then accommodate a four-car front row, Stewart was again right up there for the third race running when the British Grand Prix heralded the mid-point of his debut year. He did not keep company with Clark, Hill and Ginther for long, though, having a rather lonely race to fifth position, while Clark won as he pleased. Still, the half-term report could hardly have been more glowing: the new boy had finished every race, and what's more he had finished them all in the points. Only a victory could make the second half of his season better. It would.

Zandvoort, on 18 July, provided the third Scottish one-two of the 1965 season, with Clark having the upper hand as usual. Though Hill, by now referred to by Jackie as 'Grandpa' at every opportunity, planted his BRM on pole again, Stewart was relegated to the third row, but when Graham started losing ground midway through the race, the Dutch Grand Prix was in Clark's safe hands and it was left to Jackie to save the day for the Bourne team, passing Gurney's Brabham for second place before half-distance and holding on till the end of the 80-lap race.

Six races, four podiums, never out of the points – the law of averages dictated that Stewart must come a cropper some time. Ironically, it happened at the track that would later go down in history as the scene of his greatest drive. The fearsome Nürburgring measured no fewer than 22.81 kilometres, a distance the cars in the German Grand Prix were invited to cover fifteen times. Men such as Stewart's Ecurie Ecosse mentor David Murray had found the challenge daunting in their time; now it was wee Jackie's turn. On first acquaintance with the track in a Formula One car, Stewart showed scant respect: his early practice time of 8m 30.6s slashed a staggering nine seconds off Surtees' lap record. In preparation for this stunning effort, he had applied his usual detailed homework, including the use of a powerful Mercedes Benz, borrowed from Tony Rudd. The BRM team manager takes up the story. 'Mercedes lent me a very nice car which Jackie borrowed to learn the circuit. He felt his hired VW Beetle would not have enough steam. I could not believe my eyes when it was returned, and neither could Mercedes. There was not a mark on it, or much tread on the tyres, and the oil did not just leak, it poured out. It had also lost several speeds in its gearbox, but it was all in a good cause.' Saturday, for Jackie, brought further improvement to 8m 26.1s, a time only one man could better. No prizes for guessing who, and it was Clark's furious pace on the Sunday that proved Stewart's undoing. Trying valiantly to keep Clark, and Hill, in sight, Jackie became too closely acquainted with the Eifel scenery on lap three, bent a wishbone and chalked up a dreaded 'DNF' for the first time.

Between the inception of the world championship, in 1950, and the beginning of the 1965 season, Monza had seen eight winners in its fifteen races. Their names read like a roll of honour of Grand Prix racing at the time: first-ever world champion Giuseppe Farina, Ascari, Fangio, the two Hills Phil and Graham, and of course Clark; and alongside those six the peerless Moss, never champion but for many the greatest all-round driver of the lot, and his fellow Englishman the gifted but always understated Tony Brooks. Such was the list that Jackie Stewart was to join on 12 September.

Newly crowned world champion Clark put his 32-valve Climax to good use with pole position from Surtees, but once again Stewart was up there with them and just seven-tenths off Jim's pace. Those three and Graham Hill swapped the lead regularly in the first half of the 76-lap race, then Surtees succumbed to clutch trouble and Clark to a faulty fuel pump, leaving the two BRM drivers to go at it hammer and tongs. This they duly did, until Hill dropped a wheel on to the grass on his way out of the Parabolica. Stewart pounced, opened up a gap of 3.3 seconds, and tasted Grand Prix victory for the first time at an average speed of 209.961kph. 'Another Clark in the making?' enquired *The Times* in its report on what it called the 'race of the year'.

The *Glasgow Herald*, the daily paper closest to his home, was more prosaic and, without a correspondent of its own in Italy to record the Dumbarton boy's first victory, settled on publishing the Reuters version of events. The news agency reported that, at times, the gap between Stewart and Hill was only about 200 yards. Recalling the race later, Tony Rudd, BRM team manager and chief engineer, said he had spent much of its later stages attempting to signal to Hill and Stewart that it was stupid to race each other. 'Graham had recognised the challenge that was coming from Jackie that year,' he said. 'He never really showed it, but I could sense it. Then, at Monza, they were miles ahead of everyone else and the cars were running beautifully, and what do they do? The idiots raced each other. I tried everything I could to stop them but they just kept on at it. Graham went wide on the loose stuff, and that cost him two or three seconds, and Jackie came over the line in the lead. He won his first world championship race, but he couldn't understand why we weren't all clapping him and patting him on the back, or saying, "Wonderful!" Idiot!'

But Rudd was certainly not among those surprised to see Stewart successful in the old royal park. 'He seemed to settle into the team so well, and pretty quickly,' he remembered. 'He was obviously a bit shy and a little nervous at first, but he soon got over that. Once he got into his car, and the flag fell, you always got 101 per cent out of him. Jackie would stick his neck out. Jackie would always have a go.' This attitude in his driving also helped endear Stewart to BRM's larger-than-life chairman Louis Stanley, who was to be such a stalwart supporter of the moves, inspired by Jackie, to bring improved safety to Grand Prix motor racing. In his memoirs, he picked out Monza in 1965 as his favourite Stewart win of the era 'because of the manner in which it was achieved'. In Stanley's view, 'Hill, on the outside, made a slight error of judgement, put his wheels on the loose gravel, and lost six seconds to Stewart . . . That night at our celebration dinner, we watched a replay of the episode on slow-motion film . . . They must have been anxious moments, but there were no hard feelings.'

The tension surrounding that finish, however, took the gloss off his first win for Stewart. As he told Engel, 'Graham came up to me afterwards and said it wasn't my fault, but I wasn't sure whether he was just being nice to me, so as not to spoil my big occasion. Later on we all sat round at dinner and watched the race on television. The whole team! It was a tense moment. Fortunately, it showed that he had been slightly behind me when he went off. So it cleared my conscience. But during the time I should have been most elated I had this funny little feeling inside me that didn't quite allow my excitement to bubble over. So, although it was my first Grand Prix win, it was somewhat spoilt. In fact, the feeling of anti-climax was so strong that when I won at Monte Carlo the following May, I genuinely felt it to be my first Grand Prix win. I had forgotten Monza.'

In October, the two long-haul races that finished off Stewart's first season were incident-packed, to say the least. At Watkins Glen he qualified sixth, elbowed his way through to third by lap six, spent twenty minutes in the pits with a broken throttle cable and discovered he had bent a wishbone on a kerb while passing Ginther's Honda on the opening lap. In Mexico, he was feeling off-colour, lost an engine in practice, suffered a suspension failure and used the spare car, only to retire with clutch failure after 36 laps. Still, after qualifying eighth he had made it through to second on the opening lap.

A maiden victory, three second places, one third, one fifth and one sixth – for a new boy it was not a bad return. With the six best scores retained, Stewart dropped that historic point from his first Grand Prix at Kyalami, kept a total of 33 and finished third overall behind Clark and Hill. Not only that, he was also only the fourth driver in world championship history to win a race in his debut season, the others being Farina in the inaugural event at Silverstone, Fangio, also in 1950, and Giancarlo Baghetti in 1961. 'I never thought I would get so far this year,' Stewart had admitted amid the Monza euphoria. 'I had set out really just to learn my way very carefully.' In 1996, he put it all into perfect perspective: 'Just because he gets to Formula One, it doesn't mean a guy is home and dry. I only really came of age as a driver in 1968, and I'd been in Formula One in 1965, 1966 and 1967.' The three taps on the table as he counted out the years emphasised the point. There was still some serious learning to do.

Yet it could not have seemed that way when the 1966 season got into gear. For a handful of Grand Prix drivers, including Stewart, it began in the Antipodes with the Tasman Series, then in its heyday. In a part of the world with a magnificent motor racing heritage, the Tasman Series, which had been going since 1961, allowed international aces to try out new features and run themselves in before the world championship season began. Brabham, Moss, Gurney, Clark, Hill, Surtees – all had preceded

Stewart on trips Down Under, and Clark was the reigning Tasman champion when Stewart made his first foray at the height of summer in the southern hemisphere. Six pole positions, five fastest laps and four wins later, Stewart had succeeded Clark as Tasman Series winner.

A leading light in Australian motor racing in the same era was David McKay, who became the first Australian touring car champion in a 3.4-litre Jaguar in 1960, around the time when Jackie Stewart was taking his own first tentative steps in motor sport. McKay went on to become a considerable force in national motor racing, largely through his Scuderia Veloce and the car he fondly knew as 'The Old Lady', a Ferrari 250LM which Stewart himself would soon be driving. 'The first time I met him,' McKay recalled at his New South Wales property in 2003, 'would have been at the beginning of 1966 when he came here for the Tasman, and he was a new face. An agreeable sort of a boy, you know? In a way he reminded me of Moss in that he was springy in his walk around the place; he was always bouncing around like Moss. Moss can't ever sit still. There was the same magnetism, I suppose, for those who were watching.'

For local drivers such as McKay, the Tasman Series was an annual opportunity to pit themselves against the best in the world. For the spectators who flocked to Australian and New Zealand circuits with exotic names like Pukekohe and Warwick Farm, it was heaven. In the brief period of Stewart's involvement, from 1966 to 1967, the regulations allowed for engine capacities ranging from 1.5 to 2.5 litres and a weight limit of 450kg minimum and 500kg maximum. His BRM took its first victory of that 1966 campaign in the third round at Pukekohe on 8 January, having led all the way; his second came three weeks later at Invercargill. Though they had travelled to the other side of the world, they had not escaped from the grim realities of 1960s motor racing: that race was stopped after 45 of the planned 50 laps when local driver Bill Cadwell crashed fatally. Victories at Sandown Park, Melbourne, and Longford in

Tasmania – the place that had cost Timmy Mayer his life and opened the Tyrrell door to Jackie Stewart – made the Scot champion with 42 points from his best six placings. He would be back later in the year.

With South Africa dropping off the calendar – the race was run at Kyalami, but as a non-championship event – the world championship season began in earnest in Monaco in late May. But the pecking order was about to change. The Commission Sportive Internationale (CSI), the sport's ruling body of the period, had decreed three full years earlier that 1966 would see the 'Return to Power' in the shape of a three-litre Formula One. The drivers themselves had originally lobbied for two litres, to distinguish F1 more starkly from F2, then changed their minds and backed the three-litre option. But the announcement in 1964 of Coventry Climax's intended withdrawal at the end of 1965 had left most British teams in a state of disarray as this new day dawned. In short, 1966 was an engine year in more ways than the sport's governing body had intended. Where to get the power from, and how, became the dominant questions. With a well-fettled V12 from the sportscar arena at their disposal, Ferrari started as red-hot favourites; newcomers such as McLaren struggled with a sportscar-bred Serenissima; Dan Gurney's Eagles flew at first rather slowly with an interim 2.7-litre Coventry Climax, while waiting for Harry Weslake to perfect his own V12; Cooper turned to Maserati, by whose English concessionaire they were now owned; and later in the year a man called Brabham would mate his cars with a power unit called a Repco, the brainchild of Aussies Frank Hallam and Phil Irving, and begin rewriting history in his own fashion. Honda would also make their distinctive mark by season's end with a rasping V12.

And BRM? Well, there should have been no problem, but as usual BRM contrived to make a simple situation complex, and most of the complexity came in the form of an engine called the H16. As its name suggests, this idiosyncratic device was in fact two V8s piled one on top of the other after first being 'flattened', as it were. It was essentially two 'boxer' units mated through a common crankcase. At a time when a much-loved song was taking the Beach Boys to the top of the charts, the only vibrations to emanate from the H16 were anything but good, as they and customers Lotus would find to dispiriting effect.

But as Monaco loomed, the H16 was still in the future as far as competitive racing was concerned. Hill and Stewart went to the Côte d'Azur equipped with bored-out two-litre V8 engines as a stopgap measure, and as things turned out they were just about the only two that did not stop on that curious Monte Carlo weekend. Of the sixteen cars that lined up on the grid, only seven had three-litre engines; of those seven, not one finished, and of the twenty starters just four were classified, the smallest number ever in a world championship event. Lorenzo Bandini's second-placed Ferrari was one; the other three were all BRMs.

Practice had started well for the works twosome of Hill and Stewart, Jackie outrunning his more experienced colleague, but by the time the race came round Clark and Surtees had usurped their front-row positions and the Bourne cars took off from the second row. Which is more than Clark did from his pole position: the Lotus stuck in first, allowing Surtees to race into the lead with Stewart hard on his heels. By lap fifteen, the BRM was past the ailing Ferrari, and as the other machinery fell by the Monegasque wayside Stewart took the chequered flag by 40.21 seconds from Bandini, Hill and BRM privateer Bob Bondurant, better known for his excellent sportscar driving. Stewart had his own problems. 'I suddenly lost fifth,' he revealed, 'and had to go straight from fourth to sixth, which made things more than a little difficult on the uphill sections; but otherwise the car went perfectly.' If only his team had been able to drive around difficulties with similar ease. It was the last BRM victory for four years and sixteen days; another 46 world championship races came and went before the brilliant little

Mexican Pedro Rodriguez took the chequered flag at Spa in June 1970. It would also be another two years and one month until victory number three came along for Jackie Stewart, by which time he and BRM chairman Louis Stanley's men would have gone their separate ways.

There were nine rounds in the 1966 calendar. In the eight that followed Monaco, Stewart would have the biggest accident of his career, miss one as a result of the injuries he suffered, fail to finish five times including the last three races of the year, and score points on just two other occasions. The first of them was at Spa Francorchamps on 12 June, the fateful race described in greater detail in chapter seven. During the meet, there was time for a little badinage with the visiting David McKay. 'The next time I saw Jackie,' he recalled, 'was at Spa – always a great spot, because it was a lovely situation. I always spent a lot of time with [motor racing writer] Denis Jenkinson. I remember sitting with him at a roadside café at Burnenville and having a Stella. Jenks would be talking, and it was as though he was giving me all the insider stuff on Formula One. Coming from Australia, it was a rare thing to see it at first hand. As we watched there, the cars would drift past, within two or three feet of *our* feet, in about a 140mph drift. There was the wee Scot coming past lap after lap. When we went back to the pits, he [Jackie] said to me, "Did you like it down at Burnenville?" I said, "Did you have time to look?" "Oh yes," he said. "It's a photographic sort of thing. I could see you there with Jenks." '

The laughing stopped when Stewart broke his collarbone in a first-lap accident. That kept him out of round three in France, at Reims, but he was glad to be fit for battle again when the series reached Brands Hatch in mid-July. While England's footballers were carrying their country to fever pitch with their triumphant World Cup exploits, neither of Scotland's drivers could do the same for theirs on the race track. Brabham had chosen France to launch a four-race winning streak that virtually guaranteed him a third world title. Stewart qualified eighth at Brands and retired with a sick engine after seventeen laps. His grid position was the same a week later in Zandvoort, though this time he came home fourth; and at the Nürburgring on 7 August he used a front-row start to claim his final points of the year in fifth place. The trip to Australia to drive McKay's Ferrari in a 12-Hour race at Surfers' Paradise later that month might have been a busman's holiday, but it must have come as something of a relief.

It was Stewart's status as an already established star of the F1 scene that had prompted the call to arms, as McKay confirmed. 'The promoter got in touch with me and said, "Would you be prepared to have Jackie Stewart drive the LM in the race?" I had to think a bit, because it wasn't a BRM, it was my car, and if anything happened to it I'd be down the spout in the biggest possible way because I had the contract with a petrol company to do most of the year with it. Anyway, we came to an agreeable sum, which was very big for those days: from memory it was about $14,000, because we'd just gone to dollars in Australia. I forget how we split it up with Jackie, but I imagine it was the same as I had done with Graham Hill, which was £1,500 sterling cut up £800 to me as the owner and £700 to Graham. I said it would be a good idea, and of course he wanted Jackie there as a draw card, a big draw card, particularly in the LM. There was another LM from Britain, Jackie Epstein with Paul Hawkins; there was also a P2/P3 Ferrari prototype, for David Piper and Dickie Attwood, and the McLaren/Sutcliffe GT40 from the Ford works. So it was all building up to be quite a good thing. Jackie eventually came, and he was put into a motel on the main Gold Coast highway called the El Dorado, which, I thought, was a very appropriate thing! I went round to see him. Everyone's in their Hawaiian shirts and so on, and there's little Jackie looking very pale from overseas, but very business-like. I found it very comforting that he understood he was driving for me as a privateer and not as a big works-entered team. We went around to see the car and to practise the pit stops. He was very keen to help with the boys, and of course they all thought he was great.'

Little wonder. Towards the end of the 1966 season, despite BRM's recent mediocre showings on the Grand Prix tracks, Stewart's star was in the ascendant. He was hailed as the heir apparent to Jim Clark and the man of the future. In October of that year, in a profile written by Robert Hunter, the *Weekly Scotsman* described him in faintly archaic terms as 'The Globe Trotting Ton-Up Scot'. It was an expression that stayed around a long time. Some of the details of Jackie's life at that time make for interesting reading. 'He never smokes, and his drinking is confined to the occasional Dubonnet and lemonade or a glass of celebration champagne,' reported Hunter. 'In fact, he is so conscious of the effects of even the smallest amount of alcohol on his highly tuned nervous system that he never touches a drop of it during the two days before a race.' Even then, it seemed, Stewart was keen to establish his body as a temple of purity prepared to give of its best in support of the man's overwhelmingly Calvinistic work ethic. 'He sleeps a full eight to nine hours whenever possible, and he hired a physiotherapist to teach him how to relax his body completely at every available opportunity. In this way, he ensures that his vital store of nervous energy is not run down by his fantastic travel schedule, which last year involved flying the equivalent of eight times around the world.' He was, it also said, developing his famous techniques of mind and manners management. 'A wide range of expressions chase across his pointed features, from a wide-eyed, daft-wee-Scots-laddie innocence through a young executive beetling of the eyebrows to an impish, infectious grin that has been known to charm Princess Grace of Monaco and disarm a hard-bitten American speed cop.' In the same article, this special ability to relax, or concentrate, when required was put forward as a primary reason for his success, and the main reason why 'many people who meet him casually' were so puzzled by his occasional memory lapse.

Stewart's co-driver Down Under was Kiwi Andy Buchanan, a good head taller than the Scot. As McKay recounted, Jackie fixed him with his gimlet eye and announced that one of them was going to be very uncomfortable in a bucket seat that was difficult to adjust. Six laps down to the Ford, with two hours to run, Stewart hunted the leaders down and won the race for McKay, though it was not declared official until ten days later after a mix-up in the complex lap-charting. 'He was great,' McKay insisted. 'Right through the whole weekend, which was pretty serious sort of stuff for me . . . to have somebody like Jackie was just great. Graham [Hill] had driven for me before, but this was a different thing: there was a lot more money tied up in the 250 than there was in the Cooper or Brabhams. Particularly as I'd taken virtually all the money from the petrol company instead of putting it aside to run the team for the whole year. I'd taken a punt and spent it on the car, so I was pretty nervous. But he was very helpful.'

Back home, in that summer of 1966, Jackie took over the family garage in Dumbuck, rigging all the mechanics at the premises in green and inviting his best motor racing friends to join him at an official opening ceremony on 30 August. Not long before, he, Jim Clark and Graham Hill had been to Indianapolis where mechanical failure had deprived Stewart of a win and Hill had claimed a famous triumph. The trio met at Glasgow airport that afternoon, Clark and Hill having flown into Scotland aboard their private planes, a four-seater Piper Comanche and a six-seater Piper Aztec respectively, while Jackie had chosen a commercial flight. 'I am not convinced that a private plane is worthwhile for me,' said the man who admitted he had flown more than 168,000 miles the previous year.

On the track, at Monza (fuel leak) and Watkins Glen (engine failure), and in Mexico City (oil leak), Jackie's season continued in the doldrums. A final 1966 world championship tally of fourteen points, good enough only for seventh overall, was the second lowest of his nine-year stay in Formula One. His worst came the very next year. 'Winning isn't everything,' the incomparable Arnold Palmer once opined, 'but wanting to is.' But, much as Jackie Stewart might have wanted to win in 1967, he simply couldn't. It was the only winless season of his nine in Grand Prix racing, and he garnered just ten points from the eleven world championship rounds, with two podium finishes and a staggering nine failures to make the chequered flag. Apart from brake failure in Holland, those DNFs were all attributable to engine or engine-related problems, from crown wheel and pinion to fuel injection, vibration to throttle linkage. Only one man had taken the dreaded H16 to a race victory, and, yes, that man was Jim Clark, at Monza in 1966. While Stewart and new team-mate Mike Spence wrestled manfully with the H16, 1967 would pass into sporting legend as the year when Clark and Hill, gone to Lotus after seven years with BRM, got their eager hands on the Ford Cosworth DFV.

The second day of the year saw Stewart retire from the South African Grand Prix, for which he had qualified ninth, when his H16 cried 'Enough!' with fewer than three laps gone. From mid-January to early March they were off to the colonies again, as David McKay used to put it. This time there was to be a Scottish one-two in the Tasman Series, though Clark's five wins to Stewart's two saw Jim regain the title. Clark would return and win again in 1968, by which time Stewart's Tasman days were over. 'I found later, when he came back the next year, 1967, to defend his championship,' said McKay, 'that unlike a lot of the thin-lipped species and the rather mean-faced stars that we would get here, Jackie was always quite open and prepared to help anybody with things like tyre pressures. In those days, all we had was the tyre pressures, the roll-bar or the shock absorber setting and the gear ratio settings, and he wasn't ever backward in giving advice. It was friendly advice, and helpful, whereas some of them would say, "Oh, I don't know what it is. You'll have to ask the mechanic." And, of course, the mechanic knew that if he opened his mouth he was in big trouble. Again, it was the same as Moss, who would tell anybody the gear ratios, the tyre pressures, because he knew he'd beat the pants off them anyway. It didn't matter what he told them. They'd have no hope!'

The Tasman interludes were a break from the hard work of Europe, but they brought their own problems. 'The main thing was of course the change in temperature. It was a huge thing,' said McKay, whose English education made him fully aware of the climatic differences. 'They all came out looking so bloody pale, it was incredible. It was fun, because it was entirely different, the whole atmosphere. It was fun, tremendous fun, with lots of parties, but once the official practice began it was just as tight as any bloody Grand Prix. They had to perform, because next year was coming up, it was really cut-and-thrust stuff, but then they'd go water-skiing together, eat barbecues and play cricket matches. They liked to go out on the harbour. They were very happy to be here; it was home from home. A lot of them would pick up where they left off the year before. I can't think of anyone who wasn't welcome here.

'Most of us were fawning over them and hoping we could buy something from them, which wasn't the case with Jackie, of course, because the cars were not for sale, although I think the last time they came out the BRMs, at the end of the series at Longford, under the management of Tim Parnell – 'Large Tim' – you could have bought the two cars and what was left in their fairly large box of spares – it was all they had; they pretty well swept it all up and sent it out to the colonies – for £15,000. Now, that wasn't a lot of money, but it would have cost a lot of money to keep the bloody things going. Someone asked, "Does that include the mechanics?"

'The drivers did make the point that they felt the best meeting they had every year was Warwick Farm. That was the best run, the one they enjoyed most. Geoff [Sykes, manager and clerk of the course] was very good, first-rate; so understated, no noise or anything. I think Jackie had a great deal of confidence in himself. He could afford to take what I call the motorcycle line, the long entrance and the long exit, instead of trying to keep them out. I think he felt that if anybody else was going quicker they deserved to go past him. But they didn't go past him. He was very much the pacemaker.'

Setting the pace, however, was not the BRM's forte when it came to world championship racing in 1967, Jackie's first season as an outright number one driver following Hill's decision to leave and partner Clark at Lotus. He had spent seven years with BRM, won the championship and tutored Stewart; for him, he said, it was time to move before he felt too much like part of the furniture. Stewart was the new boy in favour, but it was not much of a year to savour. He started from sixth place on the grid but reached only lap fifteen at Monaco in May; a month later, the BRM flattered to deceive by taking him to lap 51 of the Dutch Grand Prix.

At the time, Jackie was receiving his first approaches from Ferrari, later to be rejected in no uncertain terms when Stewart was apparently played off against Jacky Ickx in a negotiating game by the Old Man. 'I did not much care for Ferrari's way of working with drivers,' Stewart told Dymock. 'In particular, I had heard about him [Enzo Ferrari] pushing drivers to be competitive with each other within the team and rather upsetting the emotional side of motor racing.' This was an understatement, given what followed. Approached by Keith Ballisat of Shell, who was keen to see him join the Scuderia, Jackie travelled unwillingly to Maranello in June. He was, he said, impressed with the place, despite his misgivings. Nothing was decided at that meeting, but on his next visit Stewart received the special treatment reserved for more revered guests. Ferrari met him at the gate, and both engine maestro Franco Gozzi and team manager Franco Lini joined their talks at the famous restaurant across the road from the works' entrance. An agreement was reached informally, and Jackie handed the work of concluding a contract to his lawyers. Then, he said, he heard the news that Ferrari had offered the drive to Jacky Ickx 'because Jackie

Stewart had asked for too much money'. Having shaken hands with Ferrari, Jackie was stunned and confused. It was just what he had feared. He called Ballisat to tell him that any deal with Ferrari was now over and done with, a move that resulted, ultimately, in Ferrari spreading anti-Stewart rumours that were untrue. Ferrari suggested he had been used to raise his price with Ford, but this, said Jackie, was wrong. 'In fact, I didn't even have a deal at the time,' he said, explaining that he was still talking to BRM because they had decided to build a V12 and had offered him very good money to stay. According to Engel, this show of loyalty was a strain on Jackie who, like Ken Tyrrell, 'didn't like doing something behind their backs'.

With all this going on in the background, Jackie's return to Spa Francorchamps in mid-June brought his first finish in seven races, and a good one it was too. Leading at one stage, after Clark had pitted, Stewart then struck gear selector problems and drove virtually one-handed while holding the recalcitrant lever in gear with the other. It was another historic day: Stewart came second in the only Grand Prix ever won by Dan Gurney in his All-American Eagle-Weslake, generally acknowledged as one of the most beautiful cars in Formula One history.

Belgium, then, accounted for six of Stewart's ten points in 1967; the next round, the French Grand Prix, provided the other four. On the almost risibly short, and boring, Bugatti Circuit at Le Mans, this was a race of attrition in which Stewart's BRM – he took Parnell's V8 version instead of the H16 car – for once held together long enough for the Scot to claim third place behind Brabham and his team-mate Hulme. Then a catalogue of disasters followed, Stewart forced to retire from six Grands Prix in a row, his one front-row start of the season coming on 6 August at the Nürburgring where he ran third before dropping out on lap six. With just those ten points, and ninth place overall, the writing was clearly on the wall, and for Stewart it did not spell 'BRM' or 'H16'. Nor did it read 'Maranello'. In fact, it was time to take the French dictionary out.

6. FRENCH LESSONS

'Those Froggies must have given you too much to drink!'
                              Jackie Stewart to Ken Tyrrell in 1965

Anyone attending a world championship round at Magny-Cours, in the rural Nièvre *département* where Charolais cows outnumber the agricultural people and their cars, might be forgiven for thinking the French have no soul when it comes to motor racing. The opposite, of course, is true. A country whose heritage includes names such as Le Mans, Bugatti, Gordini, Jean-Pierre Wimille, Maurice Trintignant and Jean Behra richly deserves its place in the pantheon of automotive competition. In the mid-1960s, however, France had no major player on the world championship stage. Two decades after leaving Fortress Europe in disarray, the British had come back, this time as a sporting army, and their invading force was sweeping all before it on four wheels. But anyone taking a look at the motor sport results from early May 1965 would have seen the signs of a French renaissance. It was May Day at Reims, but there was no SOS: Jean-Pierre Beltoise beat allcomers in the Formula Three race, though it was less the driver than the vehicle he was driving that mattered in this context.

It was an MS5, the MS standing for 'Matra Sport'. 'Matra' itself was an acronym derived from Mécanique-Aviation-Traction, Engins Matra, a French company established pre-war and now a major player in the arms and aeronautics industries. A move into the automobile sector was made when Matra aligned themselves with René Bonnet and his small Djet car in 1964. In that same year, Matra Sport was set up under the leadership of one Jean-Luc Lagardère. Establishing his headquarters at Vélizy, near Paris, Lagardère set about rebuilding France's reputation as a maker of first-class racing cars and engines.

Those halcyon days brought a smile to the face of a certain François Guiter at Magny-Cours in 2003, as he looked back on the beginnings of another French company that was to loom large in the Stewart history – Elf. Guiter was in on the ground floor when Elf embarked on what we would now call a branding offensive, just as Stewart was preparing to launch himself on to the international scene. 'We conducted a major marketing research project,' Guiter explained, 'and what came out was racing. So we looked at racing – I'd never seen a motor race in my life – and we realised the French had been pretty good at it: Delahaye, Delage, Talbot, Gordini, drivers like Wimille and Sommer. But there was nobody left. So we rather pretentiously said, "We're going to put France back on top of the racing world." We looked around for someone to do it with us, and we came across a company that was making missiles, wanted to get better known, but had the same problem as us: all they did was secret stuff, so the engineers were growing a bit frustrated. So we had talks with these Matra people, who were headed up by the brilliant engineer Jean-Luc Lagardère – who, sadly, has just died – and decided to go into a four-year deal with them three or four months before the launch of our own brand. We introduced it at the Grand Prix . . . no, the Monte Carlo Rally. We said, "Right, first we'll win in Formula Three, which no one has yet done, and build a Formula One engine; in our second year we'll win in Formula Two; in the third year we'll win in Formula One; and in the fourth we'll win Le Mans." Everyone just fell about laughing. But we did it.'

Stewart's French lessons had, in fact, already begun by that time. She might not have had a great driver or team for some time, but France boasted some of the most compelling racing in Europe in the shape of a series of Formula Two events all over the country. Veteran Swiss journalist Gérard 'Jabby' Crombac was heavily involved in organising the series. 'In 1964,' he recalled nearly four decades later, 'we set up the Trophées de France. In fact at that time we called them the French Grand Prix, because there were quite a few circuits in France and the Grand Prix alternated from Rouen to Reims to Clermont-

Ferrand. In the years when there was no Grand Prix we had to do something to keep the circuits going. So Toto Roche from Reims [a leading figure in French motor racing administration, well known in the 1960s, in Louis Stanley's words, for 'wielding the flag with unpredictable abandon' in his capacity as official starter of the French Grand Prix] had the idea of setting up these "French Grands Prix", and they were hugely successful. We had picked up from the early 1950s, when F1 became F2. France had a series of races, one of which was the ACF Grand Prix at Rouen, and the others were very successful. So we did the same thing.'

And it worked, especially from the French spectators' point of view. 'The F2 races were terrific,' Crombac enthused, 'because from the organisers' point of view you had all the best drivers in the world, all the world champions, for a lower price. Because while they got paid the same, the car they drove only cost about a quarter. We consistently had Jim Clark, Graham Hill, Jack Brabham, three recent world champions, and then we had John Surtees, Jackie Stewart – we had them all. We had virtually the same crowds as for F1 races, but fewer journalists, because it was French and mainly of interest to a French audience, even though they were largely international drivers. It caused a lot of jealousy among other race organisers. People like Clark and Hill wouldn't go, usually, unless they happened to have a free weekend, but they always came for the Grands Prix de France. It was looked upon as a Formula Two World Championship. There was a European championship, but that was only for the lesser-known drivers.'

By a happy coincidence, of course, a certain K. Tyrrell was simultaneously making his way towards the top of the motor racing tree on the opposite side of the Channel. Crombac himself was instrumental in bridging the Anglo-French divide and bringing the two parties together. Lagardère made Ken the offer of a Matra chassis in 1965, and as Crombac said, Tyrrell had nothing to lose so he agreed. 'When he got home he telephoned Jackie to tell him about the deal he'd done, and Jackie said, "Those Froggies must have given you too much to drink!" Then they sent the engine, it was installed, and they sent the Matra F3 car with the F2 engine to Goodwood in a Bristol freighter normally used for Lagardère's racehorses. Jackie got in, did three laps, stopped, and told Ken, "This is the best chassis I've ever driven. I've never had so much grip. It puts the power down better than anything." Because of the fuel tank system, borrowed from aerospace, the car was incredibly stiff, which meant you could soften the springs. It was the best chassis around, and Jackie was sold on it straight away. Ken went to Paris the next day to negotiate with Lagardère, who had also just done the deal with Elf. They set up Matra International, with Ken, and the Matra team.'

Matra and Tyrrell, then, both worked their way through the F3 and F2 categories *en route* to their common destination. Ken's Cooper BRM machinery was off the F2 pace by the end of 1965, so with Stewart and 'the other Jacky', Ickx of Belgium, at the wheel, he used Matras for his 1966 campaign. It would have made little difference what he used, though, for that year was one of total Honda domination in the hands of Brabham and Hulme. For 1967, though, when F2 grew from a one-litre to a 1600cc category, Ickx used the MS7 powered by a Ford DFA four-cylinder engine to claim the European crown. Matra were already hard at work on a racing V12, but for now it was their chassis that interested Ken. An engine called the DFV had redrawn the F1 battle-lines in 1967 and was now available to customers at a reported price of £7,500 per unit. Stewart was on the lookout for a new F1 home, Tyrrell had served his managerial apprenticeship. Sometimes things just come to-gether. In this case, it was a tale of mind over matter. Both BRM and Ferrari were bigger and better equipped, not to mention better financed, than the Tyrrell Racing Organisation, yet Tyrrell, short on ready money and running racing cars from a shed in a timber yard, was high on improvisation and imagination. He knew Stewart, he knew he wanted him in his team, and he knew that it would work. 'At one point, I thought I was going to go to Ferrari,' conceded Stewart, 'but then Ken said, "Why don't you come and drive in Formula One with me?" I replied, "But, Ken, you don't have a Formula One team," to which he said, "What if I did have one?" So I said, 'Oh, Ken, you couldn't afford what Ferrari have offered to pay." '

In our modern world of Formula One motor racing, such a scenario would be rejected as preposterous and unbelievable, but in 1967 it happened. Tyrrell had harboured ambitions of running in Formula One with Jackie throughout the final year of their Formula Two association and knew that the wee Scot was in talks with both BRM and Ferrari. He was not put off. Relying on his ability to earn trust and faith in others, Tyrrell set about persuading Stewart that, if he wished to be successful in Grand Prix racing, he needed a Ford Cosworth DFV engine in a Matra chassis; at the same time, he set about persuading Walter Hayes, the vice president of Ford Europe from 1967 to 1991, that it would be tantamount to utter neglect of the Scottish race and the British empire if he allowed Stewart to accept an offer from Ferrari without putting up the support required to keep him in Britain racing with a competitive Ford-badged engine behind him.

'I asked him [Stewart] how much he wanted,' Tyrrell recalled. 'He said £20,000. Well, I didn't have 20,000 pennies, never mind pounds, so I went to Walter Hayes and told him about Jackie's offer from Ferrari. I told him that I thought Jackie would come with me and that I felt I could find the money to do it, but that in order to get things moving I needed £20,000. I asked him if he would guarantee that amount for me, whether I found the money or not, and he said, "You're on." Then I told Jackie I'd done the deal, so we had to find the money.' Together, they persuaded Dunlop to part with £80,000 to run the team and secured the chassis from Matra. Tyrrell ordered three

Cosworth engines, and gearboxes, and did all the race preparation in Surrey; then they called Hayes, thanked him and explained they had no need for the money guaranteed. 'That's how we did it,' said Tyrrell. 'We did it together all the way. When we needed money, we'd go out together to find some.' Elf, the French fuel company in search of a new image, also supported the team as the main sponsors. 'Sponsorship covered the team and drivers at first,' said Guiter. 'And these were drivers of a different era. The first year Jackie was champion we paid him £80,000, if I remember rightly, and the next year we asked how much he wanted and he said £80,000. I think that's about what Schumacher now earns in a day . . . At first it was with the team, him included, but later we had a personal deal with him.' The new-look car was to be painted French blue (Crombac's magazine *Sport-Auto* ran a reader competition to come up with suggested liveries), though, as we shall see, it did not quite start out that way.

BRM, of course, were sorry to lose their man. Hill had left the year before, for Lotus, and now Stewart, having rejected Ferrari, left for Tyrrell. In many ways he had never left him, having continued his association with the towering Englishman in Formula Two, in one of Ken's Matras, while racing in Formula One for Sir Alfred Owen's racing organisation. 'I was sorry we were losing Jackie,' said Tony Rudd. 'We had given him the car for his first world championship win and he had stuck with us loyally through a very miserable season [1967]. He started as very much the new boy in a team dominated by Graham, but he soon developed his own style and personality, and became very much one of the team. Following his crash at Spa, he became a little more sober, but the irrepressible sense of humour was still there.'

Jackie's final year at BRM might have been disappointing, but it had compensations in unexpected areas, not least in Formula Two, where the Tyrrell–Matra relationship burgeoned and where he raced against, and developed a friendship with, the rising Austrian star Jochen Rindt. In 1967, Rindt was the man to beat in that series, winning nine of the fifteen races he entered; he finished second in four others and won both the French and the British championships. Stewart, respectful of Rindt's enormous natural talent, also noticed his singularity and determination; these were qualities he understood and later admired from close quarters when, for tax reasons, he moved to Switzerland in April 1968 and became Jochen's neighbour at Begnins, near Geneva. At first, though, he had regarded Rindt as something of an enigma, a man who mixed very little, who had set ideas, and who was a bit unyielding on and off the circuit. 'He drove in Formula Two with enormous verve and obvious pleasure, but in a wild sort of way without somehow ever arriving at the accident,' said Stewart. 'He seemed to have a flair for getting the car into apparently ridiculous positions, crazy angles, as he slid through the corners, and yet he always got it back into shape.' It was in the second half of 1967, with the introduction by Dunlop of their 970 compound tyres, that Stewart raced on terms with Rindt in Formula Two, winning four major races.

If by late 1967 Stewart was coming of age in Grand Prix terms, he was also maturing as a father and family man. His first son Paul was by then a toddler, playing in a toy car, and his second son Mark was on his way, coming into the world in January 1968. Jackie, therefore, had responsibilities beyond himself and was thinking of broader horizons than his next deal and his next race. 'I wouldn't want my son [Paul] to be a racing driver,' he revealed in an interview with the *Glasgow Herald*. 'I love him dearly and I wouldn't like to think of anything happening to him.' Tellingly, he also referred to his close relationship with Jim Clark, a friendship that was to end within a matter of months in the most abrupt and brutal way at Hockenheim. He also dismissed the notion that he was driving for the money. 'It's a good life, but it's not an easy life. I'm sure I imagined that golfers earned astronomical sums, but I think they probably work for it as well. None of us races for money.

For me, it is purely an accident that I got paid to drive a racing car. I would be paying to drive. I enjoy it immensely. There is nothing else I have ever enjoyed so much. The pleasure of driving a racing car is something I haven't been able to experience doing anything else. Being able to feel that car, and feel the road, and be able to take it to its absolute limit, right to the edge . . . I suppose, because it's dangerous, this gives the extra thrill. This is where money doesn't exist.'

As the 1968 season approached, Lagardère and his troops were hard at work on their V12, planning to run it in their own chassis under the banner of Matra Sport, while Tyrrell did his own thing (didn't he always?) as Matra International. Stewart would start the year on his own, Frenchman Johnny Servoz-Gavin stepping up to F1 later on. Matra would run their M11, Tyrrell the M10, but not in South Africa. Although intended only as a hack to do some onerous testing work, the MS9 was pressed into service by Tyrrell for the opening race on New Year's Day at Kyalami.

There have been many beautiful racing cars over the years, but the MS9 deserves no place among them. It was the ugliest of ducklings. Lagardère even sent it out with livery in a particularly distasteful shade of green in what was seen by some as an attempt to dissuade Tyrrell from actually racing the car. It had only been finished on Christmas Day, so when it appeared in practice under a week later it was still in its curious matt-green undercoat. Undeterred by aesthetic considerations, Stewart promptly parked the newcomer on the front row of the Kyalami grid in the company of world champions Clark and Hill. He then had the Scottish effrontery to put his French machine into the race lead, though he was relegated to third just past the quarter-distance and had to retire after 44 laps when a con-rod broke. The repair bill, Tyrrell's first as a Grand Prix entrant, was £1,700 for an engine rebuild.

It would be five months and one week until Jackie Stewart next contested a world championship event, a period during which the structure of his racing life was to be tipped upside down and Formula One changed utterly. The death of Jim Clark, in an incomprehensible accident during a Formula Two race at Hockenheim on 7 April, shocked everyone in the sport. Three weeks later, in a Formula Two event at Jarama near Madrid, Jackie damaged his right wrist (he suffered a fractured scaphoid) when he crashed at the end of the straight during practice. He missed the Spanish Grand Prix at that same circuit two weeks later, and was effectively sentenced to a spell during which he had more than enough time to ponder the loss of his compatriot and the brutality of his occupation. 'I was more upset by that than I have ever been over anything,' said Stewart. 'This is the part of motor racing I dislike most. We are a closely knit bunch of people and we live very much together. Sometimes, I think it is a very futile and meaningless business.' The whole world of Grand Prix racing turned out, it seemed, for Clark's funeral in the hushed churchyard at Chirnside, near his home in the Scottish Borders, on a cold spring day. If it can happen to Clark, they muttered, it can happen to anyone.

But the show went on. In Spain, Beltoise deputised. For Monaco, with the Frenchman moving back to the 'national' team, it was his compatriot Servoz-Gavin who came into the 'proper' MS10 for the still indisposed Stewart. His wasn't a bad effort, either: Servoz-Gavin qualified on the front row and led until lap four when his car's driveshaft broke. When Jackie was finally fit to race again, at the Belgian Grand Prix on the second weekend in June, the Ardennes scenery might have looked familiar, but Clark's absence meant that the F1 landscape had been altered for ever. Qualifying just behind Chris Amon's fleet-footed Ferrari, Stewart, driving with a special plastic support on his forearm, lost ground at the start but recovered to dice with Denny Hulme, the battle eventually being for the lead. Stewart won that battle but lost the war: Ken Tyrrell had gambled on running with the lightest possible fuel load, and he paid the price when his driver had to race in for a splash-and-dash on the penultimate lap. 'Pretty stupid for an oil company!' Guiter remarked with a smile 35 years later at Magny-Cours. Stewart rejoined, but the time for his final tour was more than twice as long as the fastest lap set by Surtees and the Scot wound up in a fourth place that should have been so much better.

It was simply a pleasure postponed. The long-awaited third victory of Jackie Stewart's Formula One career arrived on 23 June at Zandvoort. The wrist, thrust back into plaster by his doctor when he returned to Switzerland after Spa, was still swollen and painful enough, following practice on Friday, for Stewart to sit it out on Saturday. But someone was looking kindly on the little Scot, for rain on race day meant the steering would be much lighter and the physical challenge less daunting. That, and the use of the wet-weather Dunlops, propelled Stewart into the lead by lap four. He proceeded to lap the entire field, but allowed Beltoise in the 'French' Matra to unlap himself and complete a stirring one-two finish for the marque. Stewart was unable to shake hands with those who rushed to congratulate him. 'I am so pleased to have given Matra their first win,' he said, beaming, 'and I did not mind putting up with the discomfort of my hand to do this.' It was the first Grand Prix success for a French machine since Behra took the flag on home soil in a non-championship race at Reims in 1952; it was also the first ever Formula One World Championship victory for a French car. And it was the first of the 25 victories that F1's new perfect partnership, Stewart and Tyrrell, would amass in the course of six heady seasons together.

The French Grand Prix that followed was not, however, a day of national celebration. Not only did Stewart have to settle for third, a lap down on the triumphant Ickx's Ferrari, but the pall of tragedy again hung over Grand Prix racing as Frenchman Jo Schlesser lost his life in a blazing new Honda. Still troubled by his wrist, Stewart tussled hard with Surtees for the minor placings in the British round at Brands Hatch two weeks later, ending up sixth. He was still having his plastic cast removed and replaced regularly, and the sloping circuit with its bumps and swooping corners was not suited to his condition or his Matra's performance. He admitted later, to Eric Dymock, that he had driven with only one arm for more than half the race, and, after being lifted out of the car at the end, had been physically sick with exhaustion. Back home in Begnins, he slept for eighteen hours. It was, undoubtedly, a low-key build-up to one of the high points of his life.

In sport, the great arenas have always been the perfect stage for the greatest players. Nicklaus at Augusta, Borg at Wimbledon, Armstrong in the Tour de France – all giants of their respective games, all transcending time and place or becoming synony-mous with one time, one place. For Jackie Stewart, that time and place arrived in August 1968 at the greatest motor racing arena of them all. The Nürburgring had already staged some of the most stirring exploits in the sport's history. As recently as 1957, Juan Manuel Fangio had driven the race of his matchless career there when his Maserati picked off the Ferraris of Luigi Musso, Peter Collins and Mike Hawthorn. Thoughts of the Nürburgring brought names like Bernd Rosemeyer and Rudolf Caracciola instantly to the lips. On that August day in 1968, as the Ring and its great twin circuit Spa approached the end of their era, John Young Stewart etched his own name alongside theirs.

To add to the challenge of its 22.81 kilometres, the Eifel weather was at its unseasonal worst. Rain and mist might have added a Scottish flavour, but they made the Nürburgring an inhospitable place indeed, especially for a man with a 400hp machine in his hands. The Matra could not match the qualifying pace of Ickx's Ferrari, which took pole in 9m 4s. In fact, Stewart, wearing his plastic sleeve again to support his injured wrist, qualified sixth, on the third row, a full 50 seconds slower than the Belgian driver but the last man under the ten-minute mark. With Friday afternoon and all of Saturday washed out, he had to wait for an extra practice session staged on Sunday morning to achieve it. But would the race take place at all? It did, but only after an interminable delay. Twenty drivers lined up on the grid that day, but there was only one car in it, and it carried the number 6.

It also carried some very special Dunlop wet-weather tyres. They, and the driver's surpassing skill, propelled the Matra into the lead at the Schwalbenschwanz on the opening lap. By the end of the second lap, Stewart led by over half a minute. Vic Elford, Jean-Pierre Beltoise and Chris Amon all had accidents; John Surtees, Jo Siffert and Lucien Bianchi had problems other than the weather to worry about. By lap four, the gap – the gulf – had stretched to a full minute. Hill's late-race spin merely underscored the distance between Stewart and his closest pursuers. In the end, after fourteen laps of the Nürburgring, the Matra came home by a margin of four minutes and three seconds. Jackie Stewart was Ringmeister and Regenmeister all rolled into one, a sportsman at the very summit. 'The visibility was so poor, we were driving on instinct,' he said afterwards. 'I am a slow learner in a lot of things, but on a circuit, once I have got a thing established in my mind, it doesn't often go away, and I think it was one of the occasions when this was of enormous value.' On this performance, created on that unique stage, he would build the record-breaking career that made him one of the true greats.

Not that he was done with 1968, not by a long chalk. Monza provided his second and last DNF of the season with an engine failure; at Mont Tremblant in Canada he finished sixth despite a twenty-minute pit stop to repair his front suspension; but on 6 October at Watkins Glen win number five came along, this time by a mere 25 seconds after Stewart had moved into the lead on the opening lap. One race to go, and everything to play for: as they made their way to Mexico, Graham Hill led the title race on 39 points, Stewart was on 36 and reigning champion Denny Hulme in a McLaren Ford a further three in arrears. Before flying to Mexico, however, Stewart and Hill went back to

London for the Earls Court Motor Show where each enjoyed a chance to barb the other with public posturing and ribbing. It was all harmless fun, but a colourful part of the build-up to their title showdown at a time when their public images were growing by the day.

When they arrived in Mexico, it was the Matra man who qualified slowest of the three pretenders, his preparation hampered by a broken universal joint and subsequent suspension damage. A better time in the spare car counted for nothing as the Scot opted to use his repaired race machine on Sunday afternoon. From eighth on the grid, Stewart was through to third by the end of the first lap. A lap later, Surtees was dispensed with; by lap five so was Hill, and Stewart was in the lead, from Hill and Hulme. The New Zealander was first to give, his McLaren burying itself in the barriers after ten laps, by which time Hill had regained command. Jo Siffert thought this was all a bit much, so he threw his Lotus past both Stewart and Hill to lead before the halfway point until his throttle cable broke. For a while, Stewart and Hill were separated by no more than a second, but as the gap grew on lap 38, the Scotsman's title chances diminished. A loss of oil pressure had caused a misfire, the disconsolate driver dropping back to seventh as the victorious Hill celebrated his second title and helped console Lotus for their calamitous early-season loss. 'Graham won the race fair and square,' Stewart recalled. 'And it was a nice way for him to win the championship. Ken was terribly disappointed, more than I was really, because I had the chance to figure it all out while the race was unfolding.'

Still, 1968 had brought major breakthroughs for Jackie Stewart. His magisterial effort in West Germany had carried him to the highest ranks of Grand Prix drivers; it was his first season of multiple victories; and he ended it as runner-up after missing two rounds through injury. He had cleared the decks for a monumental effort in 1969.

* * *

It was the year of Northern Ireland and Nixon, of Kennedy and Kopechne, Manson and Tate. Cinemagoers crowded in to see McQueen in *Bullitt*, Newman and Redford in *Butch Cassidy and the Sundance Kid*. The incomparable Rod Laver carried off his second Grand Slam. Ted Heath paid Australia back by taking the Sydney–Hobart, and Tony Jacklin won the Open. A man walked on the moon. And a boy from Dumbuck became world champion.

This momentous year in the life of John Young Stewart began, however, in rather downbeat fashion. That may seem paradoxical given that he won the South African Grand Prix on 1 March by 18.8 seconds over world champion Graham Hill's Lotus 49B, but the feat merited only a passing mention (STEWART WINS and two paragraphs) in *The Times*. But if the newspaper popularly nicknamed the Thunderer had cared to read the signs, they were there, and appropriately enough they were all Anglo-French.

By a happy coincidence, that first Grand Prix of Stewart's first title-winning year took place on exactly the same day that the supersonic airliner Concorde first flew. In fact, test pilot André Turcat must have lifted the beautiful aircraft's needle nose off the Toulouse runway at almost the same moment Stewart was projecting the Matra Ford's nose into the lead on the opening lap at Kyalami. (Little did he know it at the time, but Stewart would invest almost as much money in Concorde tickets, for seat 1A, over the next 30 years as the cross-Channel governments had poured into the project to begin with.) A joint venture between Aérospatiale and British Aerospace, Concorde was a controversial but incontrovertibly impressive product of Anglo-French collaboration. So was the Matra Ford MS80 that propelled Jackie Stewart to the world crown.

The car flew in the face of F1's conventional wisdom of the time. For 1969 was supposed to be the year of four-wheel-drive, yet the all-conquering MS80 was the only new two-wheel-drive of the year. Four-wheel-drive had been in the air for some time, mark you: car-makers had considered it for over a quarter of a century; Moss had used the Ferguson P99 to run rings around his opposition at Oulton Park in 1961; Lotus and Chapman were insistent that this was the way for the future and that the Lotus 63 would prove it. And so were Matra, who tried hard to make a go of the MS84. They failed to make the point. Or at least, they made one point, scored by Servoz-Gavin in Canada, and that was that. Stewart himself had been vocal in requesting a four-wheel-drive car for his use in wet races, but his feats of 1969 would be accomplished in more conventional machinery.

His first win, in fact, came at the wheel of a 1968 MS10. Stewart ran the MS80 in Kyalami practice but opted for the older, tried and tested model, at Ken Tyrrell's insistence, when it came to race day. As usual, the canny Englishman was proved right. Though he qualified only fourth behind pole-sitter Brabham, Stewart eased into the lead on the opening lap and cruised home. It was a perfect start for Tyrrell and his wee driver, just the first outing they had wanted and planned. 'After not winning the championship the previous year, the really important thing for us was to profit from that experience,' said Stewart. 'We realised that we needed to make a better start, and to start much earlier. Most people in the first few races have new cars to settle in, or if not, they have interim models from the previous year. Graham had the championship won by the third race in 1968 whereas we had not started to score until the fourth event. So, we decided to start early for 1969, and this more than anything else was responsible for our success.'

Building on the trend begun in the middle of the previous year, Kyalami showed that Concorde's were not the only new set of wings in evidence for 1969. Twin aerofoils, front and back, were the order of the day among the eighteen starters as 'aerodynamics' began to take over as the Formula One buzz-word. Like the great aircraft itself, those wings were an experiment still in its infancy: Brabham's rear wing collapsed, and both had to be cut off the stricken car to enable him to continue. They would soon rise to the top of F1's controversial 1969 agenda.

There were two months to wait until the second round of the world championship. Stewart and Tyrrell put them to good use not only with extensive tyre testing at Kyalami, but also by trying out the new MS80 in the Brands Hatch Race of Champions in mid-March, a race they won. MS80 set the soon-to-be-universal trend of a bulbous 'Coke bottle' shape, memorably described by racing car historian Doug Nye as 'podgily pregnant-looking'. It was certainly full of potential. The bulge, of course, was caused by side fuel tanks, one of whose key benefits was to keep the weight of the fuel (housed in Matra's aviation-derived structural fuel tank system) within the car's wheelbase. Those wheels were thirteen-inch fronts and fifteen-inch rears, as Dunlop worked hard to win the war against both Firestone and Goodyear, while the car had front nose wing-planes on either side working in harmony with a suspension-mounted rear wing. It had its first world championship race at Barcelona's Montjuich Park, where two team-mates in winged cars almost had their last.

Some of the most dramatic images in Formula One history emerged from that Spanish Sunday in May when the Catalan city's F2 venue staged its first F1 event. The Lotuses appeared with wide rear wings, Rindt taking pole and team-mate Hill third, with Amon's Ferrari between them on the front row. All seemed well for leader Rindt as the 90-lap race settled down, though there were worrying signs that his rear wing was starting to flex and buckle. Those fears were confirmed when Hill's sister car came to grief on lap nine soon after passing the pits. The world champion emerged unscathed from an accident that inflicted shocking damage on his car. Not long afterwards it was Rindt's turn, an even heavier accident ending with the car upturned and the Austrian's nose broken. It was the beginning of a process of attrition that saw Stewart move through from sixth on the opening lap into the lead not far past half-distance when Amon's Ferrari blew up while a country mile in front. In the end, the Scot was a misleading two laps clear of a decimated field, the MS80 enjoying its first victory in its maiden Grand Prix. On a less happy note, the authorities must have known how lucky they were that the Lotus saga had not had far more serious consequences.

Fewer than two weeks later they all reconvened in Monaco, as did the Commission Sportive Internationale (CSI) after Thursday's first practice there. They reached a decision to ban wings with immediate effect, meaning everyone started again with first practice times scrubbed. Stewart responded with pole position. Remarkably, it was his first in a world championship event. It had taken over four seasons and 42 races to arrive, but when it did it opened the floodgates: in the next 57, Stewart would annex a further sixteen poles. But while he led and set fastest race lap, that first pole position did not help him win. On lap 21, team-mate Beltoise broke a driveshaft; two laps later it was the team leader's turn. Graham Hill was able to power ahead and claim his fifth Monaco victory. His fourteenth career win would be the last time the Hill name graced a winner's trophy until Graham's son Damon steered his Williams to success in Hungary almost a quarter of a century later.

Stewart, on the other hand, had only just over a month to wait for his next win. When the Grand Prix Drivers' Association (GPDA) and the Spa organisers failed to find a compromise over the Belgian circuit's safety, Zandvoort became the next staging post on the 1969 world tour. The four-wheel-drive Lotus 63 and Matra MS84 were readied in time to join the fray, Stewart essaying a few laps in the new conveyance in the second practice session and quickly finding it a slower mode of transport than his MS80. He used that car to qualify second, between Lotus pair Rindt and Hill. Rindt led, resisted Stewart when the Scot got past Hill, and was going away when it became his turn to suffer a driveshaft failure, leaving Stewart in the clear. Victory number eight came with a 24-second cushion over Siffert and another fastest lap to the Matra.

Comfortable winning margins were by now a Stewart trade-mark. His ninth career win came in the next race at Clermont-Ferrand on 6 July, this time by almost a full minute after taking his second pole position. In the race, he simply ran away and hid, with team-mate Beltoise exploiting the French crowd's support admirably to win a ding-dong struggle against Ickx's Brabham and claim second spot. A fortnight later it was Stewart's turn to make full use of his home advantage and reach another career landmark: his first victory in the British Grand Prix at the home of the world championship, Silverstone. By this stage, Jochen Rindt was making it clear that Stewart had a rival for the mantle of the sport's next leader. The Austrian claimed pole position, and the two of them went at it hammer and tongs in the opening laps, Stewart assuming the lead on lap six of the scheduled 84. Just ten laps later, Rindt was back in front, and he stayed there until lap 62 when he had to pit for bodywork repairs as an aerofoil endplate was rubbing on a rear tyre. Once again Stewart was a lap clear of the field, setting fastest lap in the process. He had done it in Beltoise's car, his own race car having been damaged in a Friday shunt, and he had done it with an engine that was nearly two years old.

The world championship that year was nominally divided into two parts. Silverstone brought the first half to an end after six of the eleven rounds. Jackie Stewart had won five of them for an interim total of 45 points. Next came Bruce McLaren, and he had a mere seventeen. The system also dictated that drivers count only their best nine results from those eleven races. In the second, five-race half, Stewart would rack up two DNFs to add to the one at Monaco, which meant he had eight race finishes to count, and every one of those saw the Scot accumulate points. There was only one more win, but what a win it was.

Meanwhile, if Rindt was the main threat on the horizon, there was another cloud, and its name was also Jacky. When asked how good the 'other' Jacky had been, Stewart once retorted, 'Not as good as he thought he was.' As we have seen, however, any man who could master the Nürburgring commanded respect, and that is precisely what Jacky Ickx did in the 1969 German Grand Prix. Jacky and Jackie traded blows throughout a practice build-up overshadowed by Gerhard Mitter's fatal crash, Ickx finally edging the Scot out for pole position. He threw the advantage away by fluffing his start, allowing Stewart's Matra to take command, but the 24-year-old Belgian fought back brilliantly to be second by lap three and in a position to challenge for the lead within another two laps. For two laps they staged one of the most exciting duels of the year until Stewart started to suffer from gear selection problems and dropped off the pace, eventually settling for an unchallenged second-place finish.

And so, once more, to Monza. Four years earlier, Stewart had beaten BRM team-mate Hill to the line at the Italian track; this time, his team-mate, Beltoise, would again figure in one of the closest finishes in Formula One history. Monza has always been known for the famous Parabolica, the sweeping right-hander that closes the lap by sling-shotting the field on to the wide straight past the pits. In 1969, it would prove the decisive feature of the venerable Italian venue. In this year of winged wonders, Stewart's decision to tackle Monza without them would prove decisive, in conjunction with an artful suggestion from Uncle Ken. With Rindt's Lotus on pole, a breakaway group of seven runners soon formed, with Stewart elbowing his way through from the second row into the lead, a position hotly disputed and sometimes usurped by both Rindt and Hulme in his McLaren, and even Piers Courage in the Brabham. By the time they embarked on their final circuit, they were down to four: Stewart, Rindt, Beltoise and McLaren. The late-braking and bewinged Beltoise went into the Parabolica first but paid the penalty on exit, running wide. And now Ken Tyrrell's craftiness came into play. It was only a short sprint to the line from the exit of the Curva Parabolica; why waste any of that time changing gear? He had advised Stewart to run with a

special 'tall' second gear, and the advantage paid off handsomely. Stewart outraced both Rindt and Beltoise to the line, the
leading four separated by less than one-fifth of a second. The
winning margin of eight-hundredths of a second was the
smallest Stewart enjoyed in any of his 27 world championship
victories, but in the apt setting of Monza's royal park, it was
more than enough to make Jackie Stewart king of the Grand
Prix castle. 'I had wanted to win the title in the most convincing
way possible,' he said after the race. 'We had an absolutely
terrific scrap. I feel utterly exhausted, but at this moment I
couldn't be happier.'

It little mattered that the end-of-season odyssey to the
Americas ended with two DNFs in Canada and the United
States and a fourth place in Mexico. Stewart led all three
encounters, but spun out at Mosport, suffered an oil leak at
Watkins Glen, and was outrun by Hulme, Ickx and Brabham in
the last race of the year. The short-lived Matra era in F1 was
over, as the company did what we now call 'rationalising' and
went off to focus on sportscars, but what a shockwave of
success it had sent through the sport. Six wins in a single
season, a feat that put Stewart in the exalted company of Ascari,
Fangio and Clark. In the title race, his winning margin over Ickx
was 26 points; the season had also brought the first two of his
seventeen pole positions and five of his fifteen fastest laps.
Stewart and Tyrrell had become the new Clark and Chapman.
In that year of Concorde's first flight, that year of aerofoils and
talk of aerodynamics, that year of consecration, Jackie Stewart
might not quite have been supersonic, but his speed had taken
him to new heights.

7. SAFETY FIRST AND LAST

'We accepted that Grand Prix racing was a challenge. A good analogy is mountaineering: if you provide a safety net, no challenge remains.'

Tony Brooks, winner at Spa Francorchamps in 1958

'You can't kill yourself in these cars.' It was a telling remark, but it was utterly lost on an Australian television 'personality' who might have known something about his country's football code, but was clueless when it came to motor sport. A pity: the man who said it to him was Sir Jack Brabham, in a Melbourne studio before the 2003 Australian Grand Prix. And kill yourself you certainly could in the racing cars of Brabham's era; his contemporaries frequently did. The fact that virtually no racing drivers lose their lives these days is due in no small measure to one of Brabham's contemporaries who did not, Jackie Stewart. Stewart's tireless efforts in pursuit of his goal of improving safety are as much his legacy to motor racing as the rich store of racing memories he left behind. 'In any other profession,' he once reasonably pointed out, 'a man is allowed to learn by his mistakes . . .'

Stewart was spared the dreadful baptism by fire that awaited Jim Clark when he first competed in world championship races. Clark's second event, the Belgian Grand Prix of 1960, was one of the most distressing in Formula One history. It began with Stirling Moss sustaining multiple injuries when his Lotus left the road at Burnenville. Soon after, Mike Taylor's Lotus Climax suffered steering failure and the Englishman was lucky to escape with his life after plunging into the roadside scenery. Less fortunate were his compatriots Alan Stacey and Chris Bristow. During the race itself, Bristow lost control of his Cooper as he diced with Willy Mairesse in the Ferrari and died when he was catapulted out on to the track. Minutes later, Stacey, possibly stunned after being hit in the face by a bird, crashed at Malmédy and lost his life. If we remember that Clark's first visit to the grandiose Ardennes circuit for a 1958 sportscar race had been marred by the death of fellow Scot Archie Scott-Brown, it is small wonder that the double world champion conceived a hatred of the place his four consecutive F1 victories there could never mask. In his early autobiographical book *At the Wheel*, Clark recalled that 1958 race and wrote, 'I had never seen Spa before and had only heard that it was fast. Actually, if I had known the kind of track it was, I'd never have gone.'

Coincidentally, it was Spa Francorchamps – feared, revered and indeed loved by many followers of motor sport – that was to crystallise Stewart's own feelings about the dangers inherent in the way he earned his living. Those dangers were epitomised by the two circuits that dominated the early years of world championship racing. Given the racing heritage of Belgium and Germany before that competition began in 1950, it is logical enough that those two countries should have provided two of the foremost venues for the sport. More surprising is the fact that the two greatest circuits in motor racing history, Spa Francorchamps and the Nürburgring, are separated by fewer than a hundred kilometres of European terrain. One is set in the rolling countryside of the Ardennes, the other high in the Eifel mountains to the east. More coincidental still is the fact that together they contributed perhaps the two most significant moments in Jackie Stewart's career at the wheel: one took him to the pinnacle of his professional life, the other came within an inch of ending it.

The German track measured a staggering 28.29 kilometres in its original form. Twisting and climbing – there is a difference of 300 metres between its highest and lowest points – through that mountainous terrain, it encompassed no fewer than 174 corners, some of them bearing the most evocative names in motor racing history: the Schwalbenschwanz or 'Swallowtail', the Fuchsröhre or 'Fox's Den', the Karussell, and so on. Even taken in a road car with Ecurie Ecosse driver David Leslie at the wheel in 1987, it was a daunting if thrilling experience which left a Golf GTi in a sorry state and its driver and his passenger utterly elated. Lest we be carried away on our own tide of motor racing nostalgia, we would do well to remember that this most majestic of circuits had its origins at the dawn of Hitlerian Germany as a project to alleviate local unemployment. As we shall see, the Nürburgring in 1968 was the scene not only of Jackie Stewart's greatest drive, but also of one of the most astonishing victories in Formula One history. But more of that later.

Over to the west, Spa in those days was a mere 14.12 kilometres, but the Belgian circuit reproduced virtually every characteristic of its longer German counterpart. For those unfamiliar with motor racing history, the original challenge represented by Spa Francorchamps took in, roughly speaking, a triangle that linked the small Ardennes townships of Francorchamps, Malmédy and Stavelot. Belgian motor racing people refer to the circuit as Francorchamps, rarely Spa, because it lies a fair distance to the south of the town where people came to take the waters, and heads further south from there. The circuit staged its first international race in 1925, when the great Antonio Ascari in his Alfa Romeo P2 won the 'European Grand Prix', part of a four-race 'world championship' that also embraced Indianapolis, Monza and Montlhéry in France. To Ascari's name were added, through the years, those of other Spa winners such as the Monegasque Louis Chiron, Italy's Achille Varzi and Tazio Nuvolari, and Rudolf Caracciola of Germany. But not until the inaugural Formula One World Championship of 1950 did this daunting segment of the Ardennes countryside come fully into its own.

Run on public roads conveniently closed for the purpose of high-speed motor sport, the track headed downhill and south-east from Francorchamps, through the daunting Eau Rouge and steeply uphill towards Burnenville. From there it swung right and south-west in the direction of Stavelot, tearing down to the infamous Masta left–right 'kink'. Next came the northbound stretch to the huge sweeper at Blanchimont before the road turned left to head back to La Source and its famous hairpin bend. Like any stretch of self-respecting public road, the Spa Francorchamps circuit carried all the paraphernalia of everyday motoring. Signposts, kilometre markers, ditches and the occasional wayside hut lined virtually its entire length. To those artificial hazards, nature added two more of her own. Any local map will point out the 'Bois de Ville', 'Bois Tappeux' or 'Bois de Hourt' right by the roadside. Where there are so many woods, there are naturally even more trees for cars and men to wrap themselves around. Given its topography, the Ardennes region is also notoriously vulnerable to changes in the weather. There are few things more testing of a racing driver's nerve than a circuit where it can be dry one moment, wet the next, so that what seemed like safe footing is suddenly transformed into a high-speed skating rink. So it would prove for Stewart himself.

It seems ironic that, at the time of writing, Spa Francorchamps no longer figures on the Formula One calendar because the Belgian government insists on banning tobacco advertising. It was the fear of going up in smoke of another but equally lethal kind that used to haunt those who braved the Ardennes circuit at its original 14.12-kilometre worst. For as well as water, whether from the heavens or lying on the track, another elemental force came into play with frightening regularity in the Grand Prix racing of those days. Fire was the worst nightmare for any driver, especially in an era when trackside medical centres, specialist rescue teams and all the facilities of modern Formula One were still the stuff of fantasy. In Stewart's day alone, drivers of the calibre of Bandini, Siffert and Schlesser perished in blazing cars; in 1976, Niki Lauda came close to death in the fiery accident that put an end to the 'old' Nürburgring. But in that respect, Spa Francorchamps in 1966 may fairly be said to have brought about a pivotal moment in Grand Prix history.

On 11 June that year, John Young Stewart celebrated his twenty-seventh birthday. On the 12th, for what must have seemed a lifetime, he wondered if he would ever see his twenty-eighth. Stewart came face to face with Spa at its cruellest that dismal Sunday. In this first year of Formula One's 'Return to Power' under the three-litre engine rule, the Belgian Grand Prix was the second race on the calendar after Monaco, which Stewart had won. At Spa, his BRM was one of three cars on the front row of the grid, which then occupied the downhill stretch towards Eau Rouge, round the La Source corner from the top straight where the cars take the start today. Stewart's V8-engined two-litre BRM moved into place alongside pole-sitter John Surtees in the Ferrari and the Cooper Maserati of Jochen Rindt, both three-litre cars of twelve cylinders. The BRM had been three and a half seconds adrift of Surtees' qualifying pace, but three-tenths faster than 'Black Jack' in his Brabham Repco. Alongside the Australian on the second row was Lorenzo Bandini in the other Ferrari, and behind him on the outside of row three sat Richie Ginther's Cooper Maserati. Of those six drivers, five would be the top five finishers in the 28-lap race. In fact, they would be the only five officially classified. Of the fifteen who took the start, two would not be classified: Guy Ligier, four laps down in another Cooper Maserati, and Dan Gurney, a further lap astern in his lovely Eagle Climax. The other eight, including Jackie Stewart and world champions Graham Hill and Jim Clark, would retire or crash out. The real drama was that they all crashed out on the opening lap.

'One minute the road was dry, the next it was covered with driving rain,' explained Graham Hill. 'We hit the right-hand corner at about 130mph. One car started to spin and then the others, as they tried to avoid it. Then cars started hitting each other, with four eventually involved, going in all directions.' Stewart's went in the direction of one of the many ditches around the circuit, the impact violent enough to start wrapping the wreckage around him as he sat imprisoned by his steering wheel. He sat trapped on the edge of the circuit, fuel from the BRM's ruptured tank dripping on to him, the helpless driver breathlessly waiting for the spark that would signal catastrophe. Hill, in desperation, ran to a nearby farm to beg for the tools that might help him free his trapped colleague. Half an hour later he succeeded, but worse was to come. So was an ambulance, but not for another ten minutes. When it did, its part-time driver was incapable of finding his way to the hospital where the injured Stewart needed to be treated. Not until he was flown in a private jet to London did Stewart receive the care and consideration it should have been his right to expect. It was the only major accident of Stewart's magnificent 99-race career in Formula One, but the one that caused him the most soul-searching. It triggered a Stewart-led safety campaign for which the multi-millionaires who grace today's Grand Prix circuits should nightly give their heartfelt thanks.

As recently as 18 May 2003, we had devastating proof of their indebtedness. Leading the Austrian Grand Prix at Spielberg's A1-Ring, Michael Schumacher brought his Ferrari F2003-GA into the pits for its first scheduled stop. Team-mate Rubens Barrichello, another candidate for victory that day, had seen his chances diminished by a lengthy stop two laps earlier when the fuel rig failed to work properly. As Schumacher sat in his red car, residual fuel from his rig, which the team had pressed into service on Barrichello's car, ignited. For a brief but terrifying few seconds, flames played around the nozzle through which fuel gushes at thirteen litres per second. Schumacher observed the drama in his rear-view mirror, but sat calmly throughout. Alerted over the radio by Ferrari technical director Ross Brawn, the German placed massive trust in his team, and in the protective clothing at his disposal. The requirements of that clothing – helmet, gloves, underwear, socks, shoes, balaclava – are all specified in FIA standard 8856-2000, or in FIA 1986. So confident was Schumacher in their performance and in his crew that, after going on to claim his sixty-seventh career victory, he was able to joke that his mechanics had clearly felt he was a little too cool and simply wanted to warm him up. But his brief encounter with fire had recalled, chillingly, the pit-lane inferno that had engulfed his then Benetton team-mate Jos Verstappen in 1994 at Hockenheim; coincidentally, Verstappen too, relatively unhurt in that appalling blaze, was on the grid in Austria in 2003 as his racing career stretched a decade beyond those terrifying moments in Germany.

Stewart had two natural and willing allies to support him in his campaign to improve the drivers' lot. He also had another, in the shape of a group that was perhaps less willing to work with him until cajoled by Stewart and one of his peers. The first of his willing helpmates was none other than his team principal during his years with BRM; the other would follow only after Stewart had hung up his driving boots but remained an active voice in all such issues. The BRM connection, of course, came in the unmistakable shape of Louis Stanley, one of those larger-than-life figures who seem always to bestride the historical stage.

British Racing Motors was perhaps the most enigmatically British of all racing teams. Its Formula One World Championship career began in farce, encompassed genuine triumph with drivers such as Graham Hill, Stewart and others, and petered out after its final success, in 1972, at the circuit where it always seemed to go best, Monaco. Fired up by Raymond Mays and Peter Berthon, the British Motor Racing Research Trust was created to provide a competitive British presence in a motor racing arena dominated before the war by Germany and Italy, and by the resilient Italians immediately after it. In that cumbersome title, British Motor Racing Research Trust, lay disquieting clues to what lay ahead. Redolent of committees, bureaucratic bungles and sheer inertia, it became an albatross around the neck of a well-intentioned initiative. The immensely complex, V16-engined, supercharged 1.5-litre original car proved an embarrassment, its start-line failures including one at

Silverstone in the presence of royalty. One member of the executive committee, Tony Vandervell, grew so exasperated that he left, vowing to build a Grand Prix-winning car of his own. In 1958, the Vanwall duly became the first car to secure the new Constructors' Cup. BRM's title-winning days lay several years in the future, by which time Louis Stanley's decisive hand was firmly on the tiller. When the trust was put up for sale, the successful bid came from engineering firm Rubery Owen, the Owen half of which was the organisation founded by Ernest Owen in Staffordshire more than half a century before the banshee wail of that V16 was ever heard. The husband–wife partnership was instrumental in turning BRM into a force good enough to win constructors' and drivers' titles, and to give a Formula One debut to John Young Stewart.

In the present context, however, Stanley's key contribution to the Stewart safety saga was a different kind of vehicle altogether. Think of Grand Prix drivers and a conveyance irreverently nicknamed the 'Passion Wagon' and some lurid images may well come to mind. For once, it was a jocular misnomer. This was the way the cavalier souls of those carefree days referred to the mobile hospital which rejoiced under the name of the International Grand Prix Medical Service. Stewart's Spa crash, of course, came in a BRM. As a direct consequence, Louis Stanley, who endured Stewart's Keystone Cops drive to hospital in Verviers with his young driver, set about creating a system that would give men in Stewart's position – and worse – at least a fighting chance. As well as the Scotsman's Spa misfortune, Stanley was a direct and often deeply distressed witness to many of the most gruesome moments in the motor racing of his day. The 'Passion Wagon' was in fact a state-of-the-art mobile facility and the direct precursor of the outstanding medical facilities that are now required features at any world championship venue. It had a hydraulic lift, a high-speed X-ray machine, trolleys with X-ray lucent tops so that the patient need not be moved, respirators, heart machines, blood banks – and above all it was spotlessly clean and properly ventilated. Not only that, but Stanley and the persistent Stewart helped set up a system of on-track communications which meant that by the time a driver in need of attention was delivered from the scene of his accident to the mobile hospital a reasonably complete case-file was already in existence and precious time was bought. Lives were saved, amputations avoided, broken bones repaired, proper care dispensed.

The second natural ally in Stewart's ongoing campaign for greater safety, especially around the racing circuits themselves, did not start playing his full part on the F1 stage until five years after the triple world champion's racing days were over. Like Louis Stanley, he was as far removed from the Stewart background and personality as one could possibly imagine. Professor Sidney Watkins, more often known to his many F1 friends as 'Prof' or plain 'Sid', began assuming responsibility for matters medical at Grand Prix racing in the summer of 1978, by which time one Bernard Charles Ecclestone had set about transforming the whole face of the sport. Professor of Neurosurgery at the London Hospital, Watkins, a Liverpool graduate trained at the Radcliffe, had been enriched professionally by his experience at Syracuse in New York State. He was – and remains – a motor racing aficionado whose CV already encompassed supervisory work at Watkins Glen, scene of many of Stewart's feats of derring-do, and at Silverstone on the initiative of the RAC's Dean Delamont.

Silverstone, in 1973, Stewart's last appearance in his home Grand Prix, was a turning-point, when Watkins and the 'Passion Wagon' took care of several injured drivers. Sid ran it for the next five years before the approach from Ecclestone that was to take him round the circuits of the world on a personal mission to drag driver safety into the twentieth century before we reached the twenty-first. The desperate consequences of Ronnie Peterson's accident at Monza in 1978, the Prof's first major F1 case and one that left him nonplussed by the

JACKIE STEWART

ineptitude of the initial response from the rescue team, led to
the now-standard practice of having a medical car follow the
first lap of each Grand Prix, a move supported by Stewart and
that other triple world champion with direct personal experience of a major F1 accident, Niki Lauda.

'It was in the seventies,' said Watkins, as he recalled his early
encounters with Stewart, whom he had watched in action at the
Glen, 'when he caused a certain amount of disturbance to the
medical faculties of the circuits by bringing his own resuscita-
tion expert. I remember at Silverstone, it must have been the
first time he brought this chap, a Swiss anaesthetist. But the
chief medical officer and doctors in the medical centre were
outraged at the suggestion that they were going to be super-
seded by a personal physician. They made great play of the fact
that this guy wasn't going to be qualified in the United
Kingdom, he wasn't insured in the United Kingdom, and there
was no way he ought to be allowed to have anything to do with
anything. The point of view that I expressed was that the easiest
way out of the situation was to add him to the medical team;
he didn't have to do anything *a priori*, but he could be there as
Jackie's representative if Jackie couldn't speak for himself, which
is highly unlikely given the amount of speaking he does! I
should think even when he's unconscious he'd be talking.
Anyway, that sort of eased the situation.'

By 1981, the Fédération Internationale du Sport Automobile
(FISA), then the governing body for world motor sport, had
formed its own Medical Commission. The Prof and such
distinguished and self-effacing colleagues as France's Dr Jean-
Jacques Issermann formed a partnership that advised on,
oversaw the creation of and signed off all medical facilities at
the circuits coming on to the world championship calendar.
One of Sid's closest henchmen in the early years of his tenure
in this crucial position was none other than Stewart. 'I began to
have close contact with him after Bernie came to see me in May
1978 and asked me to do every Formula One race,' Watkins

132

continued. 'I guess I went to Sweden first, to Anderstorp, where the situation wasn't all that excellent. The next race was the French Grand Prix, and there I found that the organisation was considerably better than I'd ever seen anywhere else, except when I was in Watkins Glen, when I used to take a full team of medical specialists from the University Hospital of Syracuse to the circuit, so we had everything fully covered.'

Watkins next encountered Stewart *en passant* as he was heading for the Mediterranean island where Ecclestone and his drivers used to stay for the French Grand Prix. 'I was going to the island, and I think Jack had just come off it, and he stopped me and told me how very pleased he was to hear I'd been asked to do the Formula One thing by Bernie. He said that if he could help me in any way he was always available. And that has been the case. He has helped me many times. He has even intervened when he thought that a wrong decision was made by the authorities in not allowing me to go to an accident. For example, in the accident at Long Beach with Clay Regazzoni [in March 1980], I think he wrote to [Jean-Marie] Balestre [then president of the FISA] about that. So he was always very active and wanted my authority to be increased, which it eventually was, and he has been very supportive in everything that I've done. He's one of the two people in my life who ring me up when they don't want something. He and Senna were the two people in motor racing who would ring me up just to say hello, and Jack still does that.'

In 1999, Malaysia became the first 'new' player on the Formula One World Championship stage in the Far East. By then, of course, Stewart had already dragged the country of Dr Mahathir into Grand Prix racing when he secured backing from Tourism Malaysia for the Stewart Grand Prix cars in their maiden season, 1997. But when the government-built Sepang F1 Circuit opened for business two seasons later, its commitment to safety must have warmed the cockles of the Scotsman's heart. Not only was this a state-of-the-art layout, designed by leading international course-builder Hermann Tilke, it also put safety right at the head of its long list of priorities. Visiting members of the media, in fact, were invited to attend the opening of the Sepang F1 Circuit Medical Centre on Wednesday, 19 October 1999. In the presence of chief medical officer for the Malaysian Grand Prix Colonel Dr Mohammed Zin, the FIA medical delegate our friend Professor Watkins, and his close colleague Dr Issermann, the superb facility showed how far F1 had come since those spine-chilling days at Spa and elsewhere. The staff comprised no fewer than 43 doctors, 100 medical assistants, nine staff nurses and 60 more people trained in first aid. The Race Medical Centre was a permanent structure with everything needed for two specialist trauma teams; here, diagnosis and stabilisation would take place before air or road transport to referral hospitals was called upon. Each of the four 'Fast Intervention Vehicles' carried an anaesthetist and a paramedic; each of the three 'Extrication Vehicles' carried a doctor and five paramedics; and four further small cars carried a doctor and two paramedics. In addition there were ten ambulances, three at the Medical Centre itself and seven stationed at strategic points around the 5.542-kilometre circuit. 'An excellent set-up,' beamed the Prof in the course of the opening ceremony. 'The centre and its team are well equipped to face any eventuality. I am very happy with what I see. But I will be even happier if I don't see any drivers in here this weekend!' What he did not say was that it is to men like him and Jackie Stewart that Formula One owes facilities such as Sepang's.

Through the late 1960s and early 1970s, however, Grand Prix racing continued to claim victims with grim regularity. Though Stewart could not have known it at the time of his personal Damascus at Spa, the next few years of his life would cost him dearly when it came to friends and contemporaries in motor sport. The litany makes horrific reading: in 1967, Bob Anderson and Lorenzo Bandini; the peerless Clark in 1968, as well as Ludovico Scarfiotti, Mike Spence and Jo Schlesser;

Lucien Bianchi and Gerhard Mitter in 1969; and among those lost in 1970 was one of Jackie's closest friends in racing, Jochen Rindt.

Tim Schenken is nowadays Clerk of the Course at the Australian Grand Prix and a prominent figure in the administration of his country's busy motor racing scene. At Monza on Saturday, 6 September 1970, he was a 26-year-old up-and-coming Formula One driver negotiating only his second world championship event. Rindt was killed during practice for the Grand Prix when his Lotus 72C crashed under braking for the Parabolica, the sweeping right-hander on to Monza's main straight. Looking back in his Melbourne office 33 years later, Schenken recalled the impact that experience had on him. 'Jochen was a big hero of mine. I'd raced against him in Formula Two and got to know him quite well in early 1970. So that was very hard – to sort of rationalise it. Because here you are, wanting to do something more than anything else in the world, be a Formula One racing driver, be a world champion, and somebody you admire is killed in the second Grand Prix you've competed in. One was torn apart, a little bit. Jackie was very distraught about the whole thing, I could see that. For some reason I had to talk to him on the Sunday morning of the race, and it was hard for him, very hard for him.'

Helen Stewart, also speaking some 30 years after the incident, confirmed the fear that hung so palpably over the life of every driver of the day. 'You lived with the knowledge that Jackie could walk out the door one day and never come back,' she recalled. 'The death statistics were terrible when Jackie was racing, with a driver having a two in three chance of being killed over a five-year period. Almost every season a few drivers died, and I watched their families being destroyed, knowing that it could be us next. But I just took the view that you can die anywhere, any time.'

Schenken's famous compatriot Sir Jack Brabham was himself very close to Rindt. 'Losing Jim Clark at Hockenheim was a big blow to us all,' the triple world champion recalled. 'But Colin Chapman was always able to come up with good drivers like Graham Hill and Rindt. This was a sore point with me as I had a contract with Jochen to drive for me in 1970 and I had planned to retire, but at the US Grand Prix Colin offered Jochen a lot more money. Consequently, I had to let him go, and when Jochen was killed at Monza I felt partly responsible for letting him go. I was very close to Jochen, as was Jackie, and we all had a hard time coming to grips with the loss, particularly as it was so unnecessary and through no fault of his own. If we had had a doctor at the track as we have now [Sir Jack was speaking in 2003], Jochen could have been saved. This accident really spurred Jackie on his safety campaign, and the sport has a lot to thank him for as his relentless campaign to improve track and driver safety has done a wonderful job. The GPDA [Grand Prix Drivers' Association] did a reasonable job, but Jackie is the one who really drove it home.'

Schenken in fact took part in 33 Grands Prix, starting in Austria in 1970 and finishing in Italy in 1974. In 27 of those races Jackie Stewart was also on the starting grid. Schenken was also a very fine sportscar driver, in which capacity he enjoyed great success with fellow F1 driver Ronnie Peterson, who became his great friend. Ronnie, as we have seen, also died at Monza, in 1978, so Schenken is well placed in more ways than one to describe the motor racing world in which he and Stewart worked, and the attention paid to drivers' safety and well-being. 'When you look back now,' he said with a rueful grin, 'it was ridiculous. But I think if in 20 or 30 years' time you looked back at today you'd say the same thing. It mightn't be such a difference, because there's only so far you can go, I guess, with safety, but at the time it's what you knew. When you look back now at the starting grids of the early 1970s and see how many people have died, it would have been a lot more had it not been for the likes of Jackie and [fellow racing driver] Jo Bonnier. I think Jackie was perhaps the face of the GPDA, but I think Jo

Bonnier did a huge amount there in terms of all the administrative work. In fact, I remember I was very flattered to be invited to join the GPDA when I was Formula Three racing in the late 1960s.'

The GPDA was the third, collective and slightly less eager ally Stewart found in his bid to improve safety. Fittingly enough, it was formed in late 1961 in Monaco, the principality which is now home to a gaggle of Grand Prix drivers bound together less by a concern for their collective safety than for their considerable individual wealth. It was probably no accident that two of the prime movers in stirring the GPDA from its torpor were both involved in that first-lap furore at Spa Francorchamps in 1966. One was, of course, Jackie Stewart; the other, as Schenken reminded us, was another of the BRM band of drivers, the man who gave that marque its first Grand Prix win, Joakim Bonnier of Sweden, the eventual president of the GPDA. BRM's Louis Stanley described the urbane, educated Bonnier, killed at Le Mans in 1972, as 'the ideal ambassador and spokesman for the sport throughout the world'. Set up to act as an advisory body at first, with Stirling Moss as its first chairman and Bonnier his deputy, the GPDA was called into more direct action as the 1960s wore on and its members' ranks were depleted by fatal accidents. Since Spa is where we came in, it seems only right to note that Stewart's report on safety at that circuit, his peers' increasing concerns (especially about racing there in the rain), and the sluggish response that was inevitable at a circuit where local authorities had ultimate responsibility for the roads, all conspired eventually to have Spa's world championship round cancelled in 1969.

It is staggering to note that one of the reputedly great books about Grand Prix racing, William Court's *Power and Glory*, vilifies Stewart for his part in the removal of the old Spa. Noting the lack of unanimity among the members of the GPDA, from which Belgian Ferrari ace Jacky Ickx resigned, Court passed sweeping judgement on the Scot. 'More surprising,' he wrote in his second volume, 'was the reaction of so courageous and gifted a driver as Stewart, who had proved himself as good as any man at Spa in the five races he had driven there. He would have done better to have followed the spirited examples of Jim Clark and just got on with the business of motor racing, or of Jochen Rindt, who welcomed the high-flying aerofoils he much disliked, if only because they offered the possibility of taking Burnenville flat out! There lay the attitude of a true racing driver . . .' How easy it is to be cavalier with other men's lives.

Another contemporary who survived was Jackie Oliver. Born three years after Stewart, Oliver graduated to F1 in 1967; 49 of his 50 races came between that year's German Grand Prix and the Swedish round of 1973, which makes him close to Stewart's exact racing contemporary. Speaking in 2003 at Le Mans, where he had co-driven the Gulf-Wyer GT40 to victory with Ickx in the legendary 1969 race, Oliver underlined the importance of Stewart's safety campaign, and the obstacles placed in the Scot's way. 'The most poignant thing about Jackie was when we were driving together in Formula One in the late 1960s and he was campaigning for circuit safety. The GPDA, which was run by Jo Bonnier, was a very strong group – stronger than it is now and equal in strength as a body to FOCA [Formula One Constructors' Association] and FISA of that period. There was tremendous opposition to circuit safety because a number of traditionalists were of the opinion that the danger element of motor sport had always been there and was one thing the drivers had to cope with, and the best drivers coped better than the lesser drivers. But a mistake was not just losing the race, it was losing your life. Jackie was extremely outspoken about the fact that a mistake should not cost someone their life; the best drivers were those that had other elements in their make-up, but didn't lack courage. In fact, sometimes courage in the face of stupid odds could not be measured in courage but in stupidity. I think that argument has been borne out as cars have got safer and circuits have got safer. The best drivers still win regardless of the level of their courage. And not only was Jackie a top driver of his time, he was also under considerable commercial pressure, I would think, not to make waves with regard to the circuits and the demands of the drivers in trying to win world championships.'

Stewart won the day. Reinstated in 1970, just long enough for Pedro Rodriguez to give BRM a fond final winning flourish there, Spa in its old layout was dropped from that year on. To the joy of all in Grand Prix racing, it was very successfully remodelled, with the high-speed, treacherous section through Burnenville–Malmédy–Masta–Stavelot excised, and reintroduced in 1983. There was a new section from Les Combes across to Blanchimont, incorporating a tremendous left-hand curve at Pouhon, and there were new pits on the short straight just before the hairpin at La Source. The drivers, whose opinion alone is paramount, were thrilled by what they encountered. 'It is,' announced reigning world champion Keke Rosberg on seeing the new Spa, 'the perfect track.' All very well, but tragedy came uncomfortably close to home for Stewart at Spa once more in 2001 when Paul Stewart Racing graduate Luciano Burti, by then a Jaguar Grand Prix driver, had a monumental accident. 'I spoke to Luciano last night,' said Jackie in the aftermath of the incident, 'and he was fine. He was laughing, which sounds unbelievable when you first looked at the crash. But it is also a wonderful confirmation of the risk management which has been introduced to the sport. OK, there are more people drowned fishing, killed by cricket balls, or victims of mountaineering accidents than in F1, but when I think back to my time at the wheel – when tragedy was always lurking and I lost so many friends – at least we have taken massive steps forward, be it in new restraints, enhanced protection for the head and the neck, or extractable seats, where a driver's injury is not aggravated by being dragged out of a smashed-up vehicle. I've always campaigned for these aspects, and allied to the increased safety regulations at all the circuits – tyre walls, debris fences, gravel traps and first-rate medical support under Professor Sid Watkins – I believe we can be optimistic that the risk element has been reduced to a minimum. We will never rule it out entirely, of course, and there must always be an element of danger in this sport, but Luciano Burti is alive and kicking, whereas he wouldn't have had a prayer twenty years ago.'

The extractable seat, incidentally, is a recent development that allows rescue personnel to lift the seat with the driver still in it and remove both from the car at the same time, thereby avoiding additional stress to a possibly injured human frame. 'I came up with that idea,' explained Watkins, 'and Jackie immediately saw the sense in it. I think his car was the first actually to introduce a proper one in collaboration with Lear, the seat manufacturers. Then, of course, we made it mandatory, but Jackie had shown how it could be done. Although I must say that nice Irish chap, Gary Anderson, who had been working with Jordan, he helped me a great deal in developing that seat, as did Harvey Postlethwaite at Tyrrell, by making a sort of mock-up chassis and a mock-up seat. We went down to the Tyrrell factory to inspect it and saw that the geometry would work.'

As L.P. Hartley wrote, 'The past is a foreign country. They do things differently there.' Few facets of motor racing illustrate his point more tellingly than developments on the safety front. With the inevitable benefit of hindsight, it seems easy to dismiss those days in the 1960s and 1970s, and earlier, as a time when men thought they were men and showed cavalier indifference to personal safety. Tim Schenken doesn't see it that way. 'Not so much cavalier,' he said. 'Most drivers have something in them – I certainly had – that says it's not going to happen to them. And you just don't think of it. As I said, when I came into Formula One, the second race I did was at Monza, and that was the race that Jochen Rindt was killed at. I also did a Race of Champions at Brands Hatch in October of the following year when Jo Siffert was killed. Jo had just overtaken me; he went down the hill and the car just went left and hit the marshals' post, burst into flames, bits everywhere. I went through that and got a puncture and had to come in and change the tyre. I drove around, and by that time they'd red-flagged the race. I came to the top of Hawthorn Straight and stopped there behind all the other cars, and all the drivers were sitting in their cars. Nobody got out. I was actually crying. I was sitting there with tears pouring down my face, and I suspect others were in a bit of a state as well.

'So you are affected by these things, but you then just seem to move on. It was much the same with Graham Hill. When Graham died in 1975, I went to his funeral, and I wouldn't have the words to describe what the atmosphere was like. Incredibly . . . depressing isn't the word, I don't know what the right words are. Afterwards we went back to his house, and that was the exact opposite: you went in the door and everyone was in party mood. I went in, was there for ten minutes, waited for Betty [Hill] to arrive, and left. I couldn't stand it. Yet the following weekend you're racing and it's all behind you. You either mentally block it out or . . .'

Schenken, of course, came face to face with the same challenges as Stewart on the various circuits of the period. Places like Spa and the Nürburgring are etched in his memory. 'The Nürburgring was funny,' he recalled, 'because when I first raced there, before they put guardrail all the way round, it was just hedges. You knew when someone had gone off because there was a hole in the hedge. And usually it was a hole in the hedge with a couple of marshals peering through it and looking down the slope. It was strange, because I think Jackie made himself very unpopular with his crusade for safety – because of the cost of doing the work – and he was far more effective than the CSI, because they weren't very effective at all. When one raced at the Nürburgring, when it was hedges all the way round, it was like driving through a tunnel without a roof on it: you couldn't see very far. Then, when they redid the whole circuit, which was Jackie's initiative, putting guardrails in and moving everything back, suddenly you were driving along and saying, "Oh, that's interesting! That's pretty there! What a lovely scene!" You could see the track going up valleys and so on, which you couldn't before. I went to the Nürburgring at the invitation of Ford Germany and did a race there, which I think was a 72-hour race, 36 plus 36; originally it had been the Liège–Sofia–Liège Rally, and there'd been some tragedies, some deaths on that rally, and it was run as the Marathon de la Route. The cars started in Liège, drove to the Nürburgring, did a 72-hour race and then drove back again. So I learnt the circuit that way. But what was interesting was that I learnt it in a Ford Capri, and when I went again and raced there in a racing car I suddenly realised I didn't know it that well. Just because of the difference in the height you sit at. When you're in a Formula car there are crests, and suddenly you weren't sure what was over the crest! And Spa: I raced at Spa, on the original circuit; there was a fair bit of guardrail but there were lots of places where there wasn't, and I don't know, you just didn't think about those things.'

Not unless you were someone like Jackie Stewart, who did, and acted upon it.

8. HAPPY TO BE SCOTLAND'S SECOND DRIVER

'The real identity of the Scottish flag was created by Jim Clark.'

Jackie Stewart in 1997

Of all the forms of self flagellation invented by mankind, being a Scottish sports fan is surely the cruellest. Since sporting arenas replaced battlefields as the scene of national confrontations, Scots have had precious little to shout about. For every Bannockburn – the Wembley Wizards, Allan Wells in Moscow – there have been so many Floddens, on the football field alone: 7–2 in 1955, 9–3 in 1961, not to mention Iran and Costa Rica in the World Cups of 1978 and 1990. National pride has suffered more blows from sport than from most other areas of human activity. Putting it another way, we all have our St Andrew's Cross to bear. And, as David Coulthard has pointed out, Scottish sports fans turn more readily to teams than individuals when they look for reflections of national superiority on the sporting field. 'I don't know generally if Scotland is that passionate about racing and Formula One as history might make you imagine,' said the man whose thirteen Grand Prix victories (at the time of writing) make him the closest Scotland has yet come to filling the gap left by Clark and Stewart. Looking askance, Coulthard added, 'The Scots are pretty wary like that. They say hello to you and give you a look out the corner of the eye, not "Come here and give me a hug"; they're not like the Italians, kissing and that sort of thing. I think the Scots are more nationalistic about national sides – football, rugby, things like that – than they are about an individual. I don't know what it was like when Jackie was winning in the early 1970s because I was a wee baby. But even if I was to be on the brink of winning a world championship, yes there would be a few more headlines, but I don't think you'd suddenly get the whole of Glasgow turning out if I went up there with my trophy. You'd get a few hardy race fans. I don't think it's like Finland or places like that where the whole country goes nuts for it.'

World championships in any sporting discipline have been especially few and far between. Indeed, it says much about Scotland's heritage that most of them should have come from the boxing ring. Combative Scots, though, are not confined to the canvas. How strange it seems, therefore, that this little nation should have produced two of the greatest world champions ever seen in their elected discipline. Stranger still is the coincidence that brought Jackie Stewart to prominence as the natural successor to the racing driver he most revered, compatriot and double world champion Jim Clark. It seems only right to pause for a moment at a pivotal point in Stewart's own career, and near the tragic time of Clark's death, to look more closely at two men who brought nothing but honour to their national flag.

In the spring of 1997, Jackie Stewart travelled to Scotland to keep a very special appointment. At the tiny village of Kilmany in the north-eastern corner of Fife, he was to unveil a statue. It commemorates a true prince among that ancient kingdom's sons: Jim Clark, born there on 4 March 1936. Sports stars are not known for their willingness to play second fiddle, and John Young Stewart has never been one for self-effacement. It might have surprised many of the onlookers that day, therefore, to hear him say, 'I am happy to be considered as Scotland's second driver.' In fact, that day, Stewart made one of the most gracious speeches any sportsman can ever have given to honour one of his peers as he looked back on that April day in 1968 when Clark, his friend and mentor, drove to his death in an insignificant Formula Two race in Germany.

'That day in Hockenheim,' said Stewart, 'took from Scotland one of its greatest sons, one of its greatest examples of a sportsman, and one of the greatest racing drivers the world will ever know.' Speaking, as usual, without notes, Stewart reminisced about the 'Scottish embassy', the London flat owned by Sir John Whitmore where he and Clark found occasional haven from the already hectic schedule of a racing driver's life in the swinging sixties. Their conflicting calendars that April weekend had taken Clark to West Germany with Lotus and Stewart to Madrid's Jarama circuit for, of all things, a safety inspection on behalf of the Grand Prix Drivers' Association. 'It was because I had as much exposure to Jimmy as I had,' continued Stewart, 'both as an admirer to begin with and then obviously as a competitor and sometimes team-mate, that I became the driver I did.'

That exposure began, in F1 terms, in Stewart's maiden season, 1965. By then, Clark, three years his senior, had been in Grand Prix racing for five seasons. With the guiding genius of Colin Chapman behind him, he had already amassed thirteen of his 25 Grand Prix victories, and with them the 1963 drivers' crown. But for mechanical failures he would have won the title in 1962 and 1964 as well. He would win it for the second and last time in that first year of having his compatriot on the grid with him. In all, Clark and Stewart sat on the same Grand Prix grid together 28 times. Their shared experience of Formula One was neatly framed by South Africa, where Stewart contested his first Grand Prix on 1 January 1965 and Clark his last on the same date in 1968.

If bare statistics are anything to go by, Stewart had a privileged view of the master at work. Of those 28 Grands Prix they raced in together, Clark won eleven – including the first six, from South Africa to West Germany (Clark missed the second race of that 1965 season, Monaco, in order to take care of unfinished business at the Indianapolis 500). Jim was also on pole for fifteen of those 28 races, and on the front row in a further twelve. He set the fastest race lap in twelve, and achieved F1's equivalent of the hat-trick – pole position, race win and fastest lap – on five occasions in those three-and-a-bit seasons. Stewart, by contrast, won just twice when Clark was in the same starting line-up, at Monza in 1965 and in the first race of the 1966 season at Monaco. The Mediterranean principality, in fact, was to provide the starkest contrast in the two men's fortunes: while Clark could never come up with a winning drive there in his six attempts, Stewart won three times in his eight Monte Carlo appearances in F1 and, of course, preceded that record with a fine F3 win there in 1964. In their 28 races together, Stewart was never on pole – his first, remarkably, did not come until 1969 – nor did he record a fastest race lap, the first of those coming in 1968 in his celebrated drive at the Nürburgring.

As always, however, we must avoid the mistake of reading too much into statistics. During the period they raced together in Formula One, Clark was not only the established master of his art, he almost always had the best car in the field at his disposal, whether it was the Lotus 25, the 33 or the legendary Lotus 49. Clark was also one half of arguably the most remarkable partnership in F1 history, teaming up with radically innovative designer Colin Chapman to form a fighting force based on sheer genius. Stewart, at this time, was serving his Grand Prix apprenticeship. After taking an eternity to reach the top of the F1 tree, BRM was already climbing back down: the 1962 world titles for that team and Graham Hill were already things of fairly distant memory by the time Stewart first occupied a BRM cockpit. Later, when Clark was no longer around to witness it, Stewart too forged his own unique and equally successful partnership with Ken Tyrrell. Curiously enough, Stewart claimed the same number of victories – 25 – under Ken's tutelage as Clark had under Colin's. Perhaps more pleasingly for both men, their first season of Grand Prix racing – in fact, their first five races together – yielded no fewer than three one–two finishes, for Scotland, so to speak: they were firmly in the rival camps of Lotus and BRM respectively, but united in their determination to fly the Scottish flag from the highest mast motor racing could offer.

Yet, their Scottish provenance apart, there seemed to be little, on the surface, to bring the two men together. The differences are more marked than any similarities their mutual love of motor racing might have brought out. In the first place, that most British of distinguishing marks, their accent: Clark's was the well-rounded, slightly posh-sounding voice of the east-coast public schoolboy, or private schoolboy, to use the appropriate adjective north of the border. Born into a well-to-do family of farm managers and eventually farm owners, Clark was educated at Loretto on the shores of the Firth of Forth, near the historic port of Musselburgh to the east of the nation's capital city. Stewart, on the other hand, was from the Firth of Clyde, to the west of the city that thinks of itself as the nation's first. His is more the cheerful, sing-song voice of Glasgow than Clark's slightly genteel upper-crust eastern lilt. The two were also from diametrically opposed backgrounds. Long celebrated in the popular media as a son of the land to which he would one day return, Clark was seemingly imbued with the spirit of the countryside. Stewart the car-dealer's son, despite loving the countryside around Dumbuck, dirtied his hands more with oil and grease rather than any rustic residue. Neither, however, was exactly down at heel, even in early life.

Much has been made, since Clark's death in 1968, of the fact that he and Stewart stood on opposite sides of Grand Prix racing's great divide. Blessed, as always, with hindsight, many have placed Clark in the last days of the great 'gentleman-driver' era, Stewart just as squarely in the camp of the new, hard-bitten professionals. That's certainly how Elf's François Guiter remembers it. 'For me, Jackie Stewart was the first real professional driver,' he insisted. 'For example, he would go and spend a month in South Africa testing tyres. He would do one, even two Grand Prix distances a day in tyre testing. The Dunlop people would try to catch him out by putting back on a tyre he'd already used, and he would instantly come up with exactly the same times. He was a very intelligent young man. There had been drivers before him like Clark, but they didn't have the same application.' Maybe they didn't need it. In any case, easy categorisation does scant justice to either man.

Jack Brabham, like Stewart one of the four knights of motor racing at the time of writing, raced against them both. 'Because of driving with Jimmy Clark,' he said in 2003, 'I was a lot closer to him than Jackie, particularly as we shared a common interest in flying. For sure they were the two best Scots to cross the border. As we neared the end of the 1960s it was obvious that Jackie was going to be another Clark, but when he joined Ken Tyrrell of course he really got going. The thing that really helped was that Jackie and Ken were both close to Ford. I suppose because of my Repco days beating the Cosworth, I had to put up with Jackie and Ken getting the Cosworth development DFV, and it was no longer a driver competition. I was glad to retire at the end of 1970 as it was obvious that the combination of Jackie, Cosworth and Tyrrell had become unbeatable and had entered the history books.

'If I had to say which Scot was the best,' he added, 'I would have to say that although they were both top drivers, Jackie had a better knowledge and feel for the car than Jimmy. Jimmy was very reliant on Colin Chapman, and as Jimmy drove when the Lotus was the top car with the works engines from Coventry Climax and Cosworth, that also became an unbeatable combination.'

While it may be hard to imagine Stewart allowing someone like Chapman to wriggle out of meeting his star driver's expenses, as Colin did with Clark, even in the later stages of their relationship, it would be wrong to conclude that money meant little to Jackie's illustrious predecessor. Indianapolis illustrates the point well. Clark famously remarked of America's motor racing capital, 'You get paid an awful lot of dollars for turning left eight hundred times.' He should know: he exported as many of those dollars as he could in his personal assault on the self-styled greatest race in the world. Once Jack Brabham and the mid-engined Cooper, its engine bored out to 2.7 litres and tipped left to cope with the famous banked oval, had breached the dam in 1961 by finishing ninth, the floodgates opened and it was the old-fashioned Offy roadsters that drowned as the Europeans poured in. Second twice and, memorably, winner once in four visits to the Speedway, Clark earned sums in America that even his Formula One title-winning feats could never equal. When Clark missed that 1965 Monaco race to take care of his unfinished business in the state of Indiana, victory there was worth $166,621 to the winner, of which Clark would have annexed some 45 per cent, or an approximate £46,000. That sum was not only tidy, it was also more than three times the amount Clark gleaned from all six of his Grand Prix successes en route to the F1 crown that same year. Small wonder that Stewart, the astute Scot with an eye to the bank balance at all times, followed suit. But if Jackie's Monaco record eclipsed Jim's, at the Indianapolis Motor Speedway it was very much the other way around. Stewart competed twice, in 1966 and 1967. The first time his Lola Ford should have won, but it lost its oil pressure, and with it the lead with just ten of the 200 laps to go. In 1967 he was out after 168 laps, and that was that as far as Indianapolis went.

Though Clark busied himself mentally counting up the dollar signs as Indianapolis laps in the lead ticked by, he was, by all accounts, far less directly concerned with his earnings throughout the rest of his racing career. It seems he even asked Ford's Walter Hayes if he thought Chapman was paying him enough. Just three years later, when Ken Tyrrell launched his own title-winning campaign with Ford engines and Stewart at the wheel, his racing budget for the year was £80,000, of which, as he later recalled with a grin halfway between glee and pain, no less than 25 per cent was accounted for by John Young Stewart. Clark, however, was no more of a fool when it came to money than his perky successor. Though he agonised over it longer, he was the first of them to arrive at the decision that tax exile was a necessary evil, buying a condominium in Bermuda that meant removing his belongings from his beloved Edington Mains. In 1968, Stewart followed suit. Ironically enough, his departure for Switzerland came just four days before his compatriot's last race.

Clark, some will tell you, was taciturn – a trait that Stewart could never be accused of, not during his racing days and not on any day since they ended. But Clark kept his loquacious side for those who got close to him, of whom it appears there were precious few. If there were internationals for talking, Jackie would be the most-capped player in Scottish history, and the intimacy or otherwise of the listener seems to have little impact on the flow. Hand in hand with the difference in their volubility goes the question of what would nowadays be called their smarts. Another cliché about Clark is that he was naive, too trusting of Chapman and of people in general, at least until his native nervousness got the better of his innate charm and he began to demonstrate an uncharacteristic edginess with those around him. Streetwise long before the term was invented, Stewart in his racing career and ever since, in the equally successful business of being Jackie Stewart, has used his built-in shrewdness to devastating effect in every walk of life he has entered. If Clark at times came across as a fish out of water, especially in his early days among the sophisticates of global motor sport, Stewart was already better equipped than most to cope with sharks. 'Jackie was also able to move the sport towards the professional big money and sponsorship,' Sir Jack Brabham acknowledged. 'It is hard for me to realise just how big it has got today. When I was racing, of course people like Moss and I were classed as professional, but nothing like it was in the 1970s with Jackie Stewart. He certainly got the commercial sport up and going.'

Hockenheim, April 1968, means that one intriguing question about the two Flying Scots will forever go unanswered: what would Clark have gone on to do had he, like Stewart, retired before this most unforgiving of sports took him away from us? It requires a Bob Beamon-like leap of the imagination to see Clark in tartan trousers striding down the pit lane at the head of his own F1 team, and Stewart for one is absolutely adamant that Clark would never have got into the business of team ownership. In the last analysis, and the unkindest, the difference between Scotland's two heroes is summed up in one incontrovertible fact: one died, one stayed alive. On 7 April 1968, Jim Clark was just 32 years old; at the time of writing, Sir Jackie Stewart is 64.

The day after that spring unveiling in Fife, 29 years after he lost his life, several newspapers carried photographs of the statue of Jim Clark. Stewart's gracious refusal of the limelight was symbolised by his presence in those photographs only as a slightly out-of-focus figure in the background. The statue captures Clark in a pose sculptor David Annand took from what was apparently one of Jim's mother's favourite photographs. Annand catches the remarkable spring in Clark's step as he strides purposefully down the pit lane, which highlights something else Scotland's two greatest drivers had in common. Walk alongside Stewart, too, and you will sense, still, a similar jauntiness in his gait. A touch of Scottish cockiness in both? Natural athleticism, not only in the cockpit? Or just two men, small in physical stature, seeking higher altitude? Whatever the reason, they are the two Scottish sportsmen who reached the greatest heights in their chosen field. 'He was mild, shy, modest, but he was very fast,' said Stewart. 'For me, he was the epitome of the racing driver in the way he drove. He was always smooth and elegant.'

It is to Jackie Stewart's undying credit that, in concluding his tribute to his still sadly missed friend at Kilmany, he stated firmly, 'The flag of Scotland has been flown in almost every country in the world under the motor sport banner, be it in Formula One or rallying. But the real identity of the Scottish flag was created by Jim Clark.'

9. THE MARCH OF TIME

'How can I keep up with the rest of the world? I have my own existence to contend with.'

Jackie Stewart in 1970

What goes up, must come down. In 1970, Jackie Stewart, Scotland's 'second driver', lost his French connection, and with it, temporarily at least, his world crown. Matra insisted on the development of a V12, something that was regarded with extreme suspicion by Ken Tyrrell, and they were unwilling to provide a chassis for another Ford-powered campaign. It was clear that Stewart and his mentor had to turn elsewhere, and they turned to a supplier slightly closer to home that had sponsorship backing from the other side of the Atlantic (from STP, or Scientifically Treated Petroleum) to 'get in among the big boys'. With the 1970 season due to begin in March, Stewart decided he should start his racing year in a March.

The March company, born the previous year, took its name from the initials of the group of four men – Messrs Mosley, Rees, Coaker and Herd – who had set it up. Similarly, their cars were named by year and formula: the 693 ran in Formula Three in 1969, the 701 was a Grand Prix car for the following year. For his first effort, Robin Herd – a designer with McLaren and Cosworth, according to his CV – followed the already classic and classically simple lines: monocoque chassis, with DFV slung in the back. Its side tanks, already an embryonic aerodynamic device, were one slightly distinctive note in an otherwise unexceptional car. For the first ten races of that year, Stewart campaigned in the 701. It was no epoch-making design, but it was good enough to attract a number of customers, as well as to fulfil the needs of the two 'works' drivers, Chris Amon and Jo Siffert. It was good enough, also, to secure win number twelve of the Stewart career. And what, you may ask, did Jackie drive in the other three races of that thirteen-round world championship year? Answer: a horse of an altogether different colour. Stewart knew from the outset that the 701 was no world-beater. In 1970 there would be just one in the field: it came from Colin Chapman and Maurice Philippe and was called the Lotus 72. Stewart knew the March was merely a stopgap, a temporary pause in his own, and Tyrrell's, inexorable rise.

Still, anyone watching Stewart take the third pole position of his Formula One career for the season-opener in South Africa on 7 March could have been forgiven for thinking the BUSINESS AS USUAL signs were up outside the Tyrrell garage. March also had Amon posting an identical time of 1m 19.3s, with Siffert on the fourth row and Mario Andretti, in the STP-backed 'American' March, on the fifth. But of the five 701s that started the race, only two would finish. Stewart was third. He managed to hold the lead until lap twenty, when Brabham shot past, and then lost second to Hulme just before the halfway mark. Siffert's tenth place was the only other finish for a March in the marque's first world championship outing.

'After our scepticism, our complaining to Robin Herd, our melancholia and all our bitching, a solid third' was how Jackie described his result in *Faster! A Racer's Diary*, co-written by Peter Manso. He also revealed that he had little respect or affection for the car. During dinner with Max Mosley four days before the race, he had discovered that 'all of the March people are all keyed up since this is their first outing', and added, in relation to the car, that although the design 'seemed all right, everything else was somehow lost in the manufacture ... a shortage of good engineering, parts were brittle and heavy. And it doesn't corner worth a damn.' He was buoyed, however, by the knowledge that the Tyrrell team was to have its own car later that year. 'No one knows about it except [designer] Derek Gardner, myself and Ken, and it's going to be kept a secret,' he said. 'Henceforth, it is to be referred to as the SP, code for "Secret Project".' Stewart flew to Coventry, to Gardner's home, to carry out his own examination of the SP on 23 March, a month before the Spanish Grand Prix. In Gardner's small garage he found a full-size mock-up of the SP itself. 'Seeing it in these surroundings increased the drama, as though all the secrecy somehow augurs the car's success,' he told Manso. 'More to the point, though, it's being built especially for me, to my dimensions, and it was necessary that I get inside so they could take measurements for the steering and pedal positions as well as the interior of the cockpit. I'm leery of waxing enthusiastic, but I can't help it. It looks good.'

And then it was off to Jarama. If Montjuich, and the Lotus wings, had made the Spanish Grand Prix a highly controversial event in 1969, Madrid and its first-lap mayhem matched them in 1970. Stewart qualified third, on the front row alongside the two great Antipodeans, Brabham and Hulme. It was just as well, because being at the front took them well clear of the first-lap drama. When Jacky Oliver's BRM and Jacky Ickx's Ferrari collided near the Jarama hairpin, their full tanks exploded into flames. Though both drivers escaped, the Belgian with burns to all four limbs, the inadequate marshalling meant the surviving cars had to pick their way through foam and water for the rest of the race. A spate of engine failures on other cars helped Stewart to what became an easy win, almost to his own surprise, by a full lap from Bruce McLaren. The result, with Andretti picking up third place and Stewart's team-mate Johnny Servoz-Gavin fifth in two other Marches, was largely due to the fact that only five of the original sixteen starters made it to the line.

Three weeks later, after trips to London, Silverstone, home again and Tokyo for Jackie, who was privately concerned about his son Paul's impending surgery for the removal of his tonsils, the Tyrrell team went to Monaco where its two entries met quite different fates. Stewart, who stayed as always at the Hotel de Paris in a suite with views across the Mediterranean, the harbour and the yachts, was so completely at home on those unforgiving streets that he dominated practice and took pole number four. Servoz-Gavin had an accident in his own car, borrowed Stewart's for a final desperate qualifying effort, but failed to make it on to the sixteen-car starting grid. For Jackie, Monaco was a natural challenge, an extension of his talent to find the easiest way of going fast without fighting the streets and cambers. 'For some reason, the cars never seem to react naturally at Monte Carlo,' he explained. 'It's a very special place, and the only way to get the best from a car here is to follow it rather than lead it, make allowances, and drive around its problems rather than trying to dominate them.' Stewart flew ahead from the start and was seven seconds to the good by the ten-lap mark, but a misfire forced him into Monaco's makeshift pits on lap 27, and the stop cost the world champion a full four minutes while the ignition box was replaced. He did rejoin, but the power never came back completely and the engine forced him out for good after 58 laps. It was a disappointing end to an otherwise engaging weekend for Jackie and Helen, who had been busy socialising throughout and who on the night before the race had been invited to the royal palace for drinks at ten. Greeted by Prince Rainier and his wife, Jackie reiterated his feelings about Princess Grace from 1964: 'an incredibly beautiful woman who seems ageless, still retains an American accent, and is immune from affectation, yet stately'.

Next came Spa Francorchamps, for the last time on its daunting original layout. Major work had been done on installing barriers and creating a chicane to slow down the runners through Malmédy, but times had moved on, and would do so for another thirteen years until the revised Spa circuit was welcomed back with open arms in time for the 1983 season. By an unhappy coincidence, the mortality of the racing driver had been tragically underlined on 2 June, just five days before that final 1970 race in Belgium, when Bruce McLaren lost his life in a high-speed testing accident at Goodwood. Jackie was in Paris that day to meet an old friend from Jim Clark's days, and was stunned by the news. 'I can't describe it,' he said. 'There was an emptiness, or confusion, and all I wanted was time for it to go away, to become unreal, or untrue, or simply, somehow, to settle. It was awful. I went through everything in a daze.' At Spa Francorchamps, on a track where he had stared tragedy in the face himself but never triumphed, Stewart again put his interim March on pole position. He then put it into the race lead after passing Jochen Rindt and Chris Amon by the second lap, but this was not his day: a down-on-power engine let Amon through a lap later, and on the fourteenth Stewart's DFV disgraced itself spectacularly on Spa's home straight. On a historical note, the race went to Pedro Rodriguez in a BRM, the first time the Bourne marque had taken a world championship win since Stewart's in Monaco in 1966.

The upbeat Mexican theme continued at the Dutch Grand Prix two weeks later. The date, 21 June 1970, is the day that produced perhaps the greatest World Cup final performance ever, when Brazil thrashed Italy 4–1 in Mexico City. The Dutch Grand Prix was actually brought forward to avoid a television clash, but Zandvoort would give F1 fans their own, infinitely sadder reason to remember that date. Stewart started the race from second place on the grid, his fifth consecutive start from the front row with his new car, and fought for that same position with Ickx's Ferrari as Rindt's Lotus stamped its authority on proceedings. Stewart finished second after the Belgian pitted with a puncture, but yet again the podium was a place not of joy but of mourning. Frank Williams' friend Piers Courage fell victim to the most appalling fate when his de Tomaso crashed and caught fire, the brilliant young Englishman trapped inside. It was a desperately sad way to mark the debut of Stewart's new Tyrrell team-mate François Cévert, who had taken over from his now-retired compatriot Servoz-Gavin. Zandvoort winner Rindt had just begun a four-race winning roll that would carry him clear of all challengers for Stewart's title, but the loss of his friend Courage was a severe blow to the Austrian, for whom possible retirement loomed at the end of 1970. Instead, much worse was to come.

Jackie, too, was shattered by Courage's death. He admitted he could no longer manage the task of writing his journal, which recorded his thoughts and feelings, that year. Later he did it retrospectively, noting how he and Helen had shared the chilling and monotonous regularity of the Grim Reaper's visits to the race circuits. 'Helen and I have now seen more of life and death than most people see in two lifetimes,' he observed. He cited the names: Jim Clark, then four weeks later Mike Spence; four weeks after that, Ludovico Scarfiotti, and another month later Jo Schlesser; now Bruce McLaren and Piers Courage. After confused, inaccurate and misguided reports, Jackie had Courage's death confirmed when he stepped out of his car after the race. 'Someone had given me a Coke, and I remember smashing the bottle against the ground as I went off to the transporter,' he said. 'Yet despite it all, my mind was cold. Absolutely. In neutral.' At the hotel, avoiding photographers, Jackie stayed with Piers' entrant and best friend Frank Williams, who was also shocked to the core. The next day, they returned to the circuit to reconstruct the accident. Stewart eventually went home that evening.

The racing, of course, would continue, but first there were funerals to attend. On 24 June there was a memorial service at St Paul's Cathedral in London for Bruce McLaren, the local garage man from New Zealand who became a national hero. On the same day, in the afternoon, the drivers, in their mourning coats, held a meeting of the Grand Prix Drivers' Association at the Dorchester Hotel, more concerned than ever about safety at some of the most dangerous tracks. The next day they went to a small country church in Essex and buried Piers Courage. 'At the grave, near Piers' parents' home, Sally [Courage] was distraught, destroyed, and that made me feel worse than anything,' Jackie recorded. 'I cried right there in the open. Helen, too, and most everyone else.' These were raw days when death hurt them all.

From the beginning of July, Jochen Rindt stormed to victory in France, Britain and West Germany, and Stewart's fortunes fell away with the March's reliability. In France, for the first time in that car, he qualified on the front row, running third in the race until another pit stop for an ignition box ended his chances of a decent result. At Brands Hatch, the car handled like a dog, relegating Stewart to eighth on the grid. While running in the top six he was never close to the race leaders, and it was a mercy when, pitting for a puncture, he found his clutch had given up the ghost with 53 laps gone. As Grand Prix racing went to Hockenheim for the first time – like its great twin sister Spa, the Nürburgring was being left behind in the safety stakes – Stewart qualified seventh, had gear selection trouble, was never in touch with leader Ickx and pulled out with engine failure after 21 laps of the wooded German circuit. Ironically enough, the first race at the Osterreichring on 16 August brought a halt to Austrian favourite Rindt's winning streak, Ickx's Ferrari taking the win as Stewart retired after just eight laps with a fuel leak that left his March cockpit awash. And so, after a short break, Rindt, with a healthy lead in the drivers' championship, prepared for Monza.

The fabled Italian circuit had twice already been the scene of triumph for Jackie Stewart, but in 1970 it was to provide perhaps the cruellest blow he endured in his entire racing career. It should have been a happy weekend for Stewart and the entire Tyrrell team, even an historic one, for this was the meeting at which Ken sprang his big surprise. After one race victory and three pole positions, the days of the stopgap March were numbered. Team manager Tyrrell, who had prior to March worked so hard with cars from Cooper and Matra, was now a Formula One constructor in his own right, for at Monza in September 1970 Jackie Stewart used, in practice, the SP, the Tyrrell 001. It was not the car's first outing, though. It had started active duty at Oulton Park, the same circuit where Moss, almost a decade before, had driven the four-wheel-drive Ferguson to victory. And there was a connection: the man behind the Ferguson system was Derek Gardner, the same understated Midlander to whom Ken Tyrrell had turned when Matra became a blind alley at the end of 1969.

Under conditions of almost comical cloak-and-dagger secrecy, Gardner had worked alone in a converted bedroom to draw Tyrrell 001 from scratch. In stark contrast to today's full-scale wind-tunnel models, he worked with a one-tenth scale model before having a local joiner mock up the car – all this before they even began to cut metal for the real thing. Stewart started that Oulton Park race from the back, deliberately, because he was concerned about the car's reliability following practice problems with its fuel metering and fuel injection. In the opening race his throttle jammed open, but breaking the lap record was a happy counter-balance to the teething troubles that also included an oil pick-up glitch that led to engine failure. Fuel flow was the major worry again in practice at Monza, where the steering also proved suspect. This prompted Stewart to opt for the March on the Sunday for what was to be the Tyrrell-entered car's last race.

Tragically that day, and heartbreakingly for Stewart, there was no Jochen Rindt lining up alongside him. Saturday's action had been his last. One year earlier, the Parabolica had been the springboard for Stewart's cunning last-lap sprint to the line; this year, the entrance to the famous right-hander caught Rindt out in the last Saturday practice session. As remarked upon in chapter seven, it seems likely that proper, up-to-date medical assistance would have saved the Austrian driver, or at the very least made his last hours more endurable than they must have been. Somehow, Stewart summoned up the personal reserves to race, moreover to dice with newcomer Clay Regazzoni and Jean-Pierre Beltoise for the lead. He outran the Frenchman, as he had done the previous year, from the last corner to claim second place. But losing the race was as nothing when set alongside the calamitous loss of his closest friend in racing at a place where the sport always makes legends. In 1969, one of them had returned to visit: the incomparable Juan Manuel Fangio, a lifelong Stewart hero.

Fangio had won the drivers' championship five times between 1951 and 1957. More than that, he had done it with a modesty and style that enhanced the sport. His manner and his ability impressed Jackie. They had dinner together the night before the race, with Helen and friends, at the Villa d'Este. 'The food was great, the service was flawless, and, as always, I was fascinated by Fangio, by his eyes as much as his conversation,' Stewart recalled before Fangio's death in July 1995 from pneumonia. 'He had the most fantastic eyes, really electric eyes, very clear and full of expression, and now that he's started to wear glasses, you can see that he doesn't like them. He's conscious of putting them on and criticises himself all the while he's doing it, even pitying himself a bit, though obviously he realises that at this stage of life they're a small price to pay. Still, he can't quite accept them and makes jokes about growing old. He is nearly sixty. A small but important thing was how he handled the waiters. Good Italians to the core, they were all in awe of him. They waited until we were finished eating before approaching him, and they approached him as though he were a saint. Respectfully, timidly even, to ask for his autograph. And he gave it to them in a good way, no offhandedness, no condescension, simply putting them at ease, treating them as men not children.' Fangio's legendary attention to detail and grace and dignity in life were to become essential qualities for Stewart. Such was Stewart's respect for the Argentinian maestro that in order to attend his funeral he put on hold his hectic schedule and flew straight to Buenos Aires, then on by private plane to Balcarce, the town where Fangio had been born. Alongside Stirling Moss, José Froilán González, Carlos Reutemann and the president of Mercedes-Benz Argentina, Stewart helped carry the coffin from the church to the hearse.

That same year, after winning the drivers' title, Stewart had been besieged by fans. Afraid of a riot, he had escaped in a Mercedes-Benz driven away at speed by his friend Philip Martyn, who frightened Jackie on their way back to Como, where he telephoned his father in vain to report on his championship win. After sleeping badly that night, he received a call from his father early the following morning. It was a call he said he would never forget. The old man, who was 74 years old and had had two strokes, sounded rejuvenated by his son's success, as if 35 years had fallen off his age. His father said how proud he was to have lived to experience this day. But when his mother came to the phone, it was different. All hopes of any acceptance of his career path were dashed when she said, simply, that now he could retire.

Such memories were deeply touching in the circumstances surrounding the Italian Grand Prix in September 1970, one year on from that championship euphoria and those family phone calls. In *Faster!*, Stewart admitted that 'what happened has had a profound effect on me, my attitude and my feelings for motor racing, perhaps for ever'. Jackie and Helen's close friendship with Jochen and Nina Rindt made the weekend a deeply intense, sad and draining experience. While attending to his own job, of driving the Tyrrell-entered car as fast as possible, he was caring for Nina, trying to make telephone calls to her father in Helsinki and Jochen's father in Vienna, making arrangements, weeping in his private moments, fighting to gather himself and steel his mind and body for the work ahead, and sharing his sleeping pills with Helen. It was a traumatic time, kept strictly in check by the Stewart human management system, but not entirely. He recalled lying awake, reading, wanting to sleep, thinking of his sons Paul and Mark and wishing, deeply, that they would have nothing to do with motor racing. 'How there is always the grief and the terrible pain that people go through when a thing like this happens,' he remarked. 'I lay there thinking how stupid the whole business is, how futile and painful . . .' After responding to a request from Austrian television to take part in a Jochen Rindt tribute programme, Jackie began to talk, as always, but could not go on. He had to turn away and shed a few tears. The race, he said, was not worth talking about.

Just thirteen days after Monza, Jackie Stewart made history of a happier kind by putting the brand-new Tyrrell 001 on pole position for its maiden world championship race. They had all crossed the Atlantic for the end-of-season trio of events at Mont Tremblant in Canada, Watkins Glen in the States, and Mexico City. Those throttle slides played up again as practice got going, meaning that the Tyrrell star hopped backwards and forwards between the 001 and the 'old' March, but when the latter failed towards the end of the Saturday session, Stewart 'hot-footed' it back to the pits in time for a final crack with the new car. His time of 1m 31.5s put him one-tenth ahead of Ickx and on pole position for the sixth time. Ickx and Regazzoni were the dominant forces in the second half of the season, just as Rindt and his wonderful wedge-shaped Lotus 72 had been in the first, so stealing pole was a pleasing feat indeed for Tyrrell and his Scottish ally. They were even happier when Stewart led the race, and led handsomely, by as much as sixteen seconds with less than a quarter of the race's 90 laps gone. But a sheared stub axle meant the fairy-tale beginning ended there.

But the memories of Monza and that sequence of deaths, the pall of tragedy that hung over them all, would not go away, however far they travelled. Jackie was just one of those suffering, but he felt it deeply. After Monza, he had felt strange, experienced froth in his mouth, and passed out briefly. The following Friday, Rindt's funeral had taken place in Graz, Austria, but all the time Jackie kept extraordinarily busy, working overtime in London and Scotland during the week, fighting the demons, struggling in his own mind with the desperate realisation that his friend had not needed to die. Helen, having lost so many friends – the Clarks, the Spences, the Courages, the Rindts – was also distraught and lost, but proving to be a game character. 'They're not here any more,' wrote Jackie. 'The only person left is Graham [Hill]. He is the only one. We're not close to the others. All of this must have an effect on a woman. I have an escape . . .'

At Watkins Glen at the beginning of October, a young Brazilian by the name of Emerson Fittipaldi enjoyed his maiden world championship win for Lotus. In just over a year's time, he and Jackie would wage one of the most thrilling battles for the title in world championship history. For now, though, Stewart was not yet in a reliable car. New front uprights and stub axles had taken care of one problem, but while he led again and was going away at a second a lap, an oil leak 25 laps from the end put paid to his American chances for another year. For Stewart, there was the small consolation that Fittipaldi's victory ensured Rindt would be declared world champion, the first and only time the title has been won posthumously.

Gremlins struck again in Mexico when, after another front-row start, another flaw emerged: Stewart lost a lap while a loose steering-column was repaired. The Mexican crowd had also broken loose. The huge numbers that turned up broke down barriers and sat right at trackside, prompting local hero Rodriguez and the sport's leading driver Stewart to make a pre-race tour calling for them to move back. Fortunately it was neither a child nor a grown-up that eventually invaded the track, but an animal: a dog ran across the circuit as Stewart sped past, damaging the Tyrrell's front suspension badly enough for the Scot to retire after 34 laps. Three races, one pole, two other front-row starts, twice commandingly in the lead – a dog this Tyrrell 001 most definitely was not.

As the season ended, so Stewart's life slowed down, fractionally at least. He found time to think. His experiences had frayed his mind, eaten into his energy and his ease of focus. He was heavily loaded, he admitted. People came to him with proposals. He was asked about politics, about Vietnam, but he admitted he had not had the time to study any news or politics in sufficient depth to respond. 'It's just a big green jungle,' he said. 'My own life is so intense that it's difficult to keep up with things.' He revealed that he had stopped reading, even though he loved reading light fiction to relax. He said he could no longer read on aeroplanes. 'I've been so behind with what's in my briefcase that I can't keep up with it,' he continued. 'When I'm on a flight I fall asleep immediately, because I'm exhausted. I don't have enough time for my family, for my racing, for my friends, so how can I keep up with the rest of the world? I have my own existence to contend with.'

Interestingly, perhaps significantly given how well he knew him, John Lindsay called in to see Jackie in London later that year, on 5 November, at a time when Stewart was busy between appointments with Walter Hayes, his tailors, the American Embassy for a visa and other commitments. Lindsay, his old friend from Dumbarton, his erstwhile football team-mate, who grew up with him on the garage forecourt, went with him to night school to prepare for guild exams and who shared in their early madcap racing excursions across Scotland and England, was just visiting. But he came that day to see his friend and to talk about the way in which he had seen their friendship, and Jackie's life, change down the years. A mild envy, that Stewart, not he, should have left the village and shot to fame and wealth, had always been there before, but after going to Monza for the weekend and seeing the truth of Jackie's life as a racing driver, Lindsay had reconciled his feelings with the harsh realities. He had seen beyond the glitz and the glamour and into the pain and the destruction. 'This morning,' wrote Jackie, 'he spoke to me about this, almost guiltily, almost apologising, and apart from what it meant for the two of us, it meant a great deal to me personally . . . Something's happened. I've realised it, and it's as though there's no turning away from it. It's there. The unforgettable and permanent realisation that all things have an end.'

As the winter passed and the new season approached, motor racing remained dogged by disaster. Before the 1971 world championship season began, Italian driver Ignazio Giunti lost his life at a sportscar event in Buenos Aires. Getting on with life as usual, Stewart put his Tyrrell, now Goodyear-shod, on pole position for the season-opener in South Africa and finished second to Andretti. In this season marked by a lucky number – it was Stewart's seventh in F1 – victory with the unlucky number thirteen was merely postponed for one race. As he had done a year earlier, Stewart triumphed in Spain on 18 April, this time at Montjuich Park. He came through from fourth on the grid to lead by lap six, and, keeping Ickx in careful check, won by 3.4 seconds. The day was doubly significant, of course: not only did it bring victory number thirteen for the Scot, it was number one for a car bearing the Tyrrell name. In fact, 1971 was to be the most successful year in Tyrrell's Formula One history. Over the three seasons 1971–73, Stewart would present Ken with no fewer than fifteen of the 23 world championship victories Tyrrell cars achieved. Six of them came in 1971, matching Jackie's 1969 record, and his French team-mate Cévert also registered one.

Jackie's second victory came in Monaco, where a 003 rebuilt after Stewart's Silverstone International Trophy shunt on 26 April was the class of the field. Pole position, fastest lap and a flag-to-flag victory were underlined by the 25-second margin the Scot had in hand after 80 laps – all in a car devoid of rear brakes. A champion indeed, as Roman Polanski had realised, as he decided to commit the Monaco weekend to film. Firestone's festival in Holland restored some perspective, however, when Stewart could do no better than trail home eleven laps down on winner Ickx after an 'off' on the third lap that cost him five places.

The cold shower seemed to do everyone in the Tyrrell camp good, for Stewart then embarked on a three-race winning sequence that put world championship number two all but beyond the reach of any other driver. The F1 circus's first visit to the stunning new Paul Ricard facility at Le Castellet, in the Marseille hinterland, not far from Bandol, brought another 'Grand Slam' of pole, fastest lap and victory, this time by 28 seconds. That was not enough, so Stewart extended it to half a minute in a stunning display of superiority at Silverstone; and when Ickx spun on lap two at the Nürburgring, the Tyrrell star waltzed away to win the German Grand Prix by more than 30 seconds. It mattered little that Austria caught him out, a rear stub axle triggering Stewart's first DNF of the 1971 season. With Ickx out again and Ronnie Peterson, the only other remote contender, only eighth, John Young Stewart was world champion for the second time in three years.

Italy was another low-key affair, the engine giving up after sixteen laps following a seventh-place qualifying effort, but pole positions in Canada and the United States, and victory in a rain-shortened Mosport race illuminated by his brilliant dice with Peterson, gave Stewart a more than satisfactory finish to his year. It was rounded off in America by a maiden victory for François Cévert in the second Tyrrell. Who could have foretold that this would be the only win for the dashing Frenchman, and that within two years the place of his triumph would envelop the Tyrrell team in tragedy? For now, though, Ken Tyrrell basked in the glory of the constructors' championship, achieved with a staggering 37-point margin over BRM. Stewart's six wins helped him to 62 points, just one short of his 1969 title-winning haul.

But still the year ended on another desperate note. Brands Hatch's Victory Race on 24 October, conceived as a tribute to the Tyrrell performance, turned to heartbreak when Jo Siffert, the man who had been on pole in Austria, and who had won that race, perished in the wreckage of another burnt-out Grand Prix car. And within a few months of that tragic incident there would be another death, this time much closer to home for Jackie.

10. THE LONG GOODBYE

'You cannot be romantic about motor sport and win.'

Jackie Stewart

The headline was simple, but straightforward. The news was announced in the *County Reporter*, in plain English, and it read: BOB STEWART OF DUMBUCK DIES. Jackie's father, a kenspeckle figure in his local community not only as a result of his garage business, but also thanks to his love of all things from music to motorcycles and bowls to Burns, had been ill for some months. He passed away in Duntocher Hospital just before the 1972 world championship season began, ensuring that for Jackie Stewart, in Argentina, his eighth year in Formula One kicked off under a cloud of deeply personal loss. It seemed more than usually fitting, then, that on 6 March his youngest son should record the nineteenth victory of his career at the Autodromo in the southern suburbs of Buenos Aires. Though Carlos Reutemann in his Brabham Ford kept Stewart off pole position, the fact that the Scot set fastest lap *en route* to a flag-to-flag win by more than 25 seconds suggested that while family life would no longer be quite what it had been, professional life was carrying on as normal. Not so, however: for Jackie Stewart, 1972 would prove to be one of the most difficult periods of his still young life.

The restless drive that had characterised Stewart since his early days was already much in evidence. To his Grand Prix schedule were added outings in non-championship events of the kind in which only the United Kingdom, by then, still seemed to specialise, meets such as the International Trophy at Silverstone on 23 April, which the Scot won from Ronnie Peterson in his Lotus and Clay Regazzoni's BRM. By now, too, Stewart was mid-Atlantic man personified. As long ago as 1966, he had got a taste for a racing series which has gone down in history as one of the most popular ever put together, both with fans and drivers. This was Can-Am, which took its name from Canada and America where the races were run on tracks from Mosport to Mid-Ohio, St Jovite to Laguna Seca, and many points in between. It was North America's answer to the popularity of Formula One on the other side of the Big Pond, a competition for big sports prototypes that needed big drivers to handle them. It certainly attracted some of the best Grand Prix drivers of the day, but became known best as 'The Bruce and Denny Show' as the New Zealanders McLaren and Hulme, driving distinctive papaya-coloured monsters, carried almost all before them.

In that first year, 1966, Stewart took only a brief look at this new racing sideshow, qualifying a Lola T70 fourth at California's Riverside, but not making it to the finish. As the swinging sixties ended, however, sideshow had become main attraction as the money, and the fun, both multiplied in Can-Am racing. In 1970, Stewart tasted North American-style racing in Jim Hall's thunderous Chaparral 2J, qualifying it third at Watkins Glen but being forced out of the race by brake problems after just 22 laps. It scarcely mattered. The bug had bitten. As well as taking care of F1 business with his second world championship in 1971, Stewart also put in a full season of Can-Am at the wheel of a Lola T260. It began with a pole position at Mosport – just to let everyone know he was there – but crown-wheel and pinion put paid to any hopes of turning that success into a maiden race win. It was, not for the first time, merely a pleasure postponed: at the next round, still in Canada, at St Jovite, Stewart qualified second to Mosport winner Hulme but took the first of two wins in that year's Can-Am series. He never qualified outside the top four; in fact he was only once as low as fourth, at Laguna Seca, and he took another pole on familiar territory at Watkins Glen as he, Hulme and American ace Peter Revson shared the qualifying spoils all season long. There were only three DNFs, another race win at Mid-Ohio, and

▲ Head inclined, eyes ahead, hands in control, the apprentice shows the style of a future champion as he drives his BRM at Silverstone in 1965. Note, in the background, the absence not only of Armco barriers but also straw bales. Safety, Stewart-style, had not yet been invented. (Sporting Pictures)

◄ Always ready, the meticulous preparation is reflected in a controlled and calm gaze from the cockpit as Jackie, in the early days, settles in for another day at the office, another race and, more likely than not, another success story. (Sporting Pictures)

▲ Now, listen to me: There was no one like Ken Tyrrell for giving advice and the fledgling champion listens intently.
(Sporting Pictures)

▶ Always a family man, Jackie managed to share his racing life with his wife Helen and his sons Paul and Mark even when it seemed he was rarely at home. Here he is pictured during a Ford promotional event, making sure everyone knows he is in car number one, denoting that this is the world champion at work.
(Getty Images)

▲ Brothers in arms, Jimmy and Jackie Stewart in their racing overalls long before fate and fortune separated them. Jimmy abandoned racing and stayed at home, Jackie swept all before him and ended up living a jet setter's lifestyle with a home overlooking Lake Leman in Switzerland. (Sutton Motorsport Images)

▼ Early days with BRM and the great Graham Hill whose panache, wit and style, not to mention his great skill and courage on the track, influenced Jackie heavily as he set about learning all he could and laying the foundations for one of the greatest careers in the history of motor racing. (Sutton Motorsport Images)

▲ In the season that stamped the Tyrrell name across everyone's imagination, Jackie drives his Tyrrell Ford 003 towards victory at Monte Carlo where he won by 25 seconds in a car with virtually no brakes.
(Sporting Pictures)

◄ The laurels of victory: Jackie Stewart shares his moment of glory with Ken Tyrrell. Few team owner–driver relationships were as honest, or as fruitful, as this one. They worked together and they shared their successes.
(Getty Images)

▲ Getting a few things straight: Jackie, in quintessential fashionable cap, makes his point as Ken listens and Helen looks on. (Getty Images)

▼ Let me explain: Jackie and Paul Newman, one of his and the Jaguar team's many famous guests, analyse a point in detail during the Canadian Grand Prix at Montreal. Newman, a racing driver himself and a great fan, listens intently. (Getty Images)

▲ The most memorable moment of all: victory for Stewart Grand Prix at the European Grand Prix of 1999, at the famous Nürburgring. Johnny Herbert (left) won the race, leaving Rubens Barrichello (right) always wistful about not being the man who delivered the team their most magical moment.
(Sporting Pictures)

▶ Showing the scars of a restless life in the fast lane, Jackie faces the media in his role as president of the British Racing Drivers Club. The mark on his left cheek denoted the recent surgery he underwent as the threat of cancer continued its sweep through his family. (Getty Images)

► That fabulous feeling of gaining success was shared in a flood of tears and torrential rain at the Monaco Grand Prix of 1997, when Rubens Barrichello finished second behind Michael Schumacher. (Getty Images)

◄ The launch of an adventure that was to sweep Stewart Grand Prix to triumph and tragedy as (left to right) Jackie Stewart, Rubens Barrichello, Alan Jenkins (in car), Jan Magnussen and Paul Stewart face the cameras in London in 1997. (Getty Images)

▼ On his feet, making his point and earning his money, Jackie has always believed in perfection in all things and has demonstrated his commitment by overcoming dyslexia to become an accomplished public speaker. Here, however, he is pictured explaining why he is stepping down at Jaguar. (Getty Images)

▲ Jackie and Helen share a moment,
sealed with a kiss that demonstrates
their unity and their family strength.
Together, they have achieved much in
many ways and each is fast to attribute
their successes to the other.
(Sporting Pictures)

▼ Now it is my turn! Paul makes a
point; Jackie listens. A rare and candid
shot of father and son preparing for
business in the run-in to the launch of
Stewart Grand Prix.   (Getty Images)

a couple of late-season second places at Edmonton and Laguna Seca which meant he finished on 76 points, good enough for third overall, behind series winner Revson and Hulme. It was also good enough to bring an offer to race for McLaren in the 1972 Can-Am series, but if the spirit was willing, Jackie Stewart's body had other ideas.

When the Grand Prix season picked up again in South Africa in early March, Stewart shrugged off a rear aerofoil failure in practice to post pole position number thirteen. He duly led the race from the second lap, but gearbox difficulties brought the first DNF of the season after 45. A couple of months later, at Jarama, near Madrid, for the Spanish Grand Prix, Stewart qualified fourth behind pole-sitter Ickx, fought his way to the front after only five laps, but was overhauled, first by Brazilian Emerson Fittipaldi and then by the Belgian. A spin that ripped the Tyrrell's nose off called an early halt to proceedings. The car was not the only damaged goods. A bleeding (literally) duo-denal ulcer was draining Stewart of the vitality that was his trademark, and contributing in no small measure to performances that by his matchless standards could only be described as lacklustre. Monaco, uncharacteristically, was another. The world champion qualified eighth fastest as Fittipaldi's Lotus breezed to pole position; chasing Ickx for second place, Stewart spun on lap 44 but recovered, only to lose power as the wet conditions affected the car's electrics and limp home fourth.

Racing commitments, appearances for sponsor-suppliers such as Goodyear, Elf and Ford, and a punishing personal schedule had all taken their toll. It was time for a rest. Stewart took it while his F1 colleagues fought it out at Nivelles, in Belgium; then they joined him, in enforced idleness, when the CSI decided Zandvoort was not fit to stage a world championship round that year. That meant Stewart had a seven-week break from active duty in his Tyrrell, and that could only spell danger for the rest of the field come July when a rejuvenated Scot, the bounce back in his step, returned to school in France. At

Clermont-Ferrand, team-mate François Cévert inconsiderately put the new Tyrrell 005 out of action soon after it was taken out of its box, but no matter: though third in qualifying behind Chris Amon, Stewart got right in among them in the opening stages, dicing with the New Zealander and his compatriot Hulme, profited from their misfortunes to be in command by lap twenty, and won going away with a margin of over 25 seconds. This was more like the real Jackie Stewart. On the flat, fast reaches of Silverstone a fortnight later, 005 suffered suspension failure that forced Stewart back into the arms of Tyrrell 003, and the two of them gave a pretty good account of themselves despite qualifying fourth. Held up by Beltoise in the opening laps, Stewart caught Ickx and Fittipaldi in traffic and was running second by lap 25, the position he occupied when they crossed the line.

Unfortunately for the Tyrrell camp, the car that occupied first position that day belonged to 'Emmo', who was beginning to put his stamp on this 1972 season as it passed the halfway stage. Now, three detuned performances in a row would put paid to Jackie Stewart's chances of back-to-back titles. The Nürburgring belonged to the brilliant Jacky Ickx, pole-winner and race-winner. Stewart had a coming-together with Peterson on the opening lap that relegated him to fifth, then a last-lap incident with Regazzoni saw the Scot lose not only his temper but any hope of salvaging some points, the Tyrrell slipping to eleventh and not actually running at race finish. It was Fittipaldi's turn on 13 August in Austria, where Stewart flirted with success throughout the opening lap until chronic oversteer let the Brazilian and several others through. Stewart came home seventh. One win to Scotland, three to Brazil . . . and Monza made it four. Unusually for the high-speed Italian track, it brought nothing but anti-climax so far as Stewart was concerned. Third on the grid behind Ickx, he suffered clutch failure at the start and went nowhere, which was exactly where his championship chances had already arrived as Fittipaldi again flashed across the line in his fourth first place of a brilliant 1972 for the young man from Brazil, the youngest ever to claim the F1 drivers' title.

Never let them think they've got you down, though; Jackie Stewart was not about to let Emmo get away scot-free, as it were. He might not have been able to go Can-Am racing that year, but when the F1 circus flew back to North America in mid-September, he made sure he came away with a brace of race wins under his belt as a warning shot for 1973. Victory number 21 was chalked up at Mosport, where Stewart hopped back and forth between 005 and 004 during practice then rocketed through from fifth on the grid to lead the race by lap four. The fact that he held on to win by 48 seconds merely underlined the man's return to his best form. Two weeks later, Watkins Glen brought victory number 22, enhanced by Cévert's fine drive to second place for Tyrrell too, though more than half a minute behind his team leader. His season had peaked and troughed, but with four wins, a clutch of lower places and 45 points to his name he finished a worthy runner-up to his Brazilian rival. He also had an obvious successor in the shape of a tall, dark, impossibly handsome, fun-loving and very fast Frenchman. All in all, things were looking good for 1973.

By the time Argentina rolled around again, on 28 January, Jackie Stewart was a mature man of 33, a double world champion and pretty much the monarch of all that he surveyed in motor racing terms. A new prince had emerged from Brazil, a man who was blazing a trail for the seemingly endless stream of talented drivers about to come out of that country to conquer Formula One, and a new challenger, Cévert, was fast approaching his maturity, on the track at least. Stewart was a relative old-timer, and a survivor. At a time when, as Helen recalled, drivers had a two-in-three chance (think about it!) of being killed in the course of a five-year racing career, he was going into season number nine. Some sections of the media started asking the question of Jackie Stewart that every sporting superstar most dreads. Here's another one: what lies between South Africa and Spain? The answer is, one of the most significant decisions in motor racing history. Jackie Stewart made up his mind to retire at the end of the 1973 season. He refused to tell Helen, for whom it would have meant an agony of waiting, ticking off the races as they came and went, the way Nina Rindt must have done with Jochen just over two years earlier. Instead, quietly in London, he opened his heart and mind to his great friend and mentor Ken Tyrrell, and to Walter Hayes of Ford.

By that time, Cévert had served notice of his own intentions, leading the opening race in Buenos Aires until passed by a hard-charging Fittipaldi, as Stewart was consigned to third by a slow puncture. And there were ominous signs when Fittipaldi did the trick again on home soil at Interlagos. Stewart leapt from a lowly eighth place on the grid to second by lap two, but was powerless to prevent another Emmo success. Clearly it was time to get down to business. Some of the most stirring performances in recent years, at a time when Grand Prix racing has largely become a no-overtaking zone, have come when the leading drivers of the day have for some reason found themselves down the grid: Schumacher at Spa, coming through from fifteenth to first; Barrichello, by then Michael's team-mate at Ferrari, starting eighteenth at Hockenheim, blindingly quick and bent on his maiden victory. In South Africa, in March 1973, Jackie Stewart showed how to storm to victory when he qualified sixteenth but led the race by lap seven on his way to his first win of the season. That unaccustomed grid position came about largely as a result of his Tyrrell's high-speed indiscretion, the car's brake failure occurring just as its driver was somewhere up around the 300kph mark at Crowthorne. Shaken but not stirred, Stewart swept through the field, survived a McLaren protest about overtaking under yellow flags, won by 25 seconds, told Tyrrell and Hayes of his future plans and set about leaving the stage as champion of the world.

Fittipaldi was just as determined that the title stay in Brazil. Victory at Montjuich Park, where Stewart's brakes forced him out of the race, made the score 3–1 to Emmo. By Monaco, it was 3–3. Initially at Zolder, Belgium's successor to the now departed Spa, it was Cévert who had threatened to restore the Tyrrell fortunes. The dashing Frenchman dashed too hard, however, and spun out of the lead, but he fought back superbly once Stewart had passed Fittipaldi and overhauled the Brazilian for a fine one-two finish. A major landmark now beckoned. Scotland's Jim Clark had surpassed the peerless Fangio with 25 world championship victories for Lotus; Zolder took Stewart to 24. What better place to match his great compatriot than Monaco, where Jim never won? Stewart rose to the occasion as only great champions do. His fifteenth pole position put a serious mortgage on the outcome of the event. Peterson set off as if to spoil the party, running away in the early lead as Monaco's notorious bottlenecks saw Stewart stuck behind Regazzoni, but when the Swede's fuel pressure let him down, Stewart pounced for the lead on lap eight and kept it for the next 70 circuits. He and Emmo were now on level pegging. All that remained was to secure the third world crown before releasing the pressure and calling it a day.

In fact, Fittipaldi was not to win another race that year. Hulme took the honours in Sweden on 17 June, with Stewart fifth, slowed by fading brakes; Peterson claimed his own first victory a fortnight later at Paul Ricard, where a chunking rear tyre forced Stewart in for an unscheduled stop and prompted another comeback drive from thirteenth to fourth; and Peter Revson won a memorably chaotic British Grand Prix at Silverstone, which started with Stewart's class stamped all over it. As if to slap down the young Swede who had come through so well in the previous race, Stewart for once threw caution to the winds, accelerated away from fourth on the grid and did not stop until his audacious pass at Becketts left Peterson stunned and visibly shaken. More stunned a few moments later was Jody

Scheckter, who disgraced himself by losing control coming out of the then fearsomely fast Woodcote corner and triggered mayhem. Stewart could not reproduce his thrilling start when the decimated field roared into action again, running third until a recalcitrant fourth gear sent the Tyrrell on an undignified journey through the Northampton cornfields before its indignant driver rejoined to finish tenth.

There was nothing corny about what came after that. On 29 July, a restored Zandvoort played host to a Tyrrell one-two, Stewart comfortably running home in front by sixteen seconds; and then they were all back at the Nürburgring for Stewart's final rendezvous with Formula One success. Fittingly enough, the maestro put his Tyrrell on pole for the final time, Cévert alongside him. He and his team-mate came home together in that order, with the rest nowhere to be seen. Stewart had now pushed the all-time record to 27 victories, and Cévert was hard on his team leader's heels. 'They had become very good friends,' Guiter fondly recalled. 'And although it's something that almost never happens between racing drivers, Jackie had taught François everything he knew. In that last year he said to Ken, "François can get past me wherever he likes, he's faster than I am." That's what he said at the Nürburgring, by which time they had been one-two a few times. Mind you, François's view of things was slightly different. "I tried two or three times to get up alongside him," he said, "and he just gently edged me out!" But as it was François, and he knew he was going to be [Jackie's] heir, he let him win the championship.' To suggest that in 1973 Cévert held back in order not to upset the applecart of Stewart's third world championship may be slightly overstating the case, but Stewart was certainly keen to anoint his young pupil, for whom the future held nothing but promise.

Fittipaldi's loose fuel pipe in Austria meant Stewart's second place was doubly precious, then on 9 September at Monza he produced a stunning drive that sealed world championship number three in the best possible style. It wasn't a winning drive as Peterson took the flag first, but many – Ken Tyrrell among them – ranked it as the equal of Stewart's 1968 Nürburgring epic. Sixth on the grid, he ran fourth early on before picking up a nail in the left rear tyre. Rejoining in twentieth place, he embarked on a comeback drive that had something of the crusade about it: eighth by lap 25, seventh by lap 33, sixth on lap 37, fifth on lap 41, and waved through to fourth by an understanding Cévert with eight laps to go. Tyrrell had said that 'a different kind of talent' was needed to win at Monza, as opposed to the Nürburgring; a different kind of talent was what Jackie Stewart took to every race track he ever graced. Like Clark's similar effort at the same venue all those years before, it was a masterpiece; unlike his great compatriot, Stewart saw his efforts rewarded by that year's ultimate prize. Yet within weeks, the victory champagne would lose all its taste and exhilaration in his disbelieving mouth.

If the previous year's North American foray had brought double success, 1973 was an entirely different story. In Canada, Stewart was fifth, a lap down on winner Revson, as a mix-up with tyres confounded the pre-race planning. Late in the race, Cévert and Scheckter had a coming-together that ended with the Frenchman in the barrier, the Tyrrell bent and broken and its driver fortunate not to be in the same state. It was a dreadful omen. Watkins Glen was to have been Stewart's hundredth Grand Prix. Ninety-nine races, seventeen poles, fifteen fastest laps and that all-time record of 27 wins: what a wonderful way to bow out it would have been, though still nobody knew of Stewart's decision to retire. Whether or not, as some have suggested, a Cévert still enraged about the incident with Scheckter was simply trying too hard in practice we shall never know. The simple fact is that the Frenchman was killed on the Saturday of that United States Grand Prix weekend in one of the most savage accidents ever seen in Formula One. The crown prince would never take over from the retiring king, and

Stewart would never race again, as Ken withdrew his Tyrrells from the race as a mark of respect. It was the saddest of ironies that, before savouring the relief of his own retirement, Stewart once again had to attend the funeral of a contemporary, moreover a promising young driver whose talent he had done so much to foster.

Tim Schenken, speaking three decades after that appalling day, was able to introduce a lighter note in his happy recollection of the Stewart–Cévert relationship. 'I'd say it would have been a different relationship from the one with Jochen [Rindt],' he said. 'He was a lad, François Cévert. He was a lad! I suspect Jochen and Jackie's friendship probably was something to do with the friendship of their wives. I suspect with François, Jackie saw him as taking over. And I've asked Jackie questions about racing, and he would say this was what he was doing here, that was what he was doing there – he was very open about all these things if you asked him a question, so François would have learnt a great deal from him. I don't know what their friendship was like off the track, but I tell you, Jackie would have had trouble keeping up with François. As I say, he was a lad and a half!'

Stewart's decision to retire was made public in mid-October. 'I can honestly say I am a lighter man than I have been for some time,' he said. 'I have enjoyed motor racing enormously, nobody has enjoyed it more than I have . . . and in all the years I have been involved in motor racing, at no time has Helen put on me any pressure to retire.' Light-heartedly, and perhaps tellingly, he also attributed his move to his son Paul, who had suggested his father retire. Stewart recalled, 'I said, "And Paul, what would I do? I have to earn pennies." He said, "Well, you could stay at home and write books," then added, "And to earn pennies you could always drive the school bus." ' On a more serious note, Stewart continued: 'There have been moments when I thought I might have been doing the wrong thing, but I can say, in all honesty, that I now feel a lighter man.'

Still, he deserved better than to have to carry the burden of such grievous loss into the next phase of his restless life. He was left gutted at the last by the death of Cévert. He had grown close to him; he had wanted to see him grow up and shine. 'He was different,' said Jackie. 'He was like a young fighting cock. He was so confident, with this terrific pair of eyes, deep light-blue eyes, but amazingly expressive. He was a good musician; he played the piano extremely well, classical music. He had so many skills, and he used to pull the birds. Oh, he had so many girls coming around the place . . . a busy, busy boy! He was almost too good-looking to be a racing driver, but he was.'

As a racer Stewart might have had few equals, but he was no pin-up like Cévert, even if his long hair, his thick sideburns and black corduroy cap enabled him to cut a style of his own. He was too serious about his work to be a romantic lead. He concentrated, and he sulked. He was not all smiles, with laughing eyes. 'I'm sure he drove Ken Tyrrell crazy,' said Edsel Ford in Mark Stewart's film *The Flying Scot*. 'The pits were always just the way Jackie wanted and the cars were the way he wanted. He said to me one day, "Edsel, don't talk to me. Go away, because I have to get myself psyched up for the race." He was prone to sit in the pits by himself, normally on the floor. People knew then not to bother him . . .' Jackie himself, reflecting on his racing career, spoke of the pressures he heaped on himself. 'It's easy to get to the top,' he said. 'It's fantastic. It's exciting. It's exhilarating. But to establish yourself on the top and then consolidate on the top, and to be expected to win all the time and to be the highest paid, to be the "winningest" driver . . . and to be the pole-sitter, to be the man to beat, to be the man that is the centre of attention, to sign the autographs, to see the sponsors, to make the speeches to the automobile clubs, to the television companies, to everybody . . . There comes a time when you've just done too much too often.'

Much as expected, there were tributes to Jackie Stewart from all quarters. One report stated that his plans 'for the future include testing prototype cars, not racing models, and tyres, television work and film making'. In another, in one of Scotland's leading newspapers, he was congratulated on his decision: 'Most will have accepted Jackie Stewart's retiral from racing with mixed feelings. Relief at this decision must be the first reaction, but it is equally certain that there will be a suspicion of sadness that a brilliant racing career has ended. The domination of the Scots in world racing circuits during the past ten years has been phenomenal in this exclusive sport. Stewart is arguably the most successful driver in history. Having won the world championship three times, and holding a world record of 27 Grand Prix wins out of 99 races, this supremely skilful Scot has left a void which will be hard to fill. Among his many honours was his election by the Guild of Motoring Writers as Driver of the Year in 1968. The award is presented for skill, courage, initiative and endurance. He showed all of these, but endurance must have been his greatest quality, driving as he did that year despite the pain of a fractured wrist.

'Stewart's career has been as remarkable as it has been successful,' the article continued, 'in that after ten years' [sic] Grand Prix racing he should retire unmarked – and this despite some narrow escapes such as his walking away unhurt from a 180mph crash on the Kyalami circuit while practising for the South African Grand Prix earlier this year. He is right to retire while he is clearly in the lead. There is much he can still do for the sport, and this will be achieved better, by a surviving champion, from the sidelines. Eight top racing drivers, including Stewart's team-mate Francois Cevert [sic], have been killed in the last five years. Stewart has chosen to live for his wife and family.

'While it is impossible to compare precisely the relative talents of all the leading drivers over the 24-year history of the world championship, there is no doubt that Jackie Stewart has had the greatest influence on the changing shape of motor racing. He is to continue his associations with Ford and

Goodyear and will clearly excel as a sports administrator and as an exponent of motoring safety.'

There was, of course, some speculation as to whether Stewart might be tempted back by some form of racing, if not Formula One, but during an appearance on *Parkinson* in London he told the chat-show host, 'No, I'm never going to race a car again. I've made up my mind about that. I'm always very strict with all my decisions in my life, and my disciplines are fairly severe, and I promised that I would never get back into a car again and I probably never will.' It was the end of Stewart the racer. His mother, Jeannie, so long an unwavering opponent of her second son's chosen career, also had a final word. 'When I retired,' Stewart recalled, 'I said to my mother, "Well, Mum, I've just retired from racing." She sat there, smiled, took note, gave a shriek and a laugh, and then said, "You're well out of it." '

The driving might have been over, but another racing chapter in a restless life was just about to start.

11. FROM COCKPIT TO CORPORATE MAN

'To travel hopefully is a better thing than to arrive, and the true success is to labour.'

Robert Louis Stevenson

Buenos Aires, Saturday, 12 April 1997, just before two in the afternoon. A sleek white racing car is wheeled back into its pit-lane garage. Suddenly, an object flies from the cockpit. It lands, metres from the car, at the feet of a small man dressed in a white shirt and tartan trousers. Rubens Barrichello has not tossed his toys out of the cot, as the metaphor goes, but he has given his employer, Jackie Stewart, a reminder of a gentleman's agreement that existed between them. In his third race for the fledgling Stewart Grand Prix team, the Brazilian has managed to qualify the car in the top ten for the following day's Argentine Grand Prix. He hasn't just scraped in either: his time of 1m 25.942s is just slightly less than a second and a half adrift of the fastest man, Jacques Villeneuve in a Williams, but it's still good enough for the inside of row three. So, Jackie owes Rubens a watch. And not just any old watch: a Rolex Daytona, a timepiece with a waiting list that only a Stewart can circumnavigate. In a sense, the wheel has turned full circle: Jackie Stewart himself had worn Rolex since his own days in the cockpit of a Formula One car, and now he is a member of the company's board with privileged access to its products.

Nobody would have enjoyed Barrichello's joke more than Jackie's former team boss Ken Tyrrell. Interviewed in 1989, Ken mused on the subject of driver superstitions, then much in vogue because of Stefano Modena's bizarre antics as he got in and out of a Grand Prix car. 'Jackie always used to say to me that he was superstitious about being superstitious,' Ken recalled with a laugh. 'I only ever knew of one thing that was, I suppose, a kind of superstition. When he took his Rolex off, before he drove the car, he only ever gave it to me, not simply to the nearest person around him. I think it was, or at least it became, a bit of a superstition with him. The problem was, I would always have to give it back to him!'

The point is that Stewart was perhaps the first sportsman to make, as easily as he did it, the transition from cockpit to corporate man. How many world champions in any sporting field have gone on to become internationally recognised business people? When it came to setting up Stewart Grand Prix, Stewart's public utterances were littered with stock phrases such as 'blue-chip companies' to highlight the quality of the backing he felt he was attracting to F1's newcomers. It was simply the culmination of a quarter of a century's work with, and for, such firms as Rolex, Moët et Chandon and, of course, Ford. When SGP began in earnest, Jackie would insist that two cases of vintage Moët be delivered at each race, received personally by his then PA, Andy Foster. 'He personified what those people thought their brands should be about,' Foster remarked. 'He was, and still is, an ambassador for them.'

'Looking after the brand' is, in a sense, exactly what Stewart has been doing with his own name and image since he left the cockpit. At the start of the Stewart Ford F1 partnership, the man in charge of Ford's worldwide affairs had one assistant in his personal office. Jackie had three. 'That was so typical of Jackie,' Foster continued. 'He was looking after his brand, paying attention to detail, insisting on recognising, even then, that the fans had put him where he was and therefore making sure all fan mail was answered.' His greatest coup of all, therefore, has had nothing to do with working for other people or endorsing other names. On the contrary, it has been in making a business – and an enormously profitable one at that – out of being Jackie Stewart.

Just ask Bernie Ecclestone. Sitting in an upstairs room in a gleaming gunmetal-grey motor home in the paddock at Magny-

Cours in the summer of 2003, the diminutive ringmaster of modern Formula One provided a pithy reply when asked to summarise Stewart's life and contribution to Grand Prix motor racing. 'Well, like a lot of us, he's done well for himself,' he observed with a deadpan expression that told more than his brief comment. 'He did a great job with his name and his own image. There's nothing wrong with that. He was good at that. Jochen [Rindt, who was managed by Ecclestone] wouldn't have wanted to do that. That wasn't Jochen. He was a racer. When we had our Formula Two team together, it was never supported as much as Jackie was with [John] Coombs and so on, but it was nice to blow him away a few times. Jochen ran the Jochen Rindt show, and he was happy with that. He was thinking in a commercial way, but not like Jackie did. Jochen was prepared to take risks with his money to make something happen. Jackie used his name to leverage things, like with Ford, and people like that.'

Ecclestone and Stewart have known each other for more than 30 years, both throughout in the spotlight at the top of world motor sport. Both came to racing as enthusiasts, drivers with a dream and big ambitions. One succeeded and became a triple world champion before switching to bestride the corporate world on behalf of a string of successful international companies; the other, never more than a determined, fun-seeking journeyman on the track, proved enormously adept at management and entrepreneurial business and transformed the glamorous old Formula One of the 1950s and 1960s from a sport for enthusiasts and amateurs into a slick global media show that has generated millionaires in many currencies for many decades. Stewart, to some degree, has benefited from Ecclestone's redefinition of Formula One, but he has done so in a way that has made him a pioneer among retired drivers and an example to all those who followed. This is, incidentally, what made Stewart a different animal, as far as Ecclestone was concerned, when it came to the creation of Stewart's own Formula One team: the Scot was not in any way indebted to Ecclestone, as so many team owners have been and remain. 'For me, one of Bernie's greatest strengths, in his power position and his dominance of the teams and the individuals, is that he has had to help so many of them out in times of trouble,' Stewart said in 2001. 'There were more "rain-cheques" out there that he could call in at any time than anyone would ever want. I wasn't concerned about that. I was concerned about my financial vulnerability, after having achieved all I had as a driver and having collected a large amount of money that would have kept me for the rest of my life without any difficulty. I was concerned that it could all be destroyed by a venture that some people were already saying I must have been mad to take on!'

They are, however, very different men, albeit men of the same generation in motor racing terms. Indeed, they are chalk and cheese, and there is little love lost between them, though each has respect for the other's achievements. Ecclestone's most famous hour as a racing driver was to take part in the support programme for the British Grand Prix at Silverstone in 1950; Stewart's that famous afternoon at the Nurburgring when he claimed one of his 27 F1 victories. Ecclestone had great respect for Stewart the driver and safety campaigner, but that level of respect never grew to admiration or any kind of affection, and this, in its own way, says much about both men. Both sought success in life, but identified different means and goals. 'I don't think I've ever been on the same wavelength as Jackie, actually, to be honest,' said Ecclestone. 'We are two different people. Absolutely. But I've known him for a long time. I've known him quite well. He is different to many people in that he sticks to doing things his own way. Jackie is a special sort of person from that point of view. Good or bad, he is not like most of the other guys. He has managed to be very clever in leveraging his name and his position whereas the other people haven't even bothered. Take [Niki] Lauda. He's won the same amount of world championships and hasn't done it.'

To compare and contrast these men, Ecclestone and Stewart, is to see two different faces of Formula One as it has evolved since Jackie retired as a racing driver. One is a wheeler-dealer, a man who has established an extraordinary power base and accumulated extraordinary wealth, but who dislikes fame and publicity. The other has used his fame and publicity to generate his second and third careers. Where Ecclestone's business empire sits anonymously behind dark glass and gleaming steel, answering telephone enquiries with the repetition of a number, Stewart has a 26-line entry in *Who's Who*, in which most of the space is taken up with his list of achievements and clubs. His entry dwarfs those of all the other Stewarts around him on his page, confirming to any doubters that he has most definitely joined the establishment. It is where his ferocious work ethic, extraordinary lifestyle and desire for success always seemed destined to take him.

Even during his BRM days, there were clear signs that Jackie desired more than the glory of winning races. 'Jackie was more sensible than Graham Hill,' wrote Louis Stanley in his memoirs. 'He quit as undisputed champion, having decided not to tempt fortune once too often . . . During his career, Jackie has amassed a personal fortune with luxurious homes on both sides of the Atlantic and creature comforts to match, but I sometimes wonder if the cost has been too high and he has sacrificed the freshness of those far-off days when it all began. I remember him staying with us in Cambridge. He had just bought a house outside Glasgow. The photograph showed an ugly semi-detached Victorian house with little architectural appeal, yet it was their home, their first home as a married couple, and was talked about with the genuine pride of possession. Some years later, after referring to his heavy engagement schedule, he said, "It's a real problem. When I'm home, I want to be away, and when I'm away, I am dying to be home." It was a dilemma of divided loyalties and responsibilities. But it is impossible to stay the clock. You can never return, at least not in the guise you imagine. Those who do, murder their memories. Jackie and Helen would look at that semi-detached house quite differently today, but in its stead would be a truer appreciation of what remains. In the case of Jackie Stewart, I regard him as one of the few among outstanding contemporaries who, by brilliant example, showed the way along which motor racing, and in particular Formula One, should develop. His naturalness survived attempts to mould him into a commercial package. In racing, he had an inborn ruthless will to win, but he always kept a tight rein on his emotions. In spite of phenomenal success, he never needed a bigger size in helmets. Not everyone was aware of his spontaneous warmth of humanity, which found expression in so many ways, a side of his nature surely inspired by the example of Helen. To me, Jackie Stewart remains the world champion *par excellence*.'

In June 1974, less than a year after his retirement from the cockpit, Jackie admitted that he found it difficult to reject the demands on his time that were making him busier than he had ever been. 'I've never stopped,' he conceded, 'but I'm still looking for something, a new passion in life. I know that there are deeper satisfactions than winning. What I want is something to consume me . . . where am I going to find a new all-consuming passion?' In less than three years, he had found it: it was the development and promotion of himself as an ambassador, businessman and consultant, representing a host of companies whose own brand images benefited from rubbing shoulders with the retired racing driver. By March 1977, when he was assistant marketing director for Elf and travelling almost daily to support the French oil company, Stewart was said to be earning more than £150,000 a year, mostly tax-free, according to British reports. The other companies with which he maintained long and loyal associations, alongside Ford, Rolex and Moët et Chandon, were Goodyear, British Airways and Ely Cartridges (keeping alive his clay pigeon shooting interests and helping in the creation of the Jackie Stewart Shooting School at

Gleneagles in Scotland), while at the same time maintaining his high media profile.

His readiness to work hard, travel far and overcome any challenge brought Jackie the security and sustained high levels of income that he desired for himself and his family. He had come a long way from Dumbuck and the family garage on the fork of the Loch Lomond and Dumbarton roads. His home at Begnins, outside Geneva, was his retreat from the business world and the venue of his carefully selected interviews with reporters keen to keep up with his new career. The house, set in six acres, was improved with extensions, the addition of a swimming pool, tennis courts and a guests' villa in the grounds. On one visit, for a feature article published in the January 1975 edition of *Business Scotland*, Graham Gauld noted that the music-loving Jackie had ensured that a high-quality multi-channel stereo system had been extended from the main house, along the poolside and into the villa. Gauld, an old friend of the Stewarts, noted also that the same Guy Rodgers three-piece suite Jackie and Helen had owned and used in their first flat was still retained for service in the little villa. This, it was said, was typical of Jackie Stewart: sensible and economical with all his money and possessions.

Stewart the businessman, of course, was not born on the day his racing career ended. He had been at the core of the man who drove for BRM and Tyrrell, who liaised with Dunlop, Elf and Cosworth, and who placed a higher value on his driving skills and on his life than any of his predecessors in Formula One. In effect, the transition from cockpit to corporate man was a smooth evolution. Indeed, as early as 1964 Stewart had made it plain to his friends that he realised motor racing was important to him financially as much as for the sporting satisfaction it could bring. He knew that every penny made by Dumbuck Garage had to be ploughed back into the business and that he would have little cash of his own. By the late 1960s, his negotiating skills as a driver had pushed the rate card upwards for them all. One well-known driver, according to Gauld, told him, 'Jackie has done more to jack up drivers' wages than anyone else, and at a period of his development when he wasn't even the best racing driver!' It was no accident. Nor was it an accident that Jackie's appearance changed, as Stanley put it, from that of a 'perky youngster with ordinary tastes, short hair and sensible clothes accompanied by a delightful unspoilt Scots girl as his wife' into something else. 'Commercial exploitation of his talent necessitated updating a public image to match current trends. His hair grew to an untidy bedraggled fringe hanging over his collar, and quirky clothes added a semi-continental touch, but nothing disguised the fact that here was a home-produced Scot playing it up. Later, the image changed again. His hair was cut shorter, groomed and styled. Outlandish clothes were put away with other childish things. He turned more to outlets other than racing, recognising the potential of promotional activities. Television commentating had an in-built appeal, for Jackie has always been over-talkative. He can't help it. Words just gush out.'

It might have been overlooked deliberately, but during this period it was obvious that Jackie was not only following fashions, he was also setting them, and acquiring finer tastes along the way. He had a briefcase made for him by Asprey, he had his clothes tailored personally in Savile Row, he always stayed in the same suites in the same great hotels, such as the Grosvenor House Hotel in London, and he kept a wardrobe ready for every eventuality in the English capital and in New York. He was a business consultant who was prepared for anything, and if at times it seemed he was prepared to endorse almost anything from leisure clothes in Spain to Japanese fashion, it would be wrong to presume so, because he took great care only to work with companies manufacturing the very highest-quality products. It was reported that he abandoned working for the Wrangler jeans company, with whom he had a contract said to be worth £60,000 a year for only six days' work, because he felt their jeans were not good enough any more. This was typical of the corporate man, calculating that he was better off in the long run not to allow his own brand to suffer through association with something he thought of as inferior.

His association with Ford was, of course, a natural development from his racing career, and he performed his duties as a marketing and public relations consultant with great effect, leaning on the long experience of Ford's European vice-president Walter Hayes, the man who had backed Ken Tyrrell to sign the 'wee Scot' in the first place, to give him expert advice. He also worked in the testing and development of Ford cars, a role he maintained for decades, and one in which his name become synonymous with theirs. Similarly, he built up a special association with Goodyear while, with Elf, which was little-known in France before they entered Formula One, he enjoyed great success. In seven years, Elf went from virtual nobodies to enjoying 25 per cent of the French market for engine oil.

All this was part of a snowball of success in Stewart's consultancy work as his image and reputation burgeoned in the years that followed his racing retirement, initially with a plumb position as resident expert on motor racing for the American ABC television network's key sports programme *Wide World of Sports* in the mid-1970s. This was one of the deals set up for Jackie by Mark McCormack's sports marketing and management organisation International Management Group (IMG), Stewart having been one of the first motor racing drivers to join their stable. In 1974, according to reports, he hosted 25 major sports programmes for ABC with viewing figures that showed audiences of more than 90 million were listening and trying to grapple with his Glaswegian accent. Even 30 years later, long after he had withdrawn from such demanding work on a regular basis, Jackie remained so popular that he would be identified by strangers in restaurants, streets or in any airport in the United States. His stint on American television secured his reputation and his fame in North America for the next three decades. Not so long ago David McKay was on a European trip from Australia that took him on a cruise ship from Nice to Venice. Cunning arrangements with the chief steward meant that McKay found himself seated for dinner alongside a gaggle of American beauties. 'I was amazed,' he recalled wryly, 'that they all drove Porsche 911s or something similar. When I asked if they were interested in cars, they said, "Oh yes, very much. There's a fellow called Jackie Stewart who's always on TV in the States." I was surprised that he was so much of a personality in the States, where Formula One still doesn't have much of a hold.' As early as 1975, Stewart told Gauld, 'Working for ABC projected me into a totally new market in the United States, because however many people read magazines and newspapers, the real power is in television: power of recognition by the public. Today, I am better known in the United States than I ever was as a racing driver just because of being a television commentator.'

This fame brought him a plethora of further offers. It was reported that he turned down one proposition, to give a short lecture tour in the United States for $70,000. Instead, he concentrated on being groomed to work for ABC as one of the station's elite team of commentators for several sports at the 1976 Olympic Games. During this time he was flying to the United States at least once a week, yet he still found enough spare time to add to his portfolio of consultancies by accepting an offer from Rolex, to assist in their promotional activity, and another from British Airways. Somehow, he balanced his life between brief stints at home and extensive travelling across Europe and America.

To help with the administration of his life, in 1974 he bought an apartment in Nyon, on the shores of Lac Leman, near Geneva, in which to accommodate his secretarial team, led by Ruth Kinnear, an Edinburgh-born fellow Scot whom he had persuaded to work for him instead of maintaining a less unpredictable routine in the head offices of a major Geneva-based organisation. She was to remain Jackie's personal secretary for many years, helping to arrange and oversee a schedule that might see him, in a typical week, spending successive days in America, Mexico and Australia. Never other than very busy, obeying this timetable of carefully pre-planned engagements around the globe, Stewart, it seemed, took the move into corporate life in his stride.

'He was deputy chairman (marketing) of our English company when we launched the brand in Britain,' recalled Elf's François Guiter, 'and I remember we had our Grand Prix days, which were really something. We would go to the tracks a few days early, with him in a big Ford and people like Jody Scheckter, Marie-Claude Beaumont or Patrick Depailler in smaller cars. And they took the journalists out round the circuits and explained it all to them. It was a fantastic thing for them to experience. We did that for quite a while. But we were always on the lookout for new ways to work with him. We asked if he would like to drive the top cars in the world again, and twice in a row he drove the top ten cars of the time, and put in some terrific times, too, to the point where [Colin] Chapman said he wanted to sign him up! He worked on a lot of things with us, and some of those films were shown all over the world.'

Chapman, of Lotus, was not the only man to be associated with an offer to bring Stewart out of retirement. Ecclestone, when he was owner of the Brabham team in the mid-1970s, said he was interested in hiring the three-times world champion. Thirty years later, it remained difficult to ascertain the precise truth surrounding the circumstances of the offer: Ecclestone said he recalled it was a joke, but friends and family close to Jackie said that it was a serious offer that was rejected because the new corporate man was earning more outside the cockpit than he would if he returned and raced for Brabham. 'All those years ago?' said Ecclestone. 'It was a funny thing that happened in Zandvoort. It was a joke. Reutemann was there, and we were talking about how much Fangio made, and Carlos,

who is a bit of a wind-up guy, said Fangio "made this and that".
We joked about making an offer to Jackie. That was all it was
. . . ask Herbie Blash.' Blash, a Brabham stalwart in those distant
days, confirmed it was all a joke. But John Lindsay, the
schoolfriend who took over Dumbuck Garage from Jackie and
his family, remembered it differently. 'Bernie Ecclestone offered
him nine million quid to do fourteen races for him, when he
was at Brabham. And the reason he didn't do it was that he was
earning more money not doing it! He was the first guy who did
that – finished racing and then earned more money afterwards
than he did when he was racing. He was always like that.'

Evidence of Stewart's work-rate and his persistence exists in
many memories, not least in those of all the people with whom
Stewart worked in Formula One. In March 1977, the Dunbartonshire *County Reporter* carried a full-page feature on their
famous 'local boy made good' in which the newspaper's special
correspondent admitted, 'After a few hours with him, I begin to
see why I'm not a millionaire too.' The chief reason for this, it
seemed, was that Jackie began his working day early with a five
a.m. alarm call and then proceeded through it at a rate that left
most ordinary mortals wondering if he was from the same
species – in spite of the fact that by this time he was already a
very wealthy man who lived in Switzerland in tax exile, who
had a portfolio of investments and who, in most laymen's eyes,
had little need to work in the normal sense of the word again.
That day, he took breakfast in his Grosvenor House suite at six
a.m., talked to three different journalists, posed for a photo-
grapher, conversed with two public relations men, ate a little
bran and toast, read the business newspapers, conducted an
interview with the BBC World Service, answered some questions from reporters until they were exhausted and then, at
6.40 a.m., left his suite to travel to the private jet area at
Heathrow. 'At precisely 6.46 a.m., he accepted the keys to a
Ford Cortina, registered JYS 1, fully kitted with white cloth
seats, wood trim and a telephone, opened the door for me and

fastened my seat belt,' the correspondent continued. She had already noted how Jackie had exchanged a joke with the night porter, tipped the doorman and signed an autograph for a stray taxi driver. 'I felt like Glenda Slag, assigned to "The Day I Took Princess Anne's Seat in Jackie Stewart's Car",' she wrote. But, she added, it was all done so nicely, it was all such excellent public relations, that 'I had to fight back an envy of all those ladies who regularly get their seat belts fastened in such a solicitous manner.'

Although this feature article, from a local newspaper, focused on only one day in Stewart's life, in its details it also managed to sum up his entire approach to life. By 7.22 that morning, Jackie was taking off in his plane, a rented Falcon Fan that had been hired by Elton John the previous week, to begin a working itinerary that took him, on Elf's behalf, to Birmingham, by car to Warwick and back, then to Bristol, Liverpool and Edinburgh. He talked incessantly as he travelled. He oozed pride in his work and in the businesses with which he was associated. 'He's "bionic catalogue man",' wrote the *Reporter*'s reporter. 'He'll never say "I flew to New York." It's always "I flew British Airways . . ." When he drives, he drives a Ford, which uses Elf petrol. He tells the time by a Rolex watch, shoots with Ely cartridges . . .' He also walked through puddles in hunter green Wellington boots made by Gates Rubber.

Keeping pace with Stewart during the 1970s and 1980s was a challenge to anyone, but those who employed him knew they were receiving complete value for their money. He never shirked a job, he was always properly prepared, and he always gave of his best. Even those who, in later years, did not count themselves among his personal admirers grudgingly admitted that for a man who had struggled with dyslexia his polish and delivery when talking to an audience, when making a presentation, were unparalleled. 'You see him when he is doing that,' said Niki Lauda, who also won three world championships and, in later years, ran the Jaguar team that emerged from Stewart

Grand Prix, 'and you cannot be anything but impressed. He is amazing. At this stuff, he is just fantastic.'

His schedule for that week in 1977, as recorded by the *Reporter*, took him to Los Angeles for a radio interview followed by three days of television work, then by return to London for the Motor Show, and finally to India, Australia, New Zealand and Thailand before he could return home to Geneva. Soon afterwards, however, he was off again to Lagos in Nigeria for an oil producers' conference. His trip to California, on a jumbo jet, saw him take his fabled seat 3A, 'because that's the best seat on a 747', courtesy of years of cultivating the right people in the right places to make his life run smoothly. Jackie carried then, as he nearly always did, an address book in which he collected the names and contact numbers for a wide range of people including junior airport staff, hotel officials, car park attendants, doormen, booking clerks, journalists and others who could help him live a hitch-free life. His reputation for qualities such as intelligence, respectability, reliability, sophistication and discretion played its part in his burgeoning success; after all, it was as easy to make mistakes with a carefully manicured image as it was to maintain one. Stewart worked on his media contacts to maintain his profile in the way he wanted it, giving interviews to key publications on an organised and planned basis. As a result, he continued to appear in *Time* magazine and *Newsweek*, his advertisements, for Rolex, in *Playboy*. His attention to detail was ever of formidable assistance to him. 'The PR organisation behind him is tremendous, and he's very well briefed,' noted the *County Reporter* correspondent. 'It certainly isn't every star who can find a garage owner's widow trembling shyly at the edge of the crowd and go up to say how very sorry he is to hear that her husband has died . . . Half an hour later, he was back on the plane, leafing through the Falcon handbook and talking about private jets. "The royal family should have one. Not one of these, but something bigger. A Grumman." He was clearly going to suggest it to Prince Philip the next time he saw him.'

In California, he said once, he had been tested along with several other racing drivers by a team of psychiatrists. 'They discovered that we had more positive reactions in an emergency and were able to operate under pressure to a higher degree than anyone they'd tested, including astronauts,' he explained, before adding, with a grin, 'They also said that we were utterly selfish, self-centred people . . .' Stewart did not go into detail about who the other drivers were who underwent this particular test. It didn't matter. Even his contemporaries knew that he was the leader of the pack. His success in business and in life after motor racing was no surprise to Jackie Oliver, for example. 'I think it's borne out by him being a supreme competitor. He is extremely confident, and if he believes an issue is right, or the approach is right, he will go with full confidence against the odds and win . . . He's an example of the very few drivers who have won difficult races in an extremely dangerous period in Grand Prix racing, when lots of drivers were losing their lives, and who went out at the top. Not many of them have retired and never gone back to it, after winning the world championship. It's another example of him thinking things through, making a decision and coming up with the right answer.'

Oliver, who like Stewart took the step from cockpit towards team ownership, understood the Stewart way better than many. He knew that Jackie's preparation, hard work and performance in every area of his life were critical to his success. 'He'll always spend an inordinate amount of time explaining his point of view to people who are opposing him,' he observed. 'And he's very persuasive. He gives more time to trying to persuade someone that his course is the right action than most people would.

'We socialised quite a lot, particularly when I stopped driving. We share a love of shooting. In fact, Jackie got me involved in shooting. He campaigned for the Mechanics Trust. He's always been keen on raising money for good causes and using his network of contacts to gain money for those causes, and the Mechanics Trust was a great social event at Gleneagles where he'd opened up this clay pigeon shoot. I took to the sport, and he and his people who were working there on the shoot encouraged me. He taught me how to shoot properly, and from that we went on to do game shooting. I enjoyed a number of really super shoots in Scotland, mostly during the 1980s when he helped me entertain my American sponsors. He did a good job there and helped me keep them for quite a long period of time.' But all of this was only Jackie doing what came naturally to him. He had the 'gift of the gab', a marksman's eye and a delight in making money. He knew his own talents and limitations, and he knew his value. Even when he announced his retirement from motor racing, on Sunday, 14 October 1973, he was clear in his thinking about what lay ahead. At a news conference, he confirmed that he had decided to quit, as we know, long before but had avoided telling Helen of his plans. Such controlled planning and tight management of his affairs exemplified perfectly why he would be such a successful business consultant and media figure in the future.

By 1984, his schedule was the stuff of legends in Grand Prix circles, and people mimicked his accent, pretending that like him they also arranged their diaries in such detail that telephone conversations of more than a few seconds or less than two minutes were arranged in advance. His diary, as outlined by Russell Bulgin for *Motor* in January that year, included opening the Scottish Motor Show, spending a weekend at home in Switzerland, a day driving in France, a day at Gleneagles, a day on business in London and a return two-day trip to New York on Concorde. Somehow, it also crammed in a parents' evening at his son's school and watching Genesis at Madison Square Garden. Oh, and he also shot a television commercial for someone in Atlanta in the middle of all that! He insisted to Bulgin that he enjoyed the pace and the buzz of it all. 'I know that some people will say it seems like a hell of a lot of travelling, but I take a month off at Christmas, a month off at Easter and two months off in the summer. In between times, I live very well.' It was difficult for readers to know if he was joking or not, certainly impossible to know if they should laugh or cry.

He was still broadening his horizons, mixing with politicians, captains of industry, royalty and celebrity, always networking to the benefit of the Jackie Stewart brand and all those that sailed with her. 'I enjoy all that,' he said to Bulgin. 'I recognise that there is only so much you can do in your life, and I think there are so many idealists around that all they do is talk and very little action prevails. My belief is that unless you can substantially affect a major happening, then you should not waste time by spinning your wheels. I feel I am achieving something very few people are in a position to achieve, because I go in and meet a minister of transport, or the president of a country, or a monarch, or a senior political person who can be useful to Goodyear or Ford. It could be beneficial to that country, too. It might be in highway safety, or it might be in almost any area.' He was more than a useful ambassador for these and other companies. Such was his success that he could not understand why other high-class drivers would not choose to continue earning high incomes without risking their lives in racing cars. 'I make as much money as they do,' he said in 1984, 'and I don't have to sit my arse in a race car. In fact, the money's got nothing to do with it. If somebody else is doing something that obviously is working out quite well for them, then why don't you think about using some of those ideas?'

David McKay can attest to Jackie's earning potential. 'You run out of superlatives,' he admitted in conversation in 2003. 'I suppose he's made, in sheer money terms, more than anybody out of motor racing other than [Michael] Schumacher, but *since* he gave up . . . in the latter 1980s, when he was good enough to have us up for Christmas at the place in the Canton de Vaud, he was going through his press cuttings. He had the Labrador – a gift from the Queen – lying at his feet, we'd had a pretty good meal with a lot of wine and so on. Helen and Annie [now

Mrs McKay] were talking about something else, and I said, "Jackie, what are you making these days?", because he'd been talking about his first million-dollar year. He said, "I don't really know exactly, but it's got to be between six and seven million dollars a year." '

But McKay had also been a privileged witness to some of the workload that produced such fabulous earnings. 'He was certainly a great tester,' the Australian added. 'I went with him once to a little circuit called Mireval, near Montpellier. Goodyear turned it into theirs. Jackie said to me on the Monday, "If you'd like to come with me, we're going down to Montpellier for a few days, I've got to test some tyres. I'll meet you at Geneva airport, the one where the private jets are, and we'll be picked up by the Goodyear plane from Luxembourg." I jumped at it. On the way down I said, "Tell me, what have you been doing since I saw you last?" He had almost complete recall of the last month: where he'd been, whom he'd addressed for Ford, and whatever else he'd been doing. And that would be enough to kill a black dog! Anyway, we went down there. It was pretty bloody hot. He had a 924, I think, a Mercedes 190 or something, and a Ford to test tyres on. It wasn't the safest circuit: there was a straight, then a long, sweeping right-hander which went down, and if you made a cock of it there you'd have rolled for miles. Jackie was out there pounding around, and it was very hot; he'd come in, they'd measure the tyres, he'd be wringing wet, and out he'd go again. This is 1985 or 1986, a long while since he'd been punting seriously, and he was going through there absolutely balls out. We'd finish the day, go back to Montpellier to the pub, have a bath, come down for a meal and a chat, and it was fascinating. He was really working at it. A lot of people would have said, "Well, that's enough," but he was there working at it until they were satisfied.'

Testing road cars of all sorts for Ford enabled Jackie to stay in contact with the job of driving he always loved. He applied his experience to evaluating ride, handling, chassis develop-

FROM COCKPIT TO CORPORATE MAN

ments and many other factors in the prototypes sent his way. To Stewart, this was not exactly work, rather highly remunerative play. 'I went with him once to Ford's Dearborn test circuit,' said his former PA Andy Foster. 'He was working with the people at Pi Research on some problem or other, and he had insisted that he be left enough time at the end of the session to go round with "my man", namely me. He got into the car, a V8 Mustang, and said, "Andy, I know there are some things I do that I make hard work of. But this? This is easy." And it was just amazing. At one point I looked across at him and he was totally relaxed, like a little old lady out driving on a Sunday afternoon.'

Stewart's relationship with Ford was not only long and loyal, but also fundamental to the growth of his portfolio of consultancies. It brought him recognition and respect. His relationship with Walter Hayes, the former director of public affairs for Ford of Britain who became vice-chairman of Ford Europe and a main board director of the Ford Motor Company, was also important. Stewart became so well known at the Ford test tracks, in Arizona and Florida for example, that he established equally strong relationships with rising managers and executives who, he could see, were to become major powers in the company. This gave him the confidence to go straight to the top at Ford whenever he had a problem, 'because they know I have no axe to grind and because I have known them since they were middle managers'.

Stewart was given opportunities to run his life very differently. He could have taken a Ford main dealership, or a manufacturing operation, or he could have invested in other businesses. Wisely, in his view, he chose instead to dedicate his time and energy, not to mention his awesome collection of air miles, to building his brand without risking his own savings. His clay pigeon shooting school at Gleneagles, which he developed and supported with great personal attention, became the busiest in Europe. Shooting always remained an important networking tool, means of relaxation and social function for Jackie. He used it to make introductions, meet people, enjoy himself and do business. Gleneagles was an obvious development. It was good business and good fun. In 1988, typically, he ran the Jackie Stewart Celebrity Challenge at Gleneagles, sponsored by Rolex, and invited many celebrities including the Duchess of York, as she was then, the Earl of Dumfries (otherwise known as racing driver Johnny Dumfries), Sean Connery, Steven Spielberg, Nigel Mansell, Kenny Dalglish and former BA chairman Lord King. But it always had to be bigger and better. His enlarged Jackie Stewart Shooting School at Gleneagles, with £150,000 worth of extensions, could in February 1990 boast of being the busiest clay target shooting school in the world. In a press release issued at the time, Jackie was quoted as saying that the school had attracted about 3,000 people in its first year, in 1985, and by 1989 had handled more than 12,000 customers. A celebrity shoot in 1993 had a list of guests that included Selina Scott, Mark Thatcher, Kiri Te Kanawa, Harrison Ford and Connery again, as well as several well-known members of European royal families.

Stewart also promoted himself as an ambassador for good, safe motoring, demonstrating driving skills and teaching them whenever possible all over Britain. On one occasion, he essayed a car around a small car park at Luton Town Football Club on a grey winter's afternoon with an egg in a mock eggcup on the bonnet. To prove the smoothness and accuracy of your driving, you had to complete a tricky course without losing the egg. Not easy, but Stewart, the supreme ace of driving, did so with some élan and made several impressive comments and suggestions. His audience was as spellbound in Bedfordshire as his guns and guests were charmed by his generosity in Scotland.

By the late 1980s, all this was *de rigueur* in a Stewart schedule that included eight days a month testing cars for Ford, and fending off offers to take his particular talents to rival car companies. 'I've been offered more money to go elsewhere, but

it's not loyalty that keeps me at Ford,' he told Philip Clarke of
Motor in August 1988. 'I suppose it's a case of better the devil
you know than the devil you don't. I'm a professional,
remember, and that means I've got to look after number one. If
I thought I could do better elsewhere, I'd go. It was the same
in my racing days. In those days, if my wife Helen had said it
was her or the racing, I'd have ended the marriage.' This
scarcely believable statement, given how close Jackie had always
been to Helen, was followed in the same year, 1988, by a survey
of motor sport opinions, carried out by Ford of Europe, that
discovered Jackie's reputation had made him more synonymous
with motor racing at that time – a period during which Nigel
Mansell was winning Grands Prix – than anyone else, a full
fifteen years after he had retired. It was proof, if it was needed,
of the remarkable success of the Jackie Stewart brand development programme down the years.

Even his business relationship with IMG was conducted in an
innovative Stewart style. 'I see them as partners rather than
simply as agents,' he told *Money Observer* in February 1991. 'I
think Mark [McCormack] and his merry men see it the same
way.' This portfolio of various jobs, his network of partners and
friends, his willingness to fly away for a day when one of his
corporate whistles was blown, earned him a great deal of money
and supplied the platform of experience and know-how to set
up Paul Stewart Racing, but heaped enormous pressure on his
diary and his lifestyle. 'The downside of it all,' he admitted, 'is
that I am really like a dentist or a doctor. My problem is my
diary.'

Typically, too, for someone ingrained with the virtues of fiscal
care after his early life, he was always conservative with his
investments and his spending. 'Some people would say I have
been too cautious, but that is something ingrained in a Scot like
me,' he said in early 1991, at the height of his multifarious
activities around the world, a time when he might split his week
between tyre-testing in the United States for Bridgestone (an

activity he moved into with consummate ease), evaluating prototypes in Arizona, Florida or Detroit for Ford, and, say, clay pigeon shooting in Scotland. 'I have been fortunate in that I have never had a cash flow problem, always earning more than I was spending. I own several properties, but I have never had a mortgage. A lot of people would say I have not been very bright about that and could have used my credit to make more money, but that's not my way.'

Stewart's lifestyle is certainly not one that appeals, other than in a superficial wouldn't-it-be-nice-to-be-that-rich way, to the friends who knew him in a different world. John Lindsay is one of those. 'For myself, and I thought this a few years ago,' he said, 'I know that if I had half the wealth that he's got I certainly wouldn't be doing what he's doing. He can't slow down. He can't ease off or play golf much. His diary is so booked up. He's all booked up twelve months in advance. And he can't delegate. He has to do it all himself. He makes the personal appearances. And he's got the plane, of course, the Jetstream, and that has just given him a higher gear, not made life easier! He got his PAs to make life easier and instead he pushed himself and did more. One year, I remember, he had just seventeen days at home. He does more flying than a pilot. It's stupid. But it goes back to the period he had here, I think, back home, when he had the garage himself. Between that and Harold Wilson, it gave him this feeling that things weren't going to last, and he has overreacted to it. Back in the driving days, he drove and raced everything. Anything that he could. He was afraid there was this financial hole coming up, and he was worried about it. So he just worked and worked.'

Lindsay found a willing ally in Andy Foster. 'I always thought Jackie was a paradox: his strengths were his weaknesses,' the English ex-infantryman said. 'The qualities that made him successful were his incredible energy level, his doggedness in pursuing anything he set his mind to, and an uncompromising attitude to anything that might get in the way. In later life, though, he was still using the shoot-the-crocodile-nearest-the-canoe approach to problem-solving. He is not good at prioritising, not good at keeping a lot of balls in the air. He likes to deal with one thing before moving on. I knew his priorities better than he did, but I didn't have a strategic role in the company so I had to use my judgement in my approach to managing him. "Andy," he once said to me, "I'm a nightmare to work for, I know I'm a nightmare, but it works for me and so far it's done me all right." One thing I learnt from Jackie is that if you are relentless, if you don't accept no for an answer, then if the original deal doesn't come off something else does.'

That particular gift – or irritating trait, depending on your point of view – was about to reward Stewart in the most challenging enterprise he had taken on since making his smooth transition from cockpit to corporate man.

12. PAUL STEWART RACING: A STAIRCASE TO FORMULA ONE

'But what will your mother think about that?'

Jackie Stewart to his son Paul, 1987

Albert Park, Melbourne, March 1996. The Victorian capital is about to stage its first Formula One World Championship race. There is a hum of activity among the many tradesmen scattered around the lakeside circuit. It seems almost impossible that within two days the cream of the world's drivers will be plying their own high-speed trade around this five-kilometre stretch of urban roadway. At the north end of the circuit, between what will be turns five and six, a small figure sits in the front passenger seat of a large Ford, patiently waiting while a companion gets out to deal with Australian officialdom.

'That's Jackie Stewart,' the companion explains to the man barring their way. 'I just want to let him see the track. He'll need to know all about it for next year.'

'I don't care if he's God,' the Australian official retorts. 'If he hasn't got a fucking pass, he's not coming through this gate.'

Some, it seemed, were less than impressed by the presence of a Formula One legend. They might not even have been aware of the gentleman's credentials in the first place. But one year later, the Stewart name would be back; back at this venue, back with all the right passes, back in Grand Prix racing, and back on the side of a Formula One car. The work necessary to get to Albert Park in 1997 had already begun, of course. In fact, it had been going on for the best part of a decade.

It is tempting to think that, his reading difficulties notwithstanding, Jackie Stewart knows his Shakespeare. 'It's a wise father that knows his own child,' the bard tells us in *The Merchant of Venice*. In a sense, it was because he knew his own elder child, Paul, that Jackie Stewart eventually found himself running a Grand Prix team. It was not until late September 1987 that Stewart relinquished the all-time record of 27 Grand Prix victories. He could have been forgiven for thinking that that, at last, was that; the racing side of the Stewart saga was over and done with. Helen in particular could scarcely have believed that, with her husband's record finally surpassed, within six months she would be starting all over again, this time with her first-born.

By the late 1980s, Jackie and Helen had almost completed the process of ensuring that Paul benefited from the education Jackie himself had never enjoyed. He was about to graduate from Duke University, which can be held responsible for his mid-Atlantic accent. He was also about to go racing in his own right, his tenacity on the subject – he'd started nagging at the age of seventeen – having finally worn his parents' resistance down to the point where he enrolled, under an assumed name, in the Brands Hatch Racing School. 'There was no reason to assume I could do it,' Paul has said, and he was right, for at the time his career began history offered ample proof that famous fathers do not always breed successful sons in the same line of endeavour, though the 1990s would disprove that to a certain extent with Damon Hill and Jacques Villeneuve. A racing great would not engender a racing great in Paul Stewart's case, as he is the first to admit, but at least, through the vehicle of Paul Stewart Racing, he tried. Needless to say, Jackie was not keen for his son to take up the sport to which he had lost so many of his friends. Advances in safety had taken motor racing light years beyond the deadly challenges Jackie had faced on the track, but even so . . . 'He didn't like it,' Paul baldly confirmed. 'His reaction, clearly, was that he thought he'd got away with it and that I was too old to go into motor racing. He had survived unscathed through what was a most dangerous period in racing, and now here I was all set to repeat the process.' Yet Jackie was wise enough not to put obstacles in Paul's way. After all, had he himself not followed in his brother's footsteps at Ecurie Ecosse? Had he himself not gone racing as A.N. Other to escape parental disapproval? This, clearly, was something his own son simply had to get out of his system.

The elder of the two Stewart boys duly began his own racing career in Formula Ford 2000, itself the offspring of FF1600, in the spring of 1988 at the age of 22. The name helped, of course: he had Camel backing, and the man who ran his car for him was ex-Jackie Stewart mechanic Roy Topp. Paul's first victory came at Cadwell Park in September of that year, and with that under his belt he graduated to Formula Three – the category in which his father had first come to national and international attention a quarter of a century earlier. It was time for Stewart senior to take a closer interest.

Andy Miller was perhaps closest to the origins of Paul Stewart Racing as a serious outfit. When Jackie Stewart approached him, Miller already had a wealth of experience in running Formula Three teams, though he was not doing so at the time. An initial meeting became a job interview by default, and Miller emerged as the man in charge of the engineering side of PSR. He is quick to dispel the myth that the enterprise was merely an exercise in parental indulgence. 'It definitely wasn't indulgence,' Miller stated firmly. 'I think Jackie made Paul do it the hard way. They'd set up Paul Stewart Racing in a smaller form because they were running Formula Ford 2000, and it was a case of trailer and car or van, and driving around doing Formula Ford 2000 races in England, and Paul had had to do a lot of that himself. Jackie made Paul do it that way: that was Paul's apprenticeship. Once he saw he was serious about it and he wanted to do it, he then decided to put everything in place and make money out of it. Jackie was never ashamed of that; it was always, "I'm doing this as a business." That's how it was always treated.'

How Paul was always treated, inevitably, was as the son of a famous father whose legend loomed large, especially where the

British media were concerned. Later in its life, PSR would give a Formula 3000 drive to another young Scot, Allan McNish, who saw at first hand the pressure to which Paul Stewart was subjected from the start of his racing career. 'If Paul hadn't had the intense spotlight during the early part of his career,' McNish claimed, 'if he had been allowed to maybe develop in a slightly less media-conscious fashion, purely and simply because of who he was, I think it would have been easier for him. I remember the first race I did in Formula Ford. I was on pole position, it rained for the race, and I didn't know you had to adjust the brake balance in a car. I was naive to say the least, and I locked up the front brakes at the first corner, skidded off and finished up about seventh after going off three or four times. Paul's first race was at Donington Park; he was on pole position, and he spun at the hairpin. I didn't receive a single column inch in *Autosport*, but he was all across the back pages – STEWART CRASHES CAR AT 120MPH. The fact that it was a first-gear hairpin at 50mph had nothing to do with it. That was just the difference: I was able to develop my craft without having everything scrutinised by not just the motor sport media, but also the main nationals. I think it was very hard for Paul just to get on and do things. And I had karting experience, he hadn't. When the car was right, he was quick, there was absolutely no question about that. But I think the lack of karting experience sometimes hampered him a wee bit in getting it right.'

One trait Paul had definitely inherited from his father was his dogged determination. In 1988, he was never out of the top four in ten FF2000 starts; the next year, he was campaigning in the British F3 series and outshining team-mate Otto Rensing quite consistently. Snetterton, a significant venue in Jackie's own racing apprenticeship, was the stage for Paul's first win in that significantly higher category. It came in early August in a race also graced by drivers named Hakkinen, McNish, Salo and Brabham, all of whom went on to become Grand Prix drivers for more or less lengthy spells and with widely varying degrees of success. The unique aspect of Paul's Snetterton success was that it was achieved backwards. Mika Hakkinen's accident brought out a red flag to halt the race, at the precise moment when young Stewart was indulging himself with a spin that carried his Reynard Mugen Honda 893 across the line and past the chequered flag. It was one way of making a name for himself in a season where he finished tenth overall. And doing things his own way was, apparently, a Paul Stewart principle, as Miller recalled. 'There was a finding-out period between Jackie and myself when the team was set up, because it was set up from nothing in a hurry, and it took a bit of shaking up to get the right people doing the right jobs. But then Jackie got comfortable with it, and he'd quite often channel through me what he thought Paul should be doing, because it was a father–son relationship, and Paul wouldn't listen to his father, even though he was a three-times world champion. Jackie was aware of that and didn't want to put any more pressure on Paul because he was obviously in this situation of being compared with his father all the time. Jackie didn't want to be seen as too hands-on. Obviously his main role and function was bringing in the money, and the overall direction of the team as it expanded.'

And expand it most certainly did. After a year of running the F3 team out of Egham, PSR was ready for a move. 'At the end of that year [1989],' said Miller, 'Jackie decided he'd like to create his "staircase of talent", so we drove around with his regular driver Gerry chauffeuring us, looking at various premises, and in the end we came across Tanners Drive on the north side of Milton Keynes. It was just an empty warehouse that we refurbished and set up, and suddenly we were doing three formulae! It was a bit of a rapid expansion. Jackie had a vision of what was missing in the way drivers graduated, really. He compared it very often to school: you go through school, university, whatever, and only that way were you prepared for life after university. It was the same with racing: you'd get this raw talent, and you'd impart knowledge to him over the period, he'd have the advantage of seeing what was going on in the other formulae and get to know the people, but he'd learn the Stewart way. And there was a definite Stewart way, in the way you drove, the way you presented yourself, the way you prepared yourself. That was very important to him. It always was with all the drivers – taking it to another level, involving the drivers in the commercial side of things. You needed to perform for sponsors, bring in sponsorship. Through Jackie's connections, people like David Coulthard probably established quite a few personal sponsors who stayed with them for quite a while through their careers.'

Coulthard retains fond memories of his spell with Paul Stewart Racing. 'I was doing Formula Ford in 1989,' he said. 'Then, when they had the plans to expand their team into the "staircase of talent", because I was winning I had a phone call at my father's garage and spoke to Jackie. Of course I was very excited because I knew who he was and knew what he had done in racing. I didn't know at that time that we were going to do the multi-formula set-up. We met, then fast forward to being invited out to his place in Switzerland. David Leslie was running me at the time, and my father came out, and the whole thing kicked off with Vauxhall Lotus. I stayed at PSR for three years, which were all funded drives. My father chose to sponsor the team a little bit as well, but essentially they were fully funded drives up until my fourth year, when the finance was difficult to reach and I went off to Pacific Racing.'

The 'Stewart way' also comprised Jackie's very pragmatic approach to the selection and nurturing of driver talent. Another of his old stamping grounds, Cheshire's Oulton Park, became the empty theatre in which young drivers performed their party piece for the watching Stewart, and often Miller as well, before being groomed to go on to stardom in front of bigger audiences. Jackie might go out on the track and take up station at a particular corner, watching the triallists go through, then radio back to Miller or return to the pit lane to make his observations. 'I always tried to put my point of view,' Miller recalled. 'It's difficult to divorce what the driver's doing from what the car's doing, so you had to consider what tyres they were on, what fuel load they were on and how the car was set up to find out whether they could do what he thought they should be doing. So maybe I had to change the car as well as have the drivers change what they were doing. Invariably it was the combination of the two that made it work.'

Stewart took particular pleasure in sitting with his young protégés, originally in a Cosworth Sierra, and comparing notes about technique, as Miller remembered. 'Jackie would say that you've got to do the same things no matter what the car is, because if you excite the car in the wrong way it won't respect you, it will misbehave; the way you brake, the way you turn the steering on, the way you take the steering off, the way you load and unload the car. It doesn't matter what you're driving. That's why he felt that going round Oulton Park with a rally car or a Cosworth or whatever was good to show the drivers how important their role was in what the car did. And it was very true. I sat in the back of the car, and Jackie drove it with neutral load on both wheels. Jackie seemed to have a lot more time to do things, but he was going very, very quick. David [Coulthard] was watching the rev counter and the exit speeds and thinking, "He's good!" David drove it, put the car into understeer and drove with understeer. Our Brazilian driver at the time would drive it, take one arm off and lean it on the handbrake, which really annoyed Jackie, and then he'd throw it into oversteer before the corner and drive it with oversteer through the corner. Same car, three drivers, three different techniques.

'It helped me as well to understand when they came back. To be honest, we were probably the forerunners of a lot of data acquisition. It came into being when Paul was driving for us and it just gave us an opportunity to help him, or perhaps gave me an opportunity to join in with it and analyse a circuit a bit more and be able to understand what Jackie was seeing: "Oh yes, he's losing this much here, he's gaining that, he's slow through this corner, quicker through that corner." It was on a very basic level at that time, but we made it work for us to develop Paul. It was just a question of whether the drivers were willing to listen. You could see sometimes they weren't interested. Some would just let Jackie talk, whereas others were hanging on his every word. And the ones that listened were the ones that made it, to be honest. He was very good, he still is. If he drove around Oulton Park [now] I imagine you would still be impressed by how quick he is, how hard he can be on a car. If he made a mistake going into a corner he'd tell you he'd made a mistake and he'd correct it before he got to the apex, whereas another driver would make a mistake and spend the rest of the corner correcting it. That was the difference: the mind management, and the control thing, because he gave himself time with his hands on the wheel when he needed to, and the right gears and things – it was nice to see.'

But PSR was, or was meant to be, more about Paul than Jackie. To say that Paul's own driving career kept going backwards after that F3 Snetterton success would be unkind. For the next five years he threw himself into the challenge of proving himself the rightful occupant of the cockpit rather than a professional with squatter's rights inherited from a world champion father. In 1990, when he switched horses in mid-stream from a Reynard to a Ralt chassis, he improved to seventh overall in a British F3 series dominated by the two Mikas, Hakkinen and Salo, taking nine top-ten race finishes and a podium at Silverstone. The results were encouraging enough to send him and Paul Stewart Racing into the 1991 FIA Formula 3000 International Championship. Behind that grandiose title hid the replacement for the old F2, in which Jackie Stewart had also starred, and which had come to an end in late 1984. If we were to persist on an unkind note, we might say that F3000 was devised as a market for the once glorious Ford Cosworth DFV, which by the mid-1980s was in the twilight of its F1 days; but if we were to face historical fact, the engine was at the centre of the new formula's initial success because it made for reliable and very cost-effective racing, both of which are major considerations, especially for the smaller outfits who are, or who used to be, the lifeblood of the junior categories. Its power, not far off midfield F1 pace, also made it a marvellous stepping-stone to the pinnacle of the sport.

While the boyish Scot called Coulthard was racing in British F3 for PSR and having a wonderful tussle with a Brazilian by the name of Barrichello, Paul was enduring a difficult maiden F3000 year in 1991. He failed to qualify at Pau and Mugello, failed to finish at Vallelunga and Hockenheim, and had a best placing of seventh at Brands Hatch in mid-August. The following season, Stewart and Coulthard both mounted F3000 campaigns, the latter third overall, Paul thirteenth equal. Gil de Ferran, meanwhile, claimed PSR's first British F3 title, winning seven of the sixteen races in the process. De Ferran had graduated, like Coulthard, from FF2000 after satisfying PSR's requirements in a special test at Donington Park. 'What made it even better,' he said, 'was that I knew Jackie was watching. When I came into the pits he sat on my front tyre and was talking to me. Jackie Stewart, three-times world champion, was talking to me, a young Brazilian boy, telling me I'd driven beautifully. It was like meeting a legend.' In 1993, de Ferran was promoted to the F3000 team with Paul again, the Brazilian ending up fourth, his boss ninth. Meanwhile, PSR were British F3 champions again thanks to the efforts of Kelvin Burt.

For 1994, the name of Paul Stewart was still very much present on the company letterhead, but it was missing from the side of the cars. Like Ken Tyrrell all those years before, Paul had admitted to himself first and foremost that his real strengths lay outside the cockpit. There had been moments when his name was connected with Grand Prix teams, albeit tail-end Charlies like Minardi, but the F1 door would never open. The honest acceptance of that fact merely underlined his determination to succeed in a managerial role. 'He had a lot of talent,' Andy Miller believed, 'but I think his weakness was really the application of mind management, in that he couldn't stay concentrated all the time on what he was trying to achieve. It's probably not a conscious thing, it's a subconscious thing. But at times we outraced Hakkinen, and he won races against a lot of drivers; he led four races in the year Hakkinen won the British Formula Three Championship [1990], so there was talent there, it's just that it wasn't there all the time. On a technical level, we struggled the first year as a new team and we had the wrong chassis; the second year, again we started with the wrong chassis and we switched. Paul obviously would have done better if he'd had an experienced team-mate who was winning races, he could have fed off that. That's something I said to Jackie at the time. "It will take time. I'm confident we can beat Bennetts [West Surrey Racing] or whatever, but it won't happen overnight because they've been there for a while." In the end, we did. I think Paul made up his own mind. He enjoyed what he was doing, but he saw the likes of David [Coulthard] coming, passing through and disappearing. He still felt he was quick and capable, but in the end he didn't want it enough.'

Coulthard insisted that what Paul Stewart did want was the chance to express himself in the idiom his father had made his own so many years before – and that was the real measure of the younger man. 'I actually don't think giving up racing was as difficult [for him],' Coulthard said, 'or I don't think that was as brave a decision as to start in the first place. Because he started with no karting foundations, no real reason to consider being a racing driver other than that he grew up around racing. It wasn't like Damon [Hill], who'd done bike racing; Paul suddenly decided, "I want to do a driving school," and then somehow persuaded his father he was going racing. So that was the real brave one. I think that in many ways, when you've got such a dominant person as Jackie around, Paul doesn't really get the spotlight shone on him enough, but however much Jackie was able to help – find the funding, find the mechanics, doing the things he did to start it – having the balls and the persuasiveness to get his father to accept supporting him when quite clearly he didn't want to support him to get started is remarkable. I just don't remember Jackie ever being able to talk him round. For good reason, once Jackie has made up his mind on something it's usually right, other than him being a bit forgetful with the odd word or calling people by the wrong name. So for Paul to have been able to tug on the emotional strings of Jackie as an ex-racer and get him to allow him to go racing was the deal of the century for Paul.'

On the driving front, Coulthard, who at the time of writing has amassed thirteen Grand Prix victories with Williams and McLaren, was perhaps surprisingly generous in his assessment of Paul Stewart the racing driver. Speaking at the Nürburgring on the eve of the 2003 European Grand Prix, he made some quite forceful points about the younger Stewart's ability. 'A lot of people,' said the McLaren star, 'might see it as an under-achieving career, but it wasn't underachieving on the basis of lack of talent, because it was marked at points of his career, like qualifying second at Macau, which I think was just extraordinary, an extraordinary performance over a lap of two and a half minutes against very good drivers at that time. You don't drive that lap just by having a good car. Even if some of them thought he had good cars at that time, he had to point that thing round, so clearly there was an underlying talent. The only reason it probably didn't work out is that he never had the early grounding and the self-confidence to have that come out all the time. Yes, he deserved to have his opportunity.'

It wasn't entirely Paul's decision, though, or at least it wasn't one taken without benefit of advice from older heads. His father's former on-track adversary Jackie Oliver remembered playing a part in the process. If Oliver was usually behind Jackie Stewart on a race track in the 1960s, he showed the Scot the way when it came to team management. Oliver spent years trying to turn Arrows into a successful Formula One team, and Paul Stewart was one of the drivers who came to him for a test. 'During the period I started with Arrows, Jackie helped me with sponsorship [by entertaining American sponsors together on game and clay pigeon shoots], and then I was quite close with Paul. Paul was trying to decide what he wanted to do with his career, with Formula One. Was he going to be a shadow of his father or was he going to make it in his own right like Damon did? I had a long discussion with Paul when he drove the Arrows car on a test day, judged his character, and said that in my opinion he should retire and take up managing a team. "Because I think your skills are better applied there. If the Formula Three team turns into a Formula One team and that's what you want to do, I think you'd be better placed there not as a driver, and you may have more success with your father's help, because your father can help in that business with the contacts he has. But when it comes to driving a racing car his help is extremely limited. It's a one-man job, it's only you who can succeed, and in my opinion I don't think you will succeed in following in his footsteps." '

If PSR never became the vehicle for Paul's graduation to Formula One driver, it did get something out of his filial system. 'I did go racing,' he maintained, 'and I enjoyed it enormously. I was privileged to race at Monaco in Formula Three and to outqualify Michael Schumacher at Macau – fantastic moments which gave me a great deal of satisfaction. But all these things happened because, to put it bluntly, of my father's success in motor sport. Clearly I had to represent him in the right way. I had to put in the effort and commitment, because otherwise everyone would have said Jackie's son was a waste of time and I would have looked like a joke. That I could never have lived with.'

The Stewart 'school' produced some of the outstanding talents of contemporary Grand Prix and Champ Car racing, and it was an important grounding for Paul and his father in the managerial skills they would require on the other side of the F1 fence. On the driving side, Coulthard had already become an obvious graduate. 'It's very difficult to put a percentage on the JYS influence inside and outside the cockpit,' said Coulthard, 'and it probably wouldn't be fair to either, because the fact is that Jackie is not someone who just has a little bit of input in a particular area. He is an all-or-nothing type of guy. He wants to influence each and every area. So if he was talking about driving he would be full on, if he was talking about team procedures, public speaking and all that sort of thing, then that would be full on. It would be him virtually leading you by the hand to their offices kicking and screaming and putting you through the course.

'I've got to say, given his level of success on track, and obviously his success off track as a businessman, I always find amazing his patience and enthusiasm for the trivia. Why can he be bothered investing his time in young drivers? I think he is pretty even-handed with his investment of time in that, but it's because he felt he had something to say and that hopefully young drivers would listen. So it does impress me how encompassing his influence is, from the lowest level, whether it be from a "gofer" – not to belittle, we don't have gofers nowadays because it's insulting – to a young driver to a Rocco Forte or any of these influential guys. He kind of swept you up and took you along. He would mix you with these guys, quite confident that you would do your best. It was never, "Ah well, we'll keep you away from the sponsors because you might say something that stuffs it up." He'd have the confidence that if you did pee on the carpet, as he's fond of saying – you know, puppies will make mistakes from time to time – he would use that and make it somehow endearing to the Sultan of Brunei or King Hussein of Jordan or any of these other guys we've met along the way. We didn't really have anything to say to these guys other than that we were racing drivers. But I had three very enjoyable years [with PSR], and obviously Jackie influenced greatly not only what you were doing on track but also your off-track preparation. There's an element of those people who see my career as having been heavily influenced by JYS's way of going about things, but I think I am the way I am because of my family. He didn't take a ruffian from the Gorbals and make me into a more rounded individual. I already had a fairly balanced upbringing; Jackie just helped turn the light on a number of things I would come across during my career, and that was greatly appreciated. We maintain today a close relationship.'

We ought to note in passing that, while PSR deliberately cultivated a Scottish image through its sponsorships, and especially in its driver recruitment programme, the mere fact of being a Scot did not produce any particular favours. 'When we go back to PSR in 3000,' recalled McNish, 'the negotiations were hard business negotiations. They were just exactly the same as they had been with Ron Dennis. They were very much the same as they had been with Porsche or currently [2003] with Renault. That's a fact of life. To be honest with you, I never really expected anything different. But the one thing was that there was always a gentle understanding, if you like – as soon as we'd finished, closed the deal, "Right, that's it, where are we going for dinner?" I still believe that if we had decided "No, we're not going to do it because we can't agree terms" or whatever, it wouldn't have spoilt the relationship – and that is a little bit different to a lot of other people. Certainly from my point of view, yes, the negotiations were hard, but there is a lot at stake in these things as well, so they have to be. But I didn't expect anything different. And I also came at the end of a line of other guys who had maybe gone through it a bit earlier!'

McNish, though, had experienced first-hand the counter-balancing benefit of Stewart senior's advice when it came to on-track matters. 'Just the odd comment now and then sent me off in a little direction. I was also very lucky with the Marlboro sponsorship at the time. They had their own systems in place at the time with McLaren, so at around twenty I was working with Ron Dennis on the one side and seeing Jackie at the 3000 races on the other side. I don't think I could have had two more professional people in their own environments. But I remember one time when Jackie was adamant; that was when I had an accident in practice in Formula Three at Brands Hatch. The car had rolled and I felt OK, but I couldn't race anyway because it was written off. Jackie sent me to Prof [Sid] Watkins the next day. "You must go," he told me. "But I feel fine," I said. "No, you must go." And he organised the appointment. I went to see Prof, and he said immediately, "You're not driving for a month." To me, that was ridiculous. "I feel fine! What are you talking about, pal?" The team I was driving for, West Surrey Racing, weren't very happy because that knocked me out of the championship race effectively, so they asked for a second opinion, at which point Prof said, "Well, you can have a second opinion if you like, but there's no way you're going to race – I've got your medical certificate in my pocket." Still I thought I was fine, but at Heathrow, having bought a ticket to Glasgow, I boarded the plane to Edinburgh and flew to the wrong airport. It was only when I got to Edinburgh that I realised there was something wrong. But to be honest, without Jackie's insistence, I would have raced because I didn't understand or appreciate there was anything wrong. I think at that formative stage of a driver's career, when they're not exposed to the complete safety structure or alternatively the polished teams and sponsors and the ways of Formula One, I think – well, I know that there is no one like Jackie. He tailored and polished more Scottish racing drivers than anyone else. David Leslie senior took them from karting into motor sport, taking them forward, and Jackie then polished the driving article.'

Coulthard echoed his compatriot's opinion about the harder side of Stewart the employer. 'Inevitably, you don't get that successful without stepping on a few toes along the way. I've seen it, during our contractual negotiations. The doors were open, the staircase was laid out, but at the point at which it might mean that he had to put his hand in his pocket – which of course isn't business; business is getting somebody else to pay for it – then you're under no illusions that that's not what he's doing. He's emotional and passionate about it, but the minute it involves the old pennies, all emotion, all passion disappears and it's straightforward business. If you owe him a fiver, he will expect you to pay it back. But again, you know where you stand with him, and that's one of his qualities. It's also one of the differences with the other guys in here [the F1 paddock].'

The talent of PSR's other outstanding graduate, Gil de Ferran, was lost to America. His is probably the clearest case in recent years of F1 team managers letting a star slip through their fingers. Jackie himself put the company philosophy succinctly. 'What Andy Miller and I were trying to do,' he said, 'was build a driver into more than a driver has ever been before. We thought we had done a good job with David Coulthard; we thought we did an even better one with Gil de Ferran.' The Brazilian agreed. 'I learnt a lot from being in a big, professional organisation,' he said of his F3000 days with PSR. 'Out of the car, Jackie made us work very hard. He put a lot of discipline in me. From the very start he gave us a lecture on how to behave throughout the year, in and out of the car.' De Ferran was particularly grateful for Stewart senior's guidance *en route* to the 1992 British F3 title. 'The championship is not a race,' he said, 'but a set of circumstances. You go through highs and lows, and highs again. I spoke to Jackie a lot of the time and he was aware of how easy it is to get over-confident or under-confident. He calmed me down when I was leading the championship by a large margin, guiding my thoughts. The experience I have gained at Paul Stewart Racing, both in and out of the car, has been immeasurable. Driving technique hasn't been the area of biggest gain, *attitude* has.'

And then along came Jan the Man. In 1983, a young man called Senna had won twelve of the twenty rounds that made up the British F3 Championship; in 1994, Jan Magnussen, he of the baby face and baritone voice, eclipsed Senna's record by taking fourteen wins in eighteen rounds at the wheel of a PSR Dallara Mugen. Magnussen blamed his own mistakes for costing him the other four. The young Dane would become the living proof of the viability of the 'staircase of talent' when Stewart Grand Prix was looking for its first drivers. At least, that was the theory. The driver, of course, is only the tip of the race team's iceberg; behind him is a small army of engineers, mechanics and other support staff, and they too were part of the staircase. 'Every now and then,' acknowledged Stewart in 1993, 'we lose some people to Formula One, and that's exactly how the staircase should be working. We can't be cross about that.'

But did JYS think at that time that he and his son would themselves be climbing that same staircase back to the highest level of motor sport? He was certainly already convinced that he – they – were doing things differently. 'We actually have dinner parties in the workshop,' he said. 'It's a way of showing everyone that our workshops are immaculate. No other team does that, and it really works well. We've moved into areas that, I would dare to say, maybe even F1 isn't in. Because my world is not just motor racing, as I left twenty years ago. I've lived a very big "corporate" life, if you like, since then, so I see angles that are not perhaps the norm for a racing team. And maybe because of that we are achieving some success.' (Almost the same words would leap off the Stewart tongue just three years later as he and Paul geared up for their entrance on to the F1 stage.) Paul concurred with his father. 'I believe that Paul Stewart Racing offers something that other teams do not,' he said in 1993. 'It offers companies an opportunity to do more than have their name on the side of our cars. Through my father's knowledge of the world of international corporations and his many business contacts, Paul Stewart Racing has the commercial expertise to help sponsors to maximise their input and turn it into a proper promotion or a workable networking opportunity. We know how to make the team work best for them.'

Paul acknowledged that even then the Stewart name was being touted as a future player in the F1 paddock. As Allan McNish said, PSR was not just grooming young talent and helping it climb the staircase, it was following them on their upward curve. 'As you would expect, PSR functioned very, very well. At the time I was there they were building up to go into Formula One: they had just signed the deal with Ford as the works engine team, so it was pretty much an operation that ran without Jackie at the helm – but he was always at the helm, always on the end of the phone, always wanting to know how things had gone in practice or testing or whatever, even if he wasn't there. And Paul was always there if Jackie wasn't, so there was definitely that hands-on approach, even if it was pretty autonomous within the operation of PSR. It was a Formula One team in Formula 3000 clothing.'

As 1997 approached, it was indeed time for a change of uniform and a change of name. The Stewart Grand Prix team's racing fortunes are documented in the chapter that follows; what matters here is that the skills and techniques developed by Jackie Stewart in those years of transition from cockpit to corporate man to involvement with Paul Stewart Racing were now about to be tested in the hardest arena of all.

Ford, of course, was the key to the whole business. It was a staggering 32 years since Walter Hayes had first brought a perky young Scottish F3 driver under the American company's giant umbrella – long enough for a fund of goodwill to be built up that even the questionable ethics of modern Formula One could probably not undermine. That synergy had come to a head in 1995, when Ford and Stewart agreed it was time for the Blue Oval to revise the way it was doing its Formula One business. Here, after all, was a company that had revolutionised Grand Prix racing in the late 1960s, when it made its glorious DFV available to customers as well as the 'works' Lotus team; a company whose engines had made Jackie Stewart himself world champion three times; more recently, and perhaps even more relevantly, a company that had supplied the motive power to make Benetton and Michael Schumacher world champions in 1994. When Ford spoke to Stewart in 1995, it was in the capacity of reigning world champions, after a decade of dominance by Honda and Renault in particular. Yet little had been made of that triumph. Benetton themselves had seen fit to switch from the Blue Oval to the silver diamond of Renault for the 1995 world championship campaign, during which season Ford's Zetec-R V8 was mounted in the Sauber cars that amassed just eighteen points and ended up seventh in the constructors' standings. What was going on? Ford's desire to do better led to the now famous conversation between them and Stewart on a company aeroplane from the 1995 Canadian Grand Prix back to Detroit, during which the Scot informed them they should change the way they did things or stop doing them altogether. There was never any likelihood of the latter, and Stewart himself was asked if he could help them do the former.

Andy Miller believed the impetus for this enormous step came from both sides, rather than as a plaintive cry from Dearborn. 'It wouldn't surprise me if Ford didn't know what they were doing, or why they were doing it and where they were going with it,' he said, 'but the time was right for someone like Jackie, who had the time and the passion. He waded in above these people that dithered, got to the people that really made the decisions and sold it to them. The big selling point, he always felt, was his integrity. They'd struggled with all the other teams, whereas they trusted Jackie. They certainly did at the top level.' Ford's Robert Rewey confirmed Miller's view. 'More than any other team principal before, Jackie knows how Ford does business and understands the reasons behind our motor sport involvement,' he said. Since Rewey was then a senior vice-president at Ford, his words can be taken to echo top-flight sentiment from the American side. 'There were certain elements that didn't want to do it, though,' Miller continued, 'and they didn't make it easy. I never would have got involved in Formula One unless it had happened, but because it was happening around me, and it *was* done in a different way, it was very attractive. A lot of people joined because of Jackie, because they wanted to work with a small team, not a big corporation, although we had the backing from Ford.'

As Maurice Hamilton has so carefully documented in his 1997 book *Racing Stewart*, Stewart Grand Prix was officially announced in 1996, which meant that Jackie and his henchmen – Miller included – had a year, give or take a few weeks, to make sure they had everything in place for an assault on the FIA Formula One World Championship in 1997. Miller knows just how hectic those days were, and how tough were the decisions that had to be made. Was Miller himself surprised when the moment came and Jackie let it be known that this Formula One venture was really going to happen? 'I believed him when he said he was talking about it, and in fact there were a couple of approaches before the Ford deal. We submitted a proposal to somebody and it got quite close; it was more of a shared deal where somebody else was going to build the car and we'd run it. That was looked at very seriously. It didn't come off, but at least we'd been through the three-month period of preparing everything, working out whether we could or couldn't do it, what staff we'd need if it did happen. So when Jackie finally went off and did the deal with Ford at least it wasn't totally out of the blue. I'm sure I can remember a conversation in the back of a motor home in Spa. We were at the F3000 race, and there were meetings then; it was getting really hot to trot. I think I and [team manager] Dave Stubbs both said, "You must be mad, this is big. This is not just a step up to another formula. This is a different world." And Jackie would have said, "I know that, but we will do it." It was an exciting time, no question – setting up from nothing. I set the initial drawing office up. It was a case of, "Shit, we've got designers starting tomorrow!" The truck bay at PSR was being turned into a drawing office, but it wasn't ready, so we realised we'd better get some tables and a network so they could start working. You worked the day and night before so it could happen seamlessly. But until it happened, you never thought it would. You never thought he'd manage to pull it off.'

William Parry was Stewart's personal assistant for two remarkable years in the mid 1990s. He, too, saw and experienced at first hand how much effort Jackie poured into the creation of a Grand Prix team in his name. He shared the draining effects, often working twenty hours a day for days on end as the wee dynamo from Dumbarton toiled at a massive workload, attempted to push boulders up hills and networked until his brain was sore at the edges in pursuit of the financial resources needed to support a fresh Formula One campaign. 'Montreal was in June [1995],' Parry reminded us, 'and the announcement was made the following January, so Jackie had all of that year [1996] in which to put together the team he needed and to find the budgets he was building into the business plan. There were some very strong business plans. All the final goals were put in place. The route by which he chose to do this, to find the backers, was networking. He did not like to do any cold calls. It was fantastically hard work, and I think it was far tougher than he expected it to be. I believe that he thought he would be able to call in a few favours and he would pull it all together pretty damn quickly, but it culminated in a massive amount of work and travel instead. He felt very disappointed and let down, sometimes, too. At one point he wondered what he was doing and if he was making the right decision to go on. He was badly let down by one company after being given a verbal and a written guarantee that they would take the title sponsorship of the team for five years and that they would pay up front. Then the person who had signed the letter sent it upstairs. After doing some number crunching, the person who would have had to sign the cheque realised that the numbers did not stack up, and they said they were not going to do it. Also around that time, Jackie realised he was not getting anywhere much in Malaysia, after a lot of promising earlier talk about a host of things. Jackie was as close to not doing it at all after that as I had ever seen him. I remember one weekend in Switzerland with him when he was just saying to himself, "Do I need this?" He was reacting to the about-faces he had experienced with some of the people out there, and he wondered if he could put his heart into it any more. It was incredibly difficult for him that summer.'

Enter, to the relief of all concerned but especially JYS, a financial giant by the name of HSBC. 'HSBC, to begin with, were not what I would call enthusiastic,' Stewart would later admit. 'But as the vision extended, they changed their thinking. They were creating a new brand that nobody knew the name of then. It was Midland Bank at that time in the UK and nobody knew what HSBC stood for. They'd moved back from Hong Kong. It was a British company, but nobody knew it, and they were linking up with their Canadian operation, Australian operation and various other countries. It was a great corporate statement, and it was youthful, dynamic, with big accounts. Ford Motor Company was one of their largest investors. They handle a lot of money for them. So, in the end, I presented to the 22-person board in one of the best decision-making processes I have ever experienced in business. The chairman of the board then was Sir William Purves. They had me in at ten o'clock in the morning, I did a fourteen-and-a-half-minute presentation, they asked questions for about half an hour, and when I was asked to leave the chairman said, "I will call you at three o'clock." Yes, the same day! He called me on the dot at three and said that the board had agreed to go ahead with it, subject to contract. Amazing . . .'

When HSBC signed up to a five-year deal in August 1996, Stewart Grand Prix was effectively transformed from a gleam in an ex-world champion's eye to a flesh-and-blood, metal and carbon-fibre reality. 'But it was a period of huge tension for him,' Parry insisted. 'He travelled everywhere, but especially in America. He was suffering great anxiety and working terrible hours. It was always dawn starts, to catch the European time zone when they were at their desks at nine in the morning and he was in America. He was always on the mobile phone. He managed his daily list of phone calls very carefully and always managed to remember where he was with each call when he started again the next time.' Parry's laptop and printer, secretary Ruth Kinnear on the other end of a telephone line in Geneva, and endless audio tapes all played vital roles. 'He had his tactical office with him at all times,' Parry continued. 'He did all the work in building up the team alongside his normal working life, and that was enough for more than one man! We worked from four a.m. to midnight, sometimes for ten days straight through. It was a truly punishing schedule. It never got better. He was always networking. It was the only way he believed in. It got him most of his success, too. In the first six months I really enjoyed it, but in the last six months I was dead on my feet. I could not have done another week with him like that. His family life was definitely second at that time and he just snatched moments at home and with Helen.'

As we have asked so many times already: why? 'It goes back to his schooldays and the dyslexia,' Parry believed. 'He felt he had been a failure, and he never recovered from it. He was working every day to prove himself, and it did not matter if he was wealthy or successful, he was still driven to do it. He was always in touch with that day at school. He didn't want to get fat round the sides, he wanted to be driven all the time.' Interestingly enough, Parry's successor Andy Foster wholeheartedly endorsed that interpretation, and the sheer cussedness their employer brought to the mammoth task of fund-raising for Formula One. 'The number of times everyone in that office looked at each other and raised their eyes to the heavens!' Foster recalled in enduring disbelief. 'Someone might have written back to turn down an approach categorically, and he'd say, "No. Take a letter." And bugger me if a month later he hadn't done the deal.'

The dealmaker himself admitted it was a new experience, even for a man of his standing and contacts. 'It was by far the most difficult thing I have ever undertaken,' said Stewart several years later. 'It was the most complicated, the most confusing to understand of the house rules, if you like. It was very difficult to have what I would call a strict business plan in place because there were so many unknowns. Not knowing what money would be coming in, potentially, from all of the activities that, quite clearly, nearly everybody else was taking some benefit from . . . It certainly wasn't a level playing field. For Formula One, our biggest responsibility was to secure an engine, because as a new racing team, especially a start-up team, in Formula One it was vital. All of the start-up racing teams in the history of the sport have struggled to get any economic security and balance. The one thing I felt was going to assure that for us was the securing of a factory engine. Now, for a brand-new team that had never turned a wheel before, that was a very unusual thing to expect. It was a big issue, and I spent an immense amount of time with Ford senior management going over the fact, and at the time Sauber were having a very unsuccessful period so Ford were extremely unhappy. I wasn't going against Sauber. It was them. They were disappointed by Sauber. And then the question came back: would I get personally involved?'

The rest, as they say, is history. Following on the HSBC coup, it remained to look after other carefully determined areas of the Stewart F1 image. 'Because Jackie Stewart had won three world championships and is recognisable around the world, I knew I could be marketed and used by all the companies we went to see,' he said. 'It was one of the big magnets of the whole thing. So, we decided there had to be a telecommunications company and an IT company, and I decided there had to be a financial services company. We needed fuel and oil. We needed tyres. The others we would look at, as we could see them fitting into what I called "blue-chip, high-prestige" companies.' Thus Hewlett Packard, MCI World Con, Texaco – after some alarums – and F1 newcomers Bridgestone all joined the fold, mainly thanks to Stewart's start-at-the-top-and-work-downwards approach to networking.

'I needed it like a hole in the head,' he said disarmingly, 'and I couldn't have done it without Paul [who helped with personnel recruitment, and in many other areas]. Another thing that's important to say, too, is that I couldn't have done it when I retired from racing. I wasn't ready. I didn't know enough about business. I had not been through the corporate hierarchy; I didn't know how to behave, to politic, to strategise, to present. I had to build credibility, believability and confidence that if Jackie Stewart was going to do something, he was going to do it well. All of those things are why these big multinationals bought in. The benefit of having not done it at the age of 34, or 36, or 38 even, four years after I retired when I still hadn't built up a reputation in the business world, is important. If I have a reputation in the business world today it is because I'm clean, because I deliver, because I do what I say I'm going to do, and I don't let people down. It's always dangerous to say that because somebody will say to you, "If he's going to talk about it like that, he's hiding something," but in our case, if we hadn't had that, it would not have occurred.'

In the end, like most things where Jackie Stewart is concerned, it all boiled down to people, and to a single-minded determination to turn everything in life into something of potential use. 'I am lucky, very lucky, that since 1969, when I won my first championship, I have built up a lot of important relationships,' he said. 'I have been lucky because this sport is so intoxicating to so many people in high places. I created relationships not by design, but simply because I was prepared to stick to them. I was prepared to be courteous to them and I was prepared to show them around, and I saw the potential of that, not for my advantage. If I meet somebody who's highly successful, I'm really impressed because they've done something that's far beyond anything I've ever done. Most of the friends I have in this world are considerably more successful than me, and I've always had the feeling that there's always something to learn.'

That learning curve was about to become the steepest it had ever appeared, even to Jackie Stewart, as former team owner Jackie Oliver confirmed. 'Usually your name and fame is a bit of a one-man band,' he observed. 'You think for yourself, you profile yourself, and Jackie has done that extremely well, so to make the transition into team owner, later on – which I think, in all honesty, he did because of his son Paul – was probably the steepest learning curve he had. For the first time in his life, he had to think of others within the team to bring success, such as the designers and the engineers, people who were perhaps more important within the operation than he was . . . That was probably quite difficult for him, and I did notice he aged quite a lot during that stressful period. Being a Scot, I think that the financial risks, as opposed to a personal risk, probably aged him quicker than the hairy moments in a racing car! Although he's still quite a fit sixty-odd-year-old, in those periods as a team owner I would imagine – as I turned from driver to team owner myself – he probably thought on many occasions that things weren't going well and Ford were giving him a hard time.

'He would have thought, "Is this the right thing for me to have done?"'

13. MARCHING TO A DIFFERENT DRUM: STEWART GRAND PRIX

'It's not a business like most other businesses.'

Jackie Stewart, November 1996

'Me? I'm just an old drummer, mate,' the Stewart Grand Prix guest grumbled as he clambered into the back of a team minibus midway through 1997. The self-appraisal sounded a bit modest, given that the guest's name was Phil Collins, but it was late at night, Paul Stewart had been in his ear about music for some time, the transport was less than luxurious, and we were in the heart of Germany.

The Genesis founder and rock music megastar was a guest at Hockenheim, just one of a seemingly endless cavalcade of the rich and famous who moved across the Stewart Grand Prix horizons in that first year of world championship Grand Prix racing. It seemed, at times, as if the entire contents of *Who's Who* had been given a collective paddock pass and their one essential port of call was the white-and-tartan garage. Joe Cocker, standing in overcoat and cloth cap in a corner of the temporary garage in Melbourne; Simon Le Bon at Silverstone, resplendent in his red-and-white boots; Ronaldo in Catalunya, beaming that gap-toothed smile at everyone the day after he scored a last-minute winner for Barcelona at the Nou Camp; the Duke of Kent at Spa Francorchamps, where he inconveniently forgot the royal wallet; and drivers, too, from Jody Scheckter and Emerson Fittipaldi to former Ferrari great José Froilán González. SGP's first year was, in one sense, a catalogue of calling-cards, an endless round of VIP visits, a chance to rub shoulders with the other half.

In another, and very real, sense it was quite the opposite: a seemingly endless slog for a bunch of 'ordinary' people brought together from other teams and other formulae in the common goal of establishing Stewart Grand Prix as a team that had the right stuff for Formula One. But from the first-floor offices of their unprepossessing Milton Keynes base to the furthest corners of the shop floor, where the gleaming white racing cars took shape, the effort they all put in was anything but ordinary. It was the people who made it all worthwhile, and they had been brought together in a year-long process of selection and interviews in which Paul Stewart played a prominent part. What had started eight years earlier with a handful of people at PSR had done what Topsy did: just grown and grown, to a scale that even Paul's vastly experienced father had not quite anticipated.

'There is an enormous difference between being a racing driver and being a team owner,' Stewart senior acknowledged. 'Driving racing cars is relatively easy: God gave you a talent which appeared as a natural ability. Of course, the really good racing drivers develop it and work at it to make it extend to the highest possible levels. However, creating a racing team from scratch was an immense undertaking, certainly bigger than anything I have ever attempted previously in my life. Getting the finance and the support of a major car-maker such as Ford, recruiting people, finding premises, trying to finance machine tools and extraordinarily expensive equipment – all of these things were immense hurdles to climb. Most people thought that I was being foolhardy and was risking too much, perhaps most of all the reputation I had built over a number of years, which could be immediately wiped away by continual poor performance or the failure of the team to survive – both of which had been par for the course for almost all new start-up teams.'

Jackie's longevity in the sport meant that nothing in the build-up to his re-entry into F1 as a team owner should really have come as a surprise, but that wasn't so: the scale of the modern Grand Prix circus had given even one of its greatest stars pause for thought. 'Yes, there have been moments when I felt I had bitten off more than I could chew,' he admitted in conversation late in 1996. 'Because of the complexities of Formula One motor racing. It's amazingly political, amazingly incestuous, and sometimes amazingly . . . disloyal.' The long pause for thought before that final adjective merely added impact to its use. Warming to his subject, Stewart went on: 'Everybody who's involved in it is incredibly hungry, aggressive and focused – almost at everyone else's cost. It's not a business like most other businesses. I've obviously been associated with it for a very long time, and I see it . . . but I perhaps see it in a slightly different way than most because I've also had another side to my life which is totally unrelated. It's heavily motor industry-related.' For 'motor industry', of course, read 'Ford'. 'The automotive industry,' Stewart added, 'is a giant, far bigger than anything motor racing will ever have, but at the same time it doesn't have anything like the same aggression in it or the same edge or the same intensity. And even though some of the people are making more money, or the companies are richer, there is not the same excitement, or the same electricity, or the same spirit that Formula One has. So it is unique. It can be a very good, positive thing, and then there are other times, and it's on those occasions that you say, "What is this?" '

That question must have oft sprung to the Stewart lips during that start-up year of 1997, principally during meetings of Formula One's most significant lobbies, the team owners themselves. If Jackie Stewart had his work cut out to get his own team off the ground, there was another team he didn't seem able to break into. Like that security guard in Melbourne in 1996, here was a group of individuals, it seemed, to whom the Stewart name meant nothing, as Craig Pollock can testify. As the Tyrrell fortunes waned, it was Pollock who had driven the purchase and renaming of that team as British American Racing. 'His biggest problem,' Pollock felt, 'was that he expected to be respected, instead of earning respect. The moment he came in and did that you could almost literally see a lot of the team principals just cut him off.'

Like Stewart, Pollock too would have to come to terms with the way F1 conducted its business. Sitting in the Magny-Cours paddock in 2003, Pollock's words still betrayed some of the bewilderment that had accompanied his and Stewart's 'initiation'. 'The first time I saw him,' he said, 'was in a team principals' meeting which took place at the Hilton Hotel, Heathrow terminal four, London. We were all sitting in the meeting room downstairs. Jackie was on one side of the table, I was on the other, and I didn't know what to expect. I just can't tell anybody how shocked I was at how a team principals' meeting like this was conducted. Of course, Max [Mosley] and Bernie [Ecclestone] were there, and it was definitely a system of "divide and rule": keep all the team principals fighting against one another – and they did that. To me, Jackie was quite vocal, and he did want to get his point over, but every time he tried to get his point over all the old guys in the room would raise their eyebrows and basically say, "Well, here we go again." The message that was being sent was, "You're the new guy. You sit in your corner and you listen to what we have to say." For me, it was learning lessons by watching the interaction between Jackie, the new boy, with Paul at his side, and them. It was a lesson for me on how I should react and maybe at times how I should not react, so it taught me that in my first year I should sit back and listen and basically only offer my opinion if I was asked. Which is what I did.'

But waiting to be asked to offer an opinion is not a Jackie Stewart trait. 'I have to say,' Pollock went on, 'I don't think he had anything substantial to say or anything that he could have offered to the team principals at that particular time. The only thing I can remember is, anything he did say was solid and sensible as opposed to some of the stuff that was going on in the room. There were definitely – and he noted this – different factions inside that room. You'd always get Ron [Dennis, of McLaren] and Frank [Williams] stuck together, and you'd always have Jean Todt [Ferrari] out on a limb. Then you'd have the Walkinshaws and the Jordans wheeling and dealing in the background; and then you'd get the sensible people: [Gabriele] Rumi from Minardi, Jackie, myself . . . What we wanted to do was something that was very positive for the future, make sure the sport was doing things in a very open way. And I would say that Peter Sauber fell into that category as well.' In effect, then, a Swiss cartel? 'Yes, exactly. Jackie had his permit to live in Switzerland, I was a Swiss national, and so were the other guys, so there were four Swiss in there and it was quite interesting. We very rarely had mini group meetings. Everyone kept to themselves. You would maybe get Ron and Frank talking together, but if I was going to have a mini-meeting, the ones I'd have had a mini meeting with at that time would have been Rumi, Jackie and probably Peter. To me, it was the straight team.'

Stewart himself subsequently went on record saying that he felt he was the only man in the room who wanted to conduct normal business. Pollock backed him up. 'I would totally agree. I was dumbfounded and shocked. The way that I saw the first team principals' meeting being conducted was – well, it was like when I was a prefect at school, and we held prefects' meetings, and we had agendas and there was a time restraint put on them and each agenda item had a given amount of time and you would then go through it. But I then became a teacher, and I went to a teachers' meeting and I thought it was the most disgusting meeting I had ever had because they were totally disorganised. Then I went into a team principals' meeting and I thought, "Well, the teachers' meeting was good." It was the biggest mess I've ever seen.'

Into this chaos, it seems, Stewart was trying to bring a little order. But it is in the nature of clubs to imagine they are exclusive, and Formula One fancies itself as the most exclusive of all. Stewart's own shortcomings didn't help his cause. One was his insistence on bringing Paul to meetings with him, something that Pollock says shocked him – which leaves little room for doubt as to how the other team principals would have reacted. The other was the Stewart insistence on having his say, whether others want to hear it or not. 'I would say he calmed down during the year,' Pollock conceded. 'He was far less vocal towards the end of the year than he was at the start, but again, anything he had to say would be logical. The only thing was that Jackie does tend to be a little bit long-winded. Instead of saying something in two words, he will think of fifty words to say the same thing, whereas I would probably only say my two words because I am a little bit shyer than he is. But he did calm down a lot.'

Small wonder, then, that the former world champion felt moved to ask, 'What is this?' Moving back to less rarefied heights, 'this', in mid- to late 1996, was an opportunity at which a number of people both inside and outside Formula One at the time could not resist jumping. When it came to recruiting staff for this extraordinary challenge, Jackie Stewart for once did have to stop talking and listen to others. He simply had to take advice about who was good at what, about who might be available and who might fit the Stewart Grand Prix bill. 'He went far and wide within the industry to get to who he could,' recalled Andy Miller, who witnessed the whole process, 'but it's a dangerous place to be taking advice. Most people in Formula One have got an ulterior motive; there's always a slant to it. Paul was very, very involved, to be honest. Paul got very close to the people we were taking on, he was heavily involved with the interviewing. I think he was very much Jackie's representative. That was definitely his function. But Jackie was never *not* involved, let's put it that way! Wherever Jackie is, he's only a phone call away, and the phone would ring constantly. He knew what was going on, everyone knew what his opinions were all the time.' There was, too, an element of the closed shop about it all, as team manager David Stubbs and Paul found. 'The people they were contacting and getting into the team from Formula One were very protective of Formula One and felt that only people with an intimate Formula One knowledge had anything to contribute,' said Miller.

Among the people who joined because of Jackie, one at least came from the furthest-flung corner of the globe around which Stewart had been trotting for so many years. When you speak with a Scottish accent, love Formula One and have Jackie Stewart on the other end of the line asking you to come home and work as media manager with his new Grand Prix team, it's hard to say no. Stuart Sykes, the Scots half of the two authors involved in writing this book, didn't. Given that 'home' was actually in Australia and he was already 50 years old, happily married and apparently entirely settled, it was a clear case of the heart ruling the head. 'If your heart's in it,' John Young Stewart had said from a distance of 12,000 miles, 'you should do it.' Which is all very well when you're not the one who has to move lock, stock and two smoking barrels to the opposite side of the world to do it. Still, Jackie had moved heaven and earth to get this team together; why shouldn't a fellow Scot move halfway round the earth to be a small part of it?

A personal chronology of the first year of Stewart Grand Prix would start with the sense of numbed disbelief that came from finding oneself standing at the home of British motor sport on the morning – the very early morning – of 14 January 1997. 'Numbed' can be taken literally, for Silverstone was, as usual at that and many other times of the year, a bleak, bitterly cold and utterly inhospitable place. Jackie turned up wearing something on his head that, from a distance, looked alarmingly like a dead cat but turned out on closer inspection to be a sensible fur hat. We were on the national circuit, or at least in a small marquee adjacent to it. The local identity known as Silverstone Sid was determined to impose a mid-winter speed limit, which meant SF-1 would not be able to stretch its legs, better known as the Ford Zetec-R V10 engine. But at least the car was about to run, and to perform more meaningful manoeuvres than the straight line it had described at Boreham in December when this Antipodean recruit was still in the process of winding up his affairs down under. Despite the cold, there was an undeniable feeling of warmth beneath the surface. It came principally from Messrs Barrichello and Magnussen, SGP's driving recruits, as they prepared for their first real taste of a car that would carry them into battle, Rubens for his fourth full season of Grand Prix racing, Jan for his very first. Never demonstrative, the deep-voiced Dane was nevertheless excited at the prospect. His Brazilian driving partner, however, has never been one to conceal his emotions, and the rather truncated test managed to give everyone present a sense that something big was about to happen. It nearly did just a few days later.

First, though, the perfect antidote to Northampton in January was a trip to Jerez for further testing on a circuit then still very much part of the F1 scene. Barcelona followed, enlivened by a hilarious moment when reigning world champion Damon Hill stole up behind the entirely betartaned Jackie Stewart and triggered a very loud version of 'Scotland the Brave' on his mobile phone. This second Spanish jaunt was then dampened somewhat when the Stewart Grand Prix media manager, preoccupied by some hire car document or other, walked into an overhead sign at Barcelona airport and had to return swathed in bandages later that same day to pick up Jackie and his guests, Jimmy Stewart and John Lindsay. 'What happened to you?' asked an incredulous team principal. The man being questioned could scarcely say how stupid he had been, or that the Stewart mechanics up at the Circuit de Catalunya had taken about half an hour to stop laughing and then a further nanosecond to come up with a yellow hard-hat emblazoned with the SGP logo in case of further accidents. Thanks, guys.

The next test venue was Estoril, always a personal favourite though no longer on the regular Grand Prix calendar. Formula One fans will know that the Portuguese track has a longish pit straight followed by a quick downhill right-hand plunge.

Testing is, by its very nature, a rather dull process for anyone who is not intimately involved in preparing the car or actually driving it. It was a shock, then, to be jolted out of incipient boredom by a dull crump from the right-hand end of the circuit. Jan had just gone past; we knew it could only be our boy. He was just starting to pick up the pace early in his stint; the configuration of the Estoril terrain meant there was no way of putting a gravel trap at the outside of that corner. At once there came that awful reaction, these days thankfully rare on motor racing circuits but still enough to make you catch your breath. What had happened? Was the youngster all right?

It was a desperately anxious posse of SGP members that set off on foot across the infield to find the answers to those fearful questions. The feeling of dread was only intensified by a message coming through the headsets from some member of the Estoril circuit personnel: he seemed to be saying, rather hysterically, that something dire had indeed happened. To say it was a relief to find Jan trapped in his cockpit may sound strange, but he was clearly more or less unharmed. The left rear suspension wishbone was the culprit; the car had been pitched into the unforgiving barrier on the outside, and part of the front right suspension had come through, pinning Magnussen by his overalls and leaving him with a small cut on his left calf. The ever-alert SGP chief mechanic David Redding (yes, 'Otis' to all and sundry) had stopped the enthusiastic Estoril rescue team from taking their big cutting tools to the tub, and a penknife eventually freed the Dane who walked to an ambulance and was driven off for hospital treatment. The bigger injury was to the team's first two-car test schedule. But that pit-of-the-stomach moment, when the telltale noise came and everyone in the Stewart garage exchanged thunderstruck glances, remains loud and clear in the memory.

Late in 1996, just before the launch of the SF-1, some eight months after being denied access to the Albert Park track where the Grand Prix team bearing his name would make its world championship debut, Jackie Stewart was doing what he has always done best: looking ahead. This time it was to his next visit to Australia and the moment 'his' car would join its sisters on a starting grid for the first time. Even for a three-times world champion, surely there would be room for a few butterflies? 'No question,' was the answer. 'It's a big event for us. The infrastructure that we've got is brand new. It will be the first time that we as a team will be working together on a single purpose. Everyone else in the team has some experience or knowledge in some form or another, or almost all. This will be Paul's first Grand Prix in this role. So it's going to be a big event for us all.'

By early 1997, Andy Miller had been drafted in to the Formula One team from his previous safe haven at PSR. 'I think they wanted to get somebody they could trust,' he explained. 'Formula One is such a world that it's easy to weave a web of confusion over what's going on, who's doing what, why they're doing it and how much money they're spending. Jackie likes to be in control, and I think it got to the point where he wasn't in control enough, so we restructured in such a way that he got back the control and knowledge of what was happening. Jackie's always been a workaholic. He was determined to be committed to Ford and he wanted to deliver, so he put in every effort he could and wanted everybody else to do the same to make this impossible dream, if you can call it that, actually turn into a reality.'

Dream? Anyone who was with Stewart Grand Prix in March 1997 for the team's debut weekend in the Formula One World Championship might remember it as more of a nightmare. That was the week when the magnitude of the task ahead came into stark and daunting focus. Yet the build-up had gone as well as, if not better than, anyone could reasonably have expected. Key appointments like that of Alan Jenkins, the immensely talented and experienced designer (ex-McLaren, ex-Penske, ex-Onyx, ex-Arrows), as technical director had brought the drive needed to produce a car, and the factory to build it in, in time for a December 1996 launch. Stubbs and Miller had contributed their own experience and pragmatism to the cause. And Stewart had signed the gifted Brazilian Rubens Barrichello, then still just 24 but already a seasoned Grand Prix regular, as their lead driver. Barrichello, formerly with Jordan, had done most of the negotiating himself before bringing the amiable Fred della Noce in as his personal manager later in the year. So the deal was done between the Brazilian driver and the Scottish team principal? 'Yes, and Paul as well. Paul had a good influence,' Barrichello recalled at the 2003 French Grand Prix. 'They worked very well as a family and I think the deal was well concluded. At the time I was in Japan. I was asleep actually, and I was woken up to sign the contract. I was happy with everything financially, and also I had the mind ready to help the team become bigger.' For Barrichello, in a sense, it was a golden opportunity, for all was not well with his still embryonic F1 career. 'Obviously,' he added, 'when they – and I think that's fair to say – when they contracted me they knew that I was experienced and still young and still hungry to win. But they thought that Jan Magnussen was the new Ayrton Senna.' Magnussen's F3 exploits, of course, had done much to impress all and sundry.

Inevitably, there was also media speculation that Jackie and Paul might round off the 'staircase of talent' by signing a Scottish driver. Coulthard was one of the names in the frame, though his situation never lent itself to such a move. 'It's one of those hypotheticals,' he said in 2003. 'My arrival in Formula One was at a different point, so I wouldn't have wanted to give up my opportunity at Williams or McLaren, two of the most successful teams in Formula One. Yes – as I said to Jackie, Paul, Mark, Helen, family and friends – yes, it would have been great to have mixed business with pleasure, because I think in certain circumstances it can work, but there was never that option.'

Allan McNish was another. 'Obviously we spoke about it,' the former PSR F3000 driver admitted. 'In racing, there are a lot of other influences. Rubens was regarded as a regular by then, and Jan had come through PSR and dominated F3, in fact beaten all Senna's records, so I don't think there was much of a question at that time from a marketing point of view in [Ford headquarters at] Dearborn. But certainly we discussed it.' Another seasoned pro with an eye on the Stewart seat was not a Scot, but an Englishman who has since grown very close to Jackie. 'I nearly did go to Stewart, actually, when I left Jordan at the end of 1996,' said former Tyrrell protégé Martin Brundle, now much more famous for his starring role in ITV's Grand Prix coverage. 'But nowadays we don't ever talk about it! I would quite like to have driven for them, but they'd already got Magnussen, and then it was between me and Rubens, and they took Rubens.' In McNish's view, the absence of a Scottish name from the Stewart Grand Prix drivers' roll is something the Stewarts themselves probably do regret. 'The only thing which would have been nice, I think, though circumstances didn't allow it, would have been if there was a Scottish driver racing in an SGP car, because there's been a Scottish driver in every other formula through PSR. At the end of it, though, F1 is a hard business, and if it doesn't fit, or the drivers aren't there at the time, or the sponsors don't want it . . . That's a fact of life. But I'm pretty sure it would have been a dream for Jackie and Paul.'

The non-Scots signings had been announced within three weeks of each other in October 1996, and just a few months after testing they had their baptism by fire in Melbourne. There was a huge welcome for the F1 newcomers, which that year, alongside Stewart and his team, included four-times world champion Prost and the re-badged Ligier outfit Alain had recently taken over. Australians being unreceptive to anything that doesn't speak English, however, it was understandably the Scot and his distinctive brand of the native tongue that captured most of the media attention. Maybe it was the tartan trews: Melbourne had certainly never seen the like, especially when

Stewart junior replicated the Stewart senior fashion statement. The week went by in a blur of sponsorship activity, during which Magnussen was roundly told off by the team principal for turning up at a cocktail function in his driver's overalls rather than the made-to-measure suit that made both him and Barrichello look like schoolboys dressed up for an outing with grown-ups. For the SGP mechanics there was no time for such frivolity. Some of them totalled just four hours of sleep that weekend.

Jan's car had not previously turned a wheel before it was asked to go out and do its stuff at the first Grand Prix of the season. Friday was hard: a handful of laps between them, a long night for the SGP crew members, and an anxious wait to see if gremlins had been got rid of in time for Saturday's qualifying (just the one-hour, all-or-nothing session in those days). Jan struggled to nineteenth on the grid, Rubens almost cracked the top ten – would probably have done so but for a late-session red flag and some damage from running over someone else's accident debris – but even P11 was enough to bring a tear to the eyes of Stewarts, father and son. It was also the subject of immense pride among the rest of the team, even if most of them could hardly keep their eyes open.

And then came the race. As Messrs Villeneuve, Irvine and Herbert blotted their copybooks on the opening lap, Rubens and Jan picked their way through carefully and at one stage ran together at the tail end of the top ten. But the lack of pre-season testing found the SF-1s out: Magnussen left the track with rear suspension problems, and not long afterwards Barrichello coasted to a halt with a chronically sick Cosworth. Anti-climax, all round. But at least there had been no major embarrassment, no sense of being in a place where Stewart Grand Prix did not belong – and that was more than could be said of the shambolic Lola effort from the adjoining garage. SGP had arrived. The first Grand Prix might have induced more insomnia than intoxication, but there had been promising signs before the dreaded initials DNF were pencilled in. 'Obviously it started on a low,' admitted Andy Miller. 'It was an incredibly difficult weekend in Melbourne. You go there with one car and come away with just about three, having built the things there, losing suitcases and all the logistical problems you could possibly imagine could happen in one weekend. A whole week with no sleep . . . We were in Formula One, no question about it!'

Including this Melbourne meet, from 1997 to 1999 Stewart Grand Prix contested 49 world championship races, used four drivers – Barrichello, Magnussen, Jos Verstappen when Jan was released midway through the second year, and Johnny Herbert – and scored, in successive years, six points, five points and 36 points, finishing ninth, eighth and sixth in the constructors' championship, a sequence that tells its own story with stark clarity. As we shall see in the next chapter, the three-year history of Stewart Grand Prix as a Formula One racing team in its own right reached a zenith in two key events, the twin poles of the team's achievement in that short but never uninteresting period. But there were several other highs along the way: Rubens qualifying on the third row in only the team's third Grand Prix weekend in Argentina; the Brazilian's brilliant third-fastest time in qualifying in Canada that same year; two SF-1s together on the third row when Grand Prix racing returned to Austria in September 1997; the first two-car points-scoring finish in Canada in June 1998, when his first-ever point wasn't enough to keep Jan in his Stewart cockpit; SF-3's brilliant harnessing of the equally brilliant 1999 Cosworth engine ('a little gem', as Andy Miller enthused); and the team's one and only pole position, at a wet French Grand Prix at Magny-Cours in 1999, when Rubens showed all his delicacy of touch in tricky conditions (Rubens was only twice out of the top ten in qualifying that season).

To balance that, the lows came thick and fast as well: a dismal Spanish GP in May 1997; an even more dismal maiden home Grand Prix when technical manager and media manager looked at each other as yet another engine let go in qualifying and decided all they could do was fall about laughing, because if they didn't they'd cry; a total of 26 DNFs between the two SF-1s that year; and a much poorer car, plagued by gearbox, transmission and differential problems and an inadequate engine, in 1998, when there simply hadn't been time or people enough to plan for the season while still struggling through year one. 'Being late with the [1998] car had the biggest influence,' admitted Alan Jenkins. 'But there was nothing else we could have done. We had done wind tunnel work for SF-2 quite early on, but with the grooved tyres [a new FIA requirement that season] and other issues, the job of building a new car was too big for us to start any earlier than we did.' David Stubbs was more trenchant. 'Unfortunately, the SF-2 was a blinking disaster, wasn't it? We should have developed the SF-1, but we went for a carbon gearbox and things like that, and it was a nightmare.'

And some moments were memorable for other reasons. Take that first British Grand Prix; it wasn't all about engines. From pressing the flesh with Fergie to a photo opportunity with three Rab C. Nesbitt look-alikes, it was a weekend full of human interest. In the film *Local Hero* by Bill Forsyth, a Scottish film-maker with a wonderful sense of humour, there is a running visual gag in which Gordon-John Sinclair rides a scooter around the fictional Scottish village that is the scene of the action. Time and again he appears, often in the distance as a tiny figure zigzagging his way across the rather desolate landscape. Silverstone, too, is a desolate landscape, and anyone taking the long view of the Northampton facility on the weekend of the British Grand Prix in 1997 would have seen another small figure zooming tirelessly to and fro. It was another local hero, also from Scotland, and his name was Jackie Stewart. Actually there were two small figures on the bike, and for once JYS was the passenger. The driver at that manic first home race for Stewart Grand Prix was Jackie's personal assistant, Andy Foster. Major Foster (rtd), actually. To the task of running Stewart's life like clockwork, Foster brought many years' experience in Her Majesty's armed services, an extremely practical bent, an infantryman's unflappable nature and a priceless 'can-do' attitude. But Foster was also in a privileged position to see how hard it all was. 'I worked for him during possibly the busiest year of his life,' he said. 'He tried to fit managing a Formula One team into a life that was already eighteen-hour days and seven-day weeks, who knows how many transatlantic trips, and so on. In effect he was trying to fit another full-time job into maybe 25 per cent of his time, which is where we come back to the incredible energy.

'As an ex-infantryman, one of the greatest assets JYS recognised in me was the ability to find demon routes to the airport if both SGP drivers were out of a race before the end. He used to love it. "Thanks for doing such clever things," he'd say. When we were in a real hurry, though, JYS would insist on driving while I navigated. Coming away from the Nürburgring, I told JYS to turn right, then immediately left. JYS took the right turn but was heading straight on when I screamed, "No, Jackie, left!" and we scraped round and went across a bridge on its cycle path. "Jackie," I said, "if I had done that you'd have crucified me." "Yes," said JYS, "but at least I did it smoothly." '

The other Andy, Miller, had his own take on what was good and less good during the Stewart years. One downside was the difficulty of forging a genuine working relationship between Stewart, on the one hand, and Ford as represented by Cosworth on the other. 'They didn't want to be there,' Miller thought. 'Basically they wanted Tom Walkinshaw to have the team. They didn't want Jackie Stewart. It wasn't the easiest of marriages. But by the end of the year [1997] we had some good results. Considering the lack of time and knowledge, some of the qualifying performances were fantastic. Remember Canada – it was stunning. First year! But that made the second year harder.'

Miller's sense of pride at having seen the team not only survive year one, but do so with its collective head held high, was evident. 'It's very, very difficult to enter Formula One at that level,' he maintained as he looked back in 2003. 'It had moved on quite a way technology-wise even from when Jordan came in 1991 – the complexities of the cars, the subtleties of the things, the influence of aerodynamics – and we didn't do it with a BAR-type budget. Quite the opposite: we were quite frugal in the money we had and in what we spent. I don't think people realised that; they thought it was a bottomless pit, but it wasn't, it was very carefully controlled. At the end of the year we didn't lose money, let's put it that way. We spent what we had, and we invested anything that was left. We didn't have to go to people and say, "Look, we're two million over or under," Jackie wouldn't do it that way. There were a couple of hard decisions, but we always kept it up front: if we did this we'd need to finance it properly, rather than doing it then worrying about financing it.' As for 1998, Miller put it rather more succinctly: 'Year two we were crazy. To even contemplate doing what we did with the car was just ludicrous: carbon box, torsion springs . . . it was a disastrous car, and a disastrous engine, and with that combination we were in trouble. At least the first year you had time to build and develop the car; the second year you had to do it while you were running the first car, and we didn't have enough people; we didn't have enough discipline in what we thought we could achieve. To cap it all, we didn't have enough space, so we moved. I stepped back from the racing side and did the factory move, on the hoof; they went off to Brazil and Argentina and came back to a new home. The drawing office was down at five o'clock in the evening and it was up and running at three the following morning, because we couldn't afford not to be online. But it was a bad car, simple as that.'

Long before year three was over, the writing was on the wall for Stewart Grand Prix. Negotiations for the final takeover by Ford were well in hand before those 49 races were up. But before that came those twin, spine-tingling poles of the three-year SGP adventure, with which nothing – no high, no low, no personal memory – can or ever will stand comparison. They took us back to the glory days of the man whose name the team so proudly wore. They took us back to places where his skills had shone at their brightest. They squared the circle where Stewart and Grand Prix racing were concerned. Their names were Monaco and the Nürburgring.

14. MESSAGE ON A BOTTLE: THE MOST MEMORABLE MOMENTS

'I think I got much more of a thrill winning the Grand Prix of Europe as a constructor than I ever did winning a Grand Prix as a driver, or even being world champion.'

Jackie Stewart, 2002

The bottle is dark green and shapely. Dom Pérignon, no less, and a vintage Dom Pérignon to boot. One minor flaw: it's empty. But for once what matters is not what is on the inside but what is, and will remain for as long as its owner, Stuart Sykes, can preserve it, on the outside. Across the glass and the golden label, in silver ink, in a rather upright but very legible hand, are the words 'For Stuart, my best memories and my best champagne – Monaco 1997'. Underneath is the signature of Rubens Barrichello, who chose Monaco that year as the stage for what was, at that time, the 24-year-old Brazilian's best perform-ance in a Grand Prix car. But, as with the bottle, what mattered at Monaco that May day was not the champagne but the much more lasting tonic effect Barrichello's second place had on the entire Stewart Grand Prix team.

Monaco is a tough place to go and work in. That may sound strange to someone who has only seen the Monaco Grand Prix on television: all those yachts, all that money, all those beautiful people – how can that be hard? Trust us: if you are a member of a Grand Prix team, Monaco really can be a bit of a nightmare. There's so much ballyhoo, first of all; everybody wants to be in Monaco, so how are you going to accommodate them all? It's not easy to find a hotel. The principals apart, most people at SGP found themselves along the coast at Menton in 1997, which meant a reasonable journey by car or, if schedules allowed, by train. There's so much red tape as well. This is the place where Ken Tyrrell's son Bob got so frustrated with officialdom that he took a swing with his rather heavy metal briefcase. Good job he missed . . . More than anything, though, Monaco is manifestly not a place to go Grand Prix racing. You have to work in far from ideal conditions to begin with: a crowded pit lane, cramped temporary garages, no room to swing a cat let alone a computer. And the geography of the place works against you as well. Yes, it's beautiful: the blue Mediterranean, the old houses on the hillside, the boats bobbing in the harbour. Ah yes, the harbour. Bit of a nuisance, that. Rather gets in the way when you have to come and go between the pit lane, the paddock and the press room. Every journey means skirting round the edges rather than the customary F1 beeline for the immediate destination.

It's not easy, either, when your transporters are deemed not important enough for the overcrowded F1 paddock and are sent packing – or unpacking, to be precise – to a multi-storey car park etched out of the cliff below the Royal Palace. Harder still when your motor home – hub of hospitality, haven for team technical talk, place of relative peace and quiet – is sent up there beside them. But that's how it was for Stewart Grand Prix at Monaco in May 1997. If Melbourne had shown the team that they were well and truly part of Formula One, Monaco seemed set on saying the opposite. SGP were outcasts, and there was no escaping the feeling that this was a deliberate snub. This was the weekend when Bernie Ecclestone made his now-famous crack about Jackie being happier up there because it was closer to the local royals. 'I didn't pick it out,' Ecclestone later insisted. 'He was a new kid on the block. Everybody has been through it. That's how it is. We don't give out favours, no matter who they are. But there's one thing that's important, and that is that you get rewards on how good or bad you are, and he was the new kid on the block. I think he was probably happy to be round there with the royalty – probably more comfortable.' Behind the joke lurked the sense of a statement being made, one that had something to do with upstarts and newcomers yet to learn their rightful place in this rich men's hierarchy. The reality was that it simply made a complicated place more difficult still for every member of the Stewart team. Thank goodness, once again, for Ford. The Blue Oval's motor home was well and truly part of the F1 establishment, and a major presence on the Monaco quayside with all the other members of the club.

Monaco is also a hard place to go to work if you are a racing driver. 'How many times did I win here?' Stewart had asked before the weekend began. The answer – four times, if you count that memorable F3 demonstration back in 1964 – underlined that he was one of the few to master the Monte Carlo streets. Jim Clark never did. Nor did Nigel Mansell. Graham Hill did – five times. Modern maestros by the name of Alain Prost and Ayrton Senna made it theirs, four times and six times respectively, through the late 1980s and early 1990s before Michael Schumacher began regularly to add the principality to his list of personal conquests. In this most unforgiving of sports, Monaco is perhaps the least charitable of all the venues visited. No straights to speak of where a car can clear its throat and stretch its legs while its driver takes a temporary breather; no respite from the corners, from the tunnel effect of Ste Devote to the headlong swirl through Casino Square – who are the real gamblers in Monaco? – or from the downhill right–left sequence between Mirabeau and the old Station hairpin to the treacherous Tabac; nowhere to get past another car; and no place to run when mishaps, mechanical or man-made, leave the driver looking for a way out. This was the place where Alberto Ascari plunged into the harbour, where Lorenzo Bandini perished in a ball of flames, where legends such as Jack Brabham and even Senna had famously got it wrong. How would Messrs Magnussen and Barrichello fare in their 1997 SF-1s?

Thursday brought the beginnings of an answer. That's another peculiarity of Monaco: race weekend starts a day earlier than anywhere else, meaning Friday can either be a free day to see and be seen or a frantic day to figure out where you failed the previous day. Jan Magnussen didn't fail, at least not in the thinking department. Faced with a mighty moment at the first corner, he was smart enough to keep the car out of the wall, keep its tyres close to circular by not standing on the brakes, and cruise quietly and harmlessly up the escape road. The same piece of Monegasque real estate would provide another heart-stopping moment for Stewart Grand Prix in three days' time. Rubens, meanwhile, was running consistently with the fastest of them until an engine failure relegated him to thirteenth at the end of Stewart's first day on the streets. Though Magnussen could qualify no higher than nineteenth, he had passed another crucial test by getting the car on the grid in the first place. Barrichello not only showed his own natural competitiveness, but indicated the growing self-confidence of the team by professing to be slightly disappointed with tenth spot. There was good reason for his mild dismay: tenth place meant nine cars ahead of him on a track where it was notoriously difficult to get past even one.

But cometh the hour, cometh the man, and on the first lap of the 1997 Monaco Grand Prix the Brazilian was *the* man. Under darkening skies, Stewart had had the good sense to disregard other teams' example and start on wet tyres. The decision paid dividends beyond their wildest dreams: Barrichello picked off Jean Alesi's Benetton and Mika Hakkinen's McLaren with a perfect start, then catapulted past future team-mate Johnny Herbert in the Sauber, David Coulthard in the sister McLaren and future world champion Jacques Villeneuve's Williams to slot into fifth position. P5 on the opening lap at Monaco, in a Stewart Ford, in the team's fifth world championship race. Four laps later it was P3. When Monaco produced mayhem, as it had done in its first world championship race in 1950 and so many times since, Magnussen coolly came through to join his senior team-mate in the top ten with just ten laps gone. On lap 39, Rubens, by now a comfortable second, made his one and only pit stop; Jan came in five laps later, and again the next time round after cutting across the chicane on new rubber and knocking off the nose. On lap 53, the unthinkable briefly flashed across the collective SGP mind. At Ste Devote leader Schumacher, in the Ferrari, had come to grief and disappeared into the escape road. Was Rubens Barrichello about to lead the Monaco Grand Prix for Stewart Ford? Had it been any driver other than the German, the answer would have been a resounding 'Yes!', but Michael had the presence of mind to gather it all up and press on for victory.

On the final lap, an apparently ailing Stewart Ford – there seemed to be a hydraulic leak, the telemetry insisted – eventually hove into view. Grown men wept, and all of them were wearing SGP overalls. Bugger the rain! This was brilliant! An exultant Rubens asked for his future wife Silvana to be brought to the top three drivers' press conference, and the usually unbending FIA said that was fine. He blew kisses to her as the other two answered questions. He could barely find the words to express the emotion that always bubbles just under Rubinho's calm exterior.

Alan Jenkins had the presence of mind, in this moment of elation – this was *his* car, after all; at the SF-1's launch Jenkins had worn an expression of profound satisfaction – to remind his media manager to mention in the official press release that this was a triumph for people, not just for machines, and to include the small army of people back at base. From glamorous Monaco, 24 years after his team boss had last won on the Monte Carlo streets, to mundane Milton Keynes, Barrichello had just built a bridge. More than a bridge: a bond that helped weld the fledgling Stewart team together as nothing else had or could. That's how SGP team manager David Stubbs remembered it. 'It was fantastic, brilliant,' he said. 'We'd put a hell of a lot of effort into getting the car ready, and to get that result . . . I worked for years at Williams and we used to have firsts and seconds, firsts and seconds – you were upset if you didn't get first and second or first and third. But I think that one was the one I remember the most, the one that meant most to me because of the effort I'd put into Stewart Grand Prix. And it was touch and go. We had a hydraulic problem ten or so laps from the end, so we were watching it and praying that the damned thing got across the line. Then the Ferrari spun, and it looked for a minute as if we might go into the lead, but second was fantastic. And where welding the team together was concerned, I think it helped a lot. Then we knew we were capable of doing the job, and I think it did pull everybody together.'

Rubens reinforced that togetherness just days later by bringing his second-place trophy to the factory, insisting on filling it up with champagne and pouring it out himself for everyone to taste with him. Barrichello has since gone on to bigger and, some would say, better things as a Grand Prix driver for Ferrari. Since 2000, he has been a Grand Prix winner. His best memories may now be some that have more meaning for him than a second place that was to remain his best result for the Stewart team, but the bottle with the Brazilian's message on it is still in its place of honour, and its owner will never forget the intoxication of those moments on 11 May in Monaco. It was the day when Jackie and Paul were almost out of their tartan trousers with excitement. The normally unflappable Jackie put the moment into its absolute perspective when he said, 'I've never been happier in my whole career. Not from a victory, not from a championship – never!'

That 'never' would last for another two years, four months and fifteen days . . .

On 26 September 1999 there was no bottle, but the message once again had something to do with intoxicating substances. The gleaming silver trophy referred to the Warsteiner Grand Prix of Europe and proclaimed that the sponsor's product was 'Die Königin unter den Bieren' – 'the queen of beers'. And the small man holding the trophy, just this once, was the king of the Formula One constructors' castle. Jackie Stewart was back at the Nürburgring, the scene of one of his and Formula One's most famous victories, in 1968, the scene of his 27th and final victory in 1973. But if a Stewart victory a quarter of a century before might have been an easy forecast to make, what happened in 1999 was one of the most unpredictable results in modern F1 history.

In fact, the 1999 European Grand Prix was one of the most chaotic races of recent times. Putting it another way, as Andy Miller did from a distance of four years, 'It was a shit weekend up until the race.' Most of the trouble had come during qualifying. 'We'd made a decision on the tyres which meant that we looked stupid the way we qualified, but it was just one of those situations: we had the right race tyres, no question, but because of the conditions we ended up qualifying nowhere.' In fact, Johnny Herbert, for the first time in his maiden year with Stewart Grand Prix, outqualified Rubens Barrichello, who had found himself stuck behind a Minardi on his best lap. Not that it meant much: the Stewart men were still starting from way back in fourteenth and fifteenth positions on the Nürburgring grid. 'But we still had a hope,' Miller added. 'We thought that whatever the weather we were going in with the right strategy. To actually win the race was way out of our expectations, but we might challenge for points.' The weather, of course, was the crucial factor. Stewart had spent a lifetime trying to avoid the unpredictable, but even he was powerless to control the climatic changes that affect the Eifel mountains more than any other venue on the Grand Prix calendar. People have come out of their warm hotels on a Nürburgring morning and seen the reading '0' on the thermometers mounted on the wall. Rain is always a distinct possibility. So it was that September weekend in 1999. 'And everything played into our hands,' Miller recalled. 'The two drivers kept their cars on the track. We had put one on each strategy at the stops so we were covered.'

The race started turning pear-shaped right away. Marc Gené's Minardi and Alessandro Zanardi's Williams got themselves out of sequence on the grid and the initial start was aborted. When they got going, local hero Heinz-Harald Frentzen put his pole-sitting Jordan into the lead, with McLaren duo Coulthard and Hakkinen in hot pursuit – and then the chaos really began. It was Frentzen's team-mate, Damon Hill, who inadvertently triggered it, his Jordan slowing dramatically in mid-pack with electrical failure. Alexander Wurz's Benetton had no place to go except into Pedro Diniz's Sauber, and the unfortunate Brazilian rolled spectacularly, thankfully emerging with nothing more than cuts and bruises and a wry wave to the crowd. After a brief spell behind the safety car, Frentzen roared off into the distance again, with the McLarens, Ralf Schumacher's Williams, Giancarlo Fisichella's Benetton and title contender Eddie Irvine's Ferrari all giving chase. But not for long. To cut a long story short, it all came down to tyres and track conditions as the clouds rolled in, rolled out again, then returned for the late stages of the race. Ferrari shot themselves in the foot when Irvine dived in towards a crew waiting with wet-weather tyres, but radioed to say he wanted to stay on dries instead; somehow the right rear went absent without leave, the Irishman was stranded for nearly half a minute, and his hopes disappeared. Frentzen emerged from his pit stop still in the lead, but promptly rolled to a halt more or less where Hill had; Coulthard led, but slid gently off into the barrier; and through it all, Herbert moved calmly through to the top six.

The 35-year-old Englishman's second stint was the crucial one. Between laps 35 and 47 Johnny manoeuvred himself into a lead he would not relinquish after his second stop. And what a second stop! Rubens had come in a lap before when it looked particularly black; Johnny stayed out a lap longer, spotted the rain clouds heading straight for him, came in and made the right choice. Ralf Schumacher's puncture and a distraught Fisichella's 'off' completed the picture, and Stewart Grand Prix were winners for the first and only time. Barrichello gave everything in his bid to make it a one–two, but Jarno Trulli bravely resisted everything the Brazilian could throw at him. 'Rubens was delighted we won the race,' said Miller, 'but he was split. That would have been his first win, and he *should* have won it. He was leading, he came in a lap before, and it looked as if it would stay dry; Johnny came in a lap later and it was dark and raining, so Johnny made the right call. It was very close. But then Rubens' move to Ferrari had already been announced. It was marvellous, it really was, for everybody.'

'Everybody' on that occasion included Peter Phillips, by then a Stewart employee. The Princess Royal's son had been associated with Stewart, in fact, on and off since the period of intense build-up to the launch of SF-1 nearly three years earlier. 'Fortunately enough,' he explained at the Nürburgring in 2003, as a Williams team member, 'my last race for Stewart was actually at the Nürburgring in 1999. Like everybody else, I was completely swept up in the emotion of it all. I've won a few things playing rugby and had some fantastic times, but that was one of the highlights of my sporting life. It was such a fantastic feeling – a fantastic effort from a team that really were minnows, a very small team at the time. It was an amazing day. A lot of people felt sorry for Rubens, because he'd been there for so long, and in many ways you could understand that. But Johnny Herbert had a lot of bad luck that year and it was just so nice that he ended up there. It couldn't have happened to a nicer bloke.' Barrichello himself, generous to a fault, agreed, but with more than a little chagrin. 'I miss not having won one race for them,' he said from Fortress Ferrari in the paddock at Magny-Cours in 2003. 'In a way, the Nürburgring in 1999 was fantastic, but I'm sure that even Jackie or Paul would have loved it more if I had won that race. Johnny was a super, super guy, we teamed up very well, but in a way I was there first and it was very unlucky that I made the wrong decision on the tyres. But at the end of the day Monaco 1997 was very, very high, and the team was superb in that respect. Even the engineers; we gelled very well together. I'm sure Jackie felt sorry for me that

I was leaving the team, but at the same time he was happy that I was going to other dreams.'

Of course, it wasn't the same Nürburgring that Stewart had so memorably conquered all those years before. Like the old Spa, the old Nürburgring track, the fearsome Nordschleife, had been left behind in the rush to modernise, to sanitise, to standardise; it lay behind the 'new' Ring, a brooding presence that reminded you of days gone by. But it was still the circuit in the Eifel mountains; it still bore the same name; it was still a race that counted towards the world championship. For Jackie Stewart, it was the culmination of a sporting life, as Peter Phillips confirmed. 'I mean, he'd won the world championship as a driver, and now he'd won a world championship race as a team owner – you've got to be pretty happy with that.'

In fact, a lot of people were impressed, as ex-PSR man Allan McNish pointed out. 'Looking back at it,' said the Scot, 'I think you have a different opinion now to what you had at the time. What you had at the time was a small, or smaller, independent team fighting against the might of the majors, with the backing of Ford but without the real sort of major manufacturer backing. The results they achieved were fantastic. When Jackie went into Formula One it was at a later stage of his life, and he'd been out of F1 for a while. I knew he always had his finger on the pulse, but I didn't think he'd be able to achieve those sorts of results: the second position at Monaco in the first year, a win in the third. If you look at people who are spending many, many millions more dollars in the paddock now and are nowhere near achieving that sort of result, it just proves how tenacious he was and how he, with the group of people around him, ran a very, very tight ship that was able to get results. It wasn't just there to survive. He's always been very good at business, and I'm pretty sure that every year the books balanced, because that's the only way you can do it. Well, you can do it another way, but you only survive for a few years. So the books balanced, but to be able to get the books to balance and to be able to then allow the technical departments to run and get enough performance out of the car is a very, very tricky thing. Like I said, there's one team I know very well that spend more than three times what SGP did and haven't been able to achieve that sort of result.'

Outstanding as it was, though, the result was tinged with a certain kind of sadness. The European Grand Prix was Stewart Grand Prix's forty-seventh race; their forty-ninth, at Suzuka five weeks later, was to be their last in that guise. Before Johnny Herbert guessed right and won the European Grand Prix, the sale of Stewart Grand Prix to Ford had already been announced, and the adventure was over.

15. SELLING UP AND MAKING SPACE

'To obtain a Ford sponsorship to build a race team and then sell it to them is something that could only be done by a Scot!'

Sir Jack Brabham, 2003

In the days when Paul Stewart Racing's front, or back, door was the one on which every budding racing driver in the United Kingdom knocked first, Jackie Stewart learnt a thing or two about parents. 'Fathers?' he once expostulated. 'I could write a book about fathers!' They might have been the modern breed of sporting fathers pushing their offspring, gifted or otherwise, into lucrative careers, but perhaps Stewart could have stood back and pondered his own position. After three years of Stewart Grand Prix, that is exactly what he had done. If Germany, and its famous Nürburgring, had provided the magical memory of a deeply satisfying win at the European Grand Prix, Germany and another famous automotive occasion were to be the location for an equally memorable development. On 14 September 1999, an announcement at the Frankfurt Motor Show revealed that SGP was no more: from the start of 2000 the team would be 'badged' and known as Jaguar Racing, as the owners of the Jaguar marque, Ford, set about rebuilding its image in a modern market. 'I set Stewart Grand Prix up for my son Paul,' Stewart said in Germany, 'and it hurts me that the company's now gone.'

The announcement had in fact been delayed: the deal itself was done as early as mid-1999. Because even Jackie Stewart cannot be in two places at once, SGP personnel were made aware of the decision to sell through simultaneous statements in Milton Keynes and Montreal, where the travelling members of the team were preparing for that season's Canadian Grand Prix. The man who broke the news in Canada was Andy Miller, to whom it came as no real surprise. 'Probably a couple of months before it happened, you knew,' he acknowledged. 'It was quite strange, because Ford had extended the engine contract, which seemed a daft thing to do if you were negotiating to buy a team. I'm not sure if that was a double bluff by Jackie or whatever, but it just seemed a strange move. It happened quite quickly when it did happen, though. At my level, with due diligence and things like that, it was clear that things were going on. But the people involved were just the commercial and financial people. Ford didn't seem interested in the technical side at all, which seems strange when you're acquiring a Formula One team. You'd think they'd have found out a bit more about what they needed to do. Maybe they took counsel from other people. But Jackie was very up front; he said, "I can't guarantee to bring enough money in to keep it going." The one thing we were all demanding was to build a wind tunnel, and he couldn't finance it. He wasn't prepared to commit again unless the money was in place, so the natural thing to him was to guarantee the future of the team and the people and get Ford to take a bigger responsibility.'

If Paul Stewart's personal coup in persuading his father to allow him to follow a motor racing career was, in David Coulthard's description, 'the deal of the century', what are we to say of Stewart senior's achievement in effectively selling his team back to the company that had largely made it possible in the first place? Given the date, 'the sale of the millennium' is the least it could be called. In hard cash terms, Stewart was said to have realised anything from £50 million to £65 million, depending on which news source you relied on. Ford, in turn, was committing twice as much money to the Jaguar effort as Stewart Grand Prix had been able to afford. But feelings in the Stewart camp were understandably mixed. 'The race team was already in Canada,' Miller recalled. 'Jackie was still negotiating and flying between the two. He went back to England to do the final deal; they were talking to Detroit and they flew back to Milton Keynes, and he wanted it announced simultaneously to the race team so they didn't just read about it. So we got everybody together, pulled the doors down, and I said, "Guess what's happened, chaps, we now work for Ford." There were a lot of sad people. Some people thought, "This could be good, there'll be lots of money, we'll go off and really challenge now." We'd got to a level where we knew what we wanted to do and how we wanted to expand, but we were getting held back because we couldn't afford to do it. So they thought Ford would be the opportunity. But several of them came up to me and they were very sad. "That's it," they said, "we'll just go the same way as everybody else now. It won't be the same." There were tears . . . And in hindsight, looking at the way it's gone, they were probably more right than the other people.'

The way it went, at least until 2003, was clearly backwards. Elf's François Guiter put it rather more tactfully. 'We stayed very friendly with Jackie, with whom we shared so many fond memories. We got on so well with him and Ken [Tyrrell], and later I took a close interest in what his son was doing with the team he set up and took into Formula One. He made a great success of that too, and managed to win a race; then he told me, as only Jackie can, "I've reached a ceiling now, I can't go any further without the backing of a major constructor, and I don't have that, so I'm going to sell." And I think he made a very good deal, but sadly they haven't done nearly as well since he left.'

The man himself felt sure, he said in Frankfurt that September day, that this new impetus would turn Stewart/Jaguar into Grand Prix winners almost straight away. 'We can definitely win races next year,' Jackie stated confidently. 'It would be too optimistic to consider the championship – that might take two or three years. However, race wins are a definite possibility. No, they're a probability.' For once, the Stewart crystal ball could be accused of poor reception.

Though Melbourne, once again the venue for the first race of the 2000 season, was painted green for Jaguar's first foray into modern Formula One, the occasion and the season that followed fell far short of Stewart's and Jaguar's expectations. It would be cruel to dwell upon their racing fortunes, since real achievements are so few in number. That first Jaguar season, with Ferrari refugee Eddie Irvine and Johnny Herbert in the driving seats, yielded four points and ninth place in the constructors' championship – this after a 36-point haul for SF-3 in 1999. It wasn't until 2001 that the self-advertising Irvine managed a podium finish, once more at Monaco; in that year Jaguar Racing moved up to eighth, though still in single figures with just nine points. While the position apparently improved in 2002 with seventh, the team actually scored one point fewer. No poles, no fastest laps, and certainly no race wins. Indeed, not until 2003, when promising Australian Mark Webber came on board, did the Big Cat start to score some consistent points, his sixth-place finish at Magny-Cours elevating the team to an unprecedented but still modest sixth place in the championship. There had been turmoil at the top, Ford high-ups such as Neil Ressler being followed by Ford friend Bobby Rahal, who in turn gave way to another triple world champion in the shape of Niki Lauda. A complete revamp before the start of 2003 merely served to underline the confusion that reigned.

Miller had picked up the signs as early as June 1999. 'There was a natural drift away because of the sale to Ford,' he said. 'We had this farcical situation in Canada, after I'd announced to the team that Ford were buying it: Neil Ressler stood up and said, "What we're buying is you guys, we're very pleased with what you've done, we don't want to change anything, we just want to develop it, add to what we've got," and then Richard Parry-Jones stood up and said, "You won't believe this place, we're changing everything." There was one speech after the other: that was a reflection of what had happened. Right then, from that point, there was confusion.' The only person who seemed to be thinking clearly at the time of the sale was the seller. 'I think selling it was hard for Jackie,' Miller acknowledged. 'I don't think he wanted to, but I think he was a realist;

he realised it was too big a monster for him to handle. Obviously Paul's health had suffered, and the stress of a Formula One team could well have contributed to that. That was all it needed for Jackie to make his mind up. I don't think he went into it with the intention of building it up and selling to Ford, I think the market was such that at the time he sold it Formula One teams were worth money, and it's turned around in a couple of seasons.'

Racing figures past and present expressed their astonishment and admiration at the deal Jackie Stewart pulled off. 'He probably thought on many occasions that things weren't going well,' Stewart's former on-track adversary Jackie Oliver said, 'and Ford were giving him a hard time. But as it turned out, it worked extremely well. He was one of the few people I could mention, outside FOCA, who formed a new team during those very powerful years of Bernie Ecclestone and succeeded in not only winning Grands Prix, but putting himself in there as a constructor in the Concorde Agreement and selling it on to Ford appropriately.' Craig Pollock nodded in agreement and appreciation. 'A very clever move,' he said. 'Perfect timing. I think he must have had some extremely good advisers at that particular time, seeing how the sport has turned, the big car constructors coming in. As a small team owner up until the next change in the Concorde Agreement it is very, very difficult to get any value out of a team, unless a constructor comes in and buys you. So I think he was well advised to make that move.' David Coulthard concurred. 'I think it's one of the most remarkable deals in Formula One! I don't know the figures, but to get someone else to pay for the set-up of the team, to run that team, and then to sell it back to them is just incredible, and only a Jackie and a Paul could do it with such style. An EJ [Eddie Jordan] or one of those guys could probably have done the same, but there would have been murmurs . . . He's the only one who could have done it. I think he absolutely took the right decision. He obviously did it because he felt it was right.'

The company, as Stewart put it in September 1999, might have been gone, but the Stewarts most certainly were not. Not yet, at least. There was a kind of purge of the former Stewart premises, with trappings such as tartan carpets and racing pictures and memorabilia removed to make room for the new corporate philosophy. Whether or not he was taking a hint, Stewart himself decided to make some room within a very short space of time. Cunning as ever when it comes to self-promotion, Stewart chose the 'reveal' of Jaguar's R1, the first racing car of this new era, to make his 'I cast a big shadow' announcement that promptly put cars, F1 seasons and everything else into the shade. 'I need to move over to allow the people who are really doing the job the space to do so,' said Stewart as he retired from the shortlived functions of chief executive officer of Jaguar Racing. Little did he know it, but he needed that space himself: there would soon be no room in his restless life for anything other than fear.

When Jackie and Paul Stewart had set out together on the SGP road, Stewart had said, 'There is a depth in the father/son relationship that you can never get from a friendship, but also we have a very good friendship because we're working together now.' Sooner than they thought, perhaps, the depth of that relationship would be tested to the limit. For a man who doesn't like surprises, Jackie Stewart was about to get the biggest and most unpleasant surprise of his lengthening life. 'April is the cruellest month,' wrote T.S. Eliot, and it was in April 2000 that Paul Stewart was diagnosed with cancer.

For many, it was the culmination of a ruinous process that had worn the young man down as he strove might and main to support his father in the move to Formula One. The close-knit nature of the Stewart family unit made it hard, more often than not, to see exactly where stresses and strains were being felt, but there can be little doubt that the eagerness to please and the burden of responsibility that fell on Paul Stewart's shoulders took their toll. The younger man had to measure up when Jackie, inevitably, was not on hand to do things all by himself. 'It's difficult to delegate when you're Jackie Stewart,' said Miller, 'because you take him out of it and it's not the same. When he only flits in and out, a bit of confusion can set in. And I think it did. The financial demands were so great, the technical demands were so confusing, because Jackie wasn't that strong on the technical side, so he had to rely on other people, and maybe that was where we were weakest. Maybe the top team principals would have got a bit closer to the technical side; Jackie left Paul to do that, and that wasn't Paul's personal forte either. But it was the enormity of it all: we went from starting with 45 people to, when he sold it to Ford, over 200. That's a lot of people to manage.'

Helplessness is not a feeling Jackie Stewart has often experienced, but now he found himself wallowing in it. Cancer is the most insidious of diseases, an invasive, literally malignant force that offends the sufferer by its very surreptitiousness. Modern technology actually allows patients to look in on their own bodies and see the cancerous cells attacking them; the reaction is both disgust and, more positively, indignant anger. Perhaps surprisingly, its treatment still strikes us as quite primitive: weeks, often months, of radiotherapy for the luckier ones; aggressive chemotherapy and its attendant evils for those who have been more seriously afflicted. It is, too, a lonely disease: the moments after a session of treatment, when nausea sets in and all the sufferer can do is rest and hope, are long. Luckily for Paul Stewart, his father's long-standing connection with America's world-famous Mayo Clinic meant that from the outset he was in the very safest of hands. 'His mother and I, his brother Mark and his wife Victoria,' said Stewart, 'all have complete confidence in his doctors. We are optimistic that he can overcome this illness and carry on living life to the full.' Sure enough, drawing strength from fellow sufferers such as Tour de France champion cyclist Lance Armstrong, and inspired no doubt by the life-affirming christening of his third child Zac just two weeks after the diagnosis, the younger Stewart has, subject to regular checks and continuing good fortune, done just that.

But if April was cruel, autumn was crueller still. Autumn 2001, that is, when Helen Stewart required an operation for breast cancer. Like a Stewart, the disease doesn't give up. Helen, too, is happily restored, but the waiting – when it was she who so often had to wait for him in the deadly days of the 1970s – is etched forever in the lines on Stewart's face. 'It has changed my whole approach to life,' he said, although there are those in his circle of intimates who may raise an eyebrow at the thought of a rearrangement of the Stewart priorities. 'Definitely in Paul's case,' thought Allan McNish. 'When SGP was running it was just flat out for him. I think that shook Jackie probably more than anyone. I don't have a child, but I can imagine what it would be like for my father for me suddenly to have something so serious . . . He was lucky that he knew the best people to go to . . . I think that started to reprioritise things in Jackie's mind. Then Helen following on the back . . . I'm a bit of a believer that these things are related to circumstances. They can be totally separate, they can be generic, but sometimes they are related to circumstances, and the intelligent people are the people who, when something does happen, react to it and don't just fall back into the same habits. The intelligent people are the people that keep on reacting. I do believe that if that had happened ten years ago SGP wouldn't have taken off.'

As Andy Miller so memorably remarked, Formula One consumes everything it can get its hands on.

For Jackie Stewart, family has always been a very big word and a very important one. It is the most significant thing in his life. His family has played a huge role in many ways in his career, in all of its phases, and it has continued to do so in different ways. All through his life, despite the massive demands made on his time, he has found moments for his mother, his father, his brother, his friends back in Dumbarton and the surrounding areas, his wife Helen and his sons Paul and Mark and their families. He even managed to embrace many other families and join them to his own, working in harmony with people from all walks of life and all backgrounds. He became close to the royal family, particularly Princess Anne and her children. 'There isn't a man who is so tied to his family,' said Peter Phillips, Princess Anne's eldest son, to whose sister, Zara, Helen Stewart, a practising Presbyterian, stood as godmother in 2003. 'Anyone who knows him knows that. He's very proud of both his sons, he's amazingly proud of his grandchildren, and he loves having them around. And he's never afraid to show his affection towards them. They're such fantastic people; there's not a bad ounce of anything in any of them. My parents keep in regular contact; both consider him a very close friend who, if ever they needed to, they would turn to for advice in certain situations.'

This sense of duty, loyalty and pride has been with Jackie throughout his life. It might have been inspired by his parents' example, his brother Jimmy's earliest achievements as a singer, and his decision to abandon his racing career to appease his mother, or it might simply have come from a deeper source, within the man himself, a need not only to achieve great things in sport and the world but to accomplish them in a way that mattered and permitted him the greater satisfaction of providing everything, from comfort to education to the best health specialists in the world, when the time required them. The most likely candidate, however, is that deep-rooted need to be recognised and praised which came from the initial sense of rejection and despondency he experienced at school.

Many people over the years have accused Jackie of cultivating his royal or celebrity friends in a deliberate way, but this is an allegation firmly dismissed by those who know him well. It has to be remembered that his life has been spent, for more than 35 years, in echelons of society where he has met famous, royal and wealthy people on a regular basis, and that it is his nature to be friendly, engaging and loyal to anyone with whom he becomes friends. 'I don't think he was a jock-sniffer,' said Andy Foster. 'He was part of the establishment; it's a chicken-and-egg situation. He befriended Princess Anne in the days when they were both involved in top-flight sport; he was friendly with Juanito [later King Juan Carlos of Spain] when he was a prince. If you were the best, people wanted to know you. And he's a loyal friend. To an extent, the establishment has come to him. And who, in his position, would try to stop it? One thing has made him what he is: 40 years of being told you're a genius is bound to rub off on you and affect the way you interact with the world.'

John Lindsay told an anecdote that showed how easy and genuine Jackie's relationship with the royal family has become. '[Their friendship] started when Princess Anne was at the BBC Sports Personality of the Year show. I think they met and got on. It's partly success and money. The extension of it all is the social ladder, isn't it? And at the top of the social ladder are the royals. That's the way I read it. I remember sitting here [in Dumbuck] a few years ago, and I knew he was coming up to Gleneagles for something. His plane was delayed, and he rang up and said he would still drop in on the way through. It was a Sunday afternoon, I think, and he drops in through the back door, as he always does, and behind him is Mark Phillips. I'd never met a royal in my life at that time, so I felt a bit of a chump. "Oh, Mark, so nice to see you," I said, but I thought, "What am I doing here?" ' But this was to be the first of many occasions on which Lindsay, one of Stewart's long-standing friends, was to be embraced within the same extended 'family' and friendship circle.

Lindsay recalled another illustrative episode. 'I was introduced to the Duke of Kent at one of the Grands Prix, it might have been at Silverstone. At Spa, I always used to disappear out into the country, but this time Jackie asked me to take His Royal Highness with me, so I said to the Duke, "Which corner would you like to go to?" He said, "Which is the best one?" I said, "Rivage." "How far is that?" he said, and I replied, "It will take you a good half an hour to get there, sir. It's a good hike." He said, "No, a bit too far, I think, a bit too far." Then someone else suggested the Bus Stop, because it's quite close to the paddock. It was the first day of practice so there was a three-quarter-of-an-hour session. I was about to say "But it's very busy out there" when the Duke said, "Ah, the Bus Stop!" and moved away with a royal stride.

'We got out of the paddock, just the two of us, and it was wet. We were trying to walk up the back, away from the worst of the water, and when we got to the Bus Stop the Duke said, "Oh, it's not too bad, is it?" I was about to explain that the section of track he was looking at was the run-off up towards the pits, and the track itself he couldn't see because of the masses of people. They'd been there since four o'clock in the morning, as it turned out, with McLaren jumpers and Graham Hill hats on. And they turned around and clocked him! Suddenly, it's ten-deep with people. They said, "Oh, we've got a place for you guys right here." And they had brought in their televisions and everything. It was ten o'clock in the morning, they'd been there for six hours, and they were offering their space to His Royal Highness, just like that.

'So we got right in there, and one of them – well, they couldn't believe it, that the Duke was there with them – took his jacket off and went up the bank at the back to take a photograph. We stayed there for the full three-quarters of an hour. They knew who was on what tyres and what was going on, and it was quite a good banter all the way through. And he joined in, the Duke; it was quite amusing. Later we went back to the pits, and then we had lunch after the next session. I was still with the Duke, and I said, "I don't know if you observed it, but one of those chaps was taking some photographs of you down there at the Bus Stop." He said, "They should have asked me to turn round for that!" I laughed. Then I said, "Actually, that might not be a bad place to go and see the Grand Prix from." He said, "Do you think they'll still be there?" And the whole weekend went on like that.

'Well, that was just typical of a weekend at a race with Jackie. Things like that just kept on happening. He loved it. He just seemed to fit into it. Now, you go with him into a room, a restaurant, and people will always turn and stare and recognise him. He gets a lot of that. In America, it is amazing. It is just embarrassing. When you think that he stopped racing 30 years ago, it's incredible.'

But fame is a poor second to family in Stewart's life. For him, everything in some way is about family, including the Stewart Grand Prix team, his shooting school at Gleneagles, and his relationships with Ford, Goodyear, Rolex and the rest. He never seemed to have any need to reach for an off switch, or to relax totally, though of course he did – but only when he had planned for it in advance. This kind of personal management often made life work for him, but it set an example that was difficult for others to follow, including his own son Paul. 'That's the difference between Jackie and Paul, isn't it?' Miller said. 'Jackie was fully engaged in everything all the time, no matter what it was. He gave everything, whether it was the Mechanics Trust, whether it was the Formula Three team, whether it was the Vauxhall team. When he was there, that was all he was there for. Whereas with Paul, Paul would be very good for a short period, then he'd be over here doing something else, and I think that's the mind management business. He didn't have it, compared with Jackie, and that's the biggest difference. If he'd had that, or been able to develop it . . . It's an enormous thing. I think you'd find that the guys on the shop floor, the mechanics and everything, they had great respect for Jackie and they really enjoyed him walking round the workshop, trying to set things up for them and do things.'

It has always been that way for Jackie, but the value of his family to him was driven home more in the 1990s and in the new millennium by the recurring incidences of illnesses that threatened to take his nearest and dearest away. And cancer wasn't the only enemy; Jimmy, Jackie's only brother, struggled after a failed first marriage to beat alcoholism until Jackie came to his assistance. Jimmy credited him with saving his life, and the two men, for so long distanced by the geography between Glasgow and Geneva and the history that came with one retiring from motor racing to stay 'at home' while the other raced and 'flew the nest', rekindled a warm fraternal relationship that has meant much to Jackie. Indeed, he has said that it was the most important thing he has ever done in his life.

James Robert Stewart was born in March 1931. As a boy, Jimmy was a fine soprano singer who was good enough to secure a recording contract with BBC Radio Scotland and to earn a reputation for the great quality of his voice. In a musical household he was a star turn, and, being the eldest son and a good-looking boy, he enjoyed his formative years. While attending Milton Primary School, a music teacher, Miss L. Hogg, identified his voice and his talent and encouraged him. 'She saw something in my voice and once a week she gave me singing lessons,' said Jimmy. 'She entered me for the Glasgow and the Paisley Singing Festivals. I auditioned for the BBC in Glasgow and after that I appeared in a number of *Children's Hour* programmes. The man in charge of the BBC Scottish Orchestra, Ian White, also chose me to do a number of recitals for other programmes, broadcast at home and abroad.' When he was only twelve years old, he received glowing reviews. One report said that 'his Vaughan Williams (*Linden Lea*) was altogether a really first-class bit of singing . . . a large, round voice of telling quality'; another said 'his natural gift of song places him far beyond his years . . . a Cathedral voice'. 'I really enjoyed my music as a boy,' Jimmy summed up, 'and singing in front of critical audiences created a real build-up of excitement and tension. Interpreting, or trying to interpret, Bach, Schubert, Handel or Haydn gave me a wonderful feeling which I couldn't again recapture.'

He tried, though. When his voice broke, at fifteen, he developed other interests and began to turn to motor racing to find the same kind of adrenalin rush he had experienced in preparation for, and anticipation of, major stage appearances as a singer. In this, too, as we know, he was successful. 'I do think that the sport has much in common with the arts,' he said. Bob Stewart, his father, supported his racing, and after supplying him with a second-hand MG TC to compete in hillclimbs at Rest and Be Thankful and other places, he bought him his first Healey Silverstone, and then helped him build a racing career. Before long, the *Lennox Herald* was announcing, 'Lance Corporal James Stewart has been approached to drive for Ecurie Ecosse, the crack Scots Grand Prix racing team. Subject to the Army granting permission, he will spend next year touring Europe on the international motor racing arenas.' The following year, he suffered a complicated compound fracture of his right elbow after crashing heavily while driving an Aston Martin DB3S at Le Mans. 'I was thrown clear as the car split in two,' he recalled. 'I badly fractured my elbow, so that indisposed me for the season and it took me a while to get back on to the circuit.' Only the week before this accident, Jimmy had reeled off a superb win in his Ecurie Ecosse Jaguar at Goodwood, but in the weeks afterwards he had little choice but to plunge himself into learning the management of the family garage business when he was away on leave.

When he came out of the army the following year, 1955, he was to suffer a double disappointment. Not only did he discover that his voice had been ruined by shouting and barking orders in the army, he also missed out on one of his motor racing dreams. In that fateful year of the tragic accident at Le Mans involving Pierre Levegh's Mercedes 300 SLR, as a result of which Levegh died along with 83 spectators and more than a hundred other people were injured; in a summer that also saw the deaths of Alberto Ascari, at Monza in a Ferrari sportscar, and Bill Vukovich, at Indianapolis, Jaguar offered Jimmy a factory drive at Le Mans, sharing a D-type with Mike Hawthorn. Unfortunately, it was an opportunity he was not to realise as at the Nürburgring, where Jackie was later to experience such glories, Jimmy had an accident during practice and suffered a serious and complicated breakage of the same arm again. 'Jaguar had a new model out and they were having trouble with the braking system,' explained Jimmy. 'During the practice, I crashed and I was trapped underneath the car. Stirling Moss was the first man to reach me and he managed to get me out.' The problem the Jaguars were suffering from was known as 'knock-back'. It consisted of a total loss of braking because the pads of the disc brakes could retract to the extent that at the first pump of the pedal the driver sensed there was nothing there, leaving him, it was said, only with a strange feeling in the pit of his stomach. Jimmy's car had run out of road on a bend at 90mph and, without any apparent brakes, swept down a bank. In an incident that foretold his brother Jackie's experiences at Spa Francorchamps in later years, Jimmy was trapped and left there for 25 minutes, lying in hope, drenched in petrol, but still blessed with the presence of mind to reach out and switch off the ignition and so avoid the danger of a fire. (For the record, Hawthorn raced that year at Le Mans and enjoyed some glory with the winning Jaguar.)

A doctor subsequently warned Jimmy that if he broke his arm a third time, he might lose it. Taking this and his mother's disaffection for his racing into account, he retired. It was a big decision, taken easily, but after full and due consideration. In those days, as Jimmy explained later, family mattered to everyone and he wanted to please his mother. He had no inkling then, of course, that the brother who was eight years his junior – and who throughout this time was looking and listening, watching and learning – was to follow his racing example and go on to become one of the greatest drivers of all.

Jimmy returned to the family motor business, then joined John Coombs in Guildford, then went back to Glasgow. His life became a series of half-hearted projects, much to the anxiety and disappointment of his younger brother, none of which could fully satisfy him after the brushes with fame and success he had experienced as a singer and racing driver. In her book *Mostly Men*, Lynn Barber offered several telling insights into both Jackie and Jimmy in a chapter written about Jackie and a day spent with him in October 1983 in a 'splashy marsh on Lord Montagu's estate at a pheasant shoot'. Not only did she note that Jackie was, above all at that time, a PR man – 'It is important to realise that almost every minute of Jackie Stewart's time is owned by someone: Goodyear, Ford, Britax, Simoniz, Rolex, Moët et Chandon and several other companies all pay him a retainer to act as their "PR consultant" for so many days a year' – she also revealed that he charged £5,000 for a speech, had purchased an apartment in New York so that Helen could indulge her interests in art and dance, and had grown up in his brother Jimmy's shadow until he broke clear. Indeed, until he was fifteen or sixteen, Jackie's only claim to fame was that he was Jimmy Stewart's brother. Barber explained that even when Jackie became successful as a clay pigeon marksman and was British champion, at nineteen, his position within the family was clear to visitors, such as Allan Jones, whose father was Jackie's coach on visits to the Jones family estate in North Wales. 'Whenever I went to stay with his family in those early days,' said Jones, 'I always thought Jackie was totally over-shadowed by his brother. The conversation was always "Jimmy this and Jimmy that", and the sideboard was covered in Jimmy's trophies. I think that made Jackie more competitive. He wanted a slot on that sideboard.'

After his accidents and his retirement, life was bleaker for Jimmy, but his upbringing and stoical good nature enabled him to hide his feelings even as Jackie began to sweep him off that sideboard with his own steady flow of achievements. When the family business was sold and his first marriage broke up, Jimmy was in limbo. Jackie helped him to start up a new business in Florida, in the hope of building a new life, but it was not a success and he disliked the heat and humidity, among other difficulties. Jackie was frustrated, and sometimes, in slightly out-of-character revelations, he made unkind remarks. 'Jimmy didn't really make anything of himself,' he was once reported to have commented. It was not a remark that stood easily alongside his affectionate support for his brother during his troubles. Jackie stood by and was loyal and supportive, by and large, as Jimmy embarked on a second marriage. The failure of this marriage, however, was a more grievous blow that left Jimmy deeper in the shade, a place where he felt overlooked and despondent, and from where he reached out for alcohol.

Even as early as 1972, when Bob Stewart died, it was clear to see the shadow cast by Jackie Stewart. When the *County Reporter* announced the death, following his passing on 22 January, it was in terms that made Bob the 'father of Jackie Stewart, the world champion racing driver'; Jimmy, his eldest son, was relegated to the ninth paragraph for his first mention in the fifteen-paragraph obituary. The sting, however – if such a word can be used in this context – came in the final three: it was recorded that Bob Stewart had told his local newspaper in 1970 that, in his opinion, Jim could have been just as successful a racing driver as his younger brother. 'Jim gave up racing, but he could have been great if he had continued,' the *Reporter* quoted.

How all this affected Jimmy Stewart, it is hard to know. In his pomp, behind the wheel, he was known as 'Big Jimmy', his brother as 'Wee Jackie'. Like Jackie, Jimmy had spent his childhood in close proximity to cars, Jaguars in particular, and men of speed. His first means of transport, he recalled, was a pedal car that provided 'unforgettable pleasure', and some dangerous moments, too. 'Many a time my escape from serious injury was more or less a miracle,' he said. 'When I whizzed in and out among the cars parked on our premises, I was oblivious of everything else going on around.' Dangers and speed were to be part of his life, perhaps too big a part. He was one of the most accomplished drivers ever produced by Scotland, but his racing accidents were not his only ones, alas. He suffered a further major crash in January 1978, when he almost lost the sight in both eyes. Jimmy lost control of his car on the Great Western Road in Glasgow, crashed, and was sent flying through the windscreen. Surgeons fought for four hours to rescue his left eye at Glasgow's Western Infirmary, and were successful, but it was a longer job with the right eye. Only two weeks later did he regain its use. The accident, reported in the *Lennox Herald*, was given scant attention, but having taken place in the days when drinking-and-driving was not the crime it became in later years, it may be fair to presume that alcohol played a part.

Jackie, living close to Geneva, was of course made aware of his brother's roller-coaster of experiences as they happened. He tried to stay close, and they both needed each other in different ways, but it was only once Jackie had succeeded in persuading Jimmy to come off the bottle that their relationship settled down properly. Evidence of Jackie's efforts came in May 1991 when in an effort to cheer up his sibling and mark his sixtieth birthday with a memorable celebration, Jackie paid to fly him to Geneva, along with John Lindsay, to stay with him overnight and then to travel down to Monte Carlo for the Monaco Grand Prix, where, as usual, they resided in sumptuous comfort at the Hotel de Paris. A tour of the pits and paddock, during which Jimmy met Nigel Mansell, Alain Prost and Ayrton Senna among others, confirmed to him that his brother belonged in the sport's hall of fame and among Europe's fashionable establishment, a fact underlined the evening after the race: while Jimmy and John went to the post-event dinner at the International Sporting Club of Monaco, Jackie had to send his apologies – because he had a conflicting engagement with Prince Rainier for dinner at the palace. 'Jackie started off pumping gas at Dumbuck for two or three pounds a week, and now he's earning millions a year,' Jimmy later told the *Herald*. 'But when I'm with him, he's still the same Jackie I remember as a wee boy. He hasn't changed one iota.'

This assessment is common among those around Jackie Stewart, whose generosity towards his brother was to become ever more significant and led, beyond all other things, to his successful efforts to save him from alcoholism. Jackie described this victory in his family life as his greatest achievement, far and away a more satisfying triumph than anything he ever achieved on a motor racing circuit. Jimmy, the beneficiary of his brother's dogged determination, could do nothing but agree, and said he would forever recall 9 October 1999 with a special clarity. That was the day he checked into the Priory Clinic in London, the first day of the rest of his life, *sans alcool*. Not long before, Jimmy had been attracting interest because, as the brother of a world-famous figure, it was deemed of curiosity value that he should have volunteered to be a Meals on Wheels driver in Dumbarton.

'I'm sure he saved my life,' said Jimmy, sitting in his comfortable flat in Rhu in early 2003. 'I don't think I'd have lived without that help. Jackie has done so much for me. He has saved me really from myself and from a serious drink problem. He came to me and he was worried about me. He said, "I am offering you the help you need and I want you to think about it." I thought about it a lot that night, and I rang him back. I said yes. Immediately, he said he wanted me to report to the Priory the next day at nine o'clock. That was it. It was done, and it was worth it. John and Nan Lindsay took me. I was there for four weeks, and then I came home and it was up to me. I knew I had to adjust to life without it. I'd made up my mind, and I succeeded. More than anything I've never wanted to let myself down, or to let Jackie down. I know it cost £350 a day and I know he paid. All of this happened four years ago [1999], and since then I've made a new man of myself. Jackie has told me that he is very proud of me, and he has told other people too. I still have drinks here, in the house, but I don't touch them. I've stuck to it. I've got my demon under control. What Jackie did was to give me the guts to do it. Someone up there helped me, and so did Jackie. I am so grateful that he had time to think of me. I was in a really bad state; I had only two years left to live. He really saved me, and that is something very marvellous.'

Jimmy went on to confirm that his unsuccessful married life had contributed to his alcoholism, adding that it was the loss of his children Jane and Ian, who went to Germany with his second wife Elizabeth, which had hurt him the most. Jackie, who was building his hugely successful business career at the time, had found it difficult to get on with Elizabeth, said Jimmy, but always did his utmost to keep his brother's life secure and intact. This loyalty paid off for them both in the end, leaving Jimmy apparently cured and far more contented, and the old trio of friends – Jimmy, Jackie and John – almost as happy as they were in the old, innocent, lost days of their childhood in Dumbuck.

Jackie's pride and satisfaction in the companionship he enjoys with family and friends was never better expressed than at private family suppers like one that took place in an Italian restaurant in London in early 2002 following the preview showing of Mark Stewart's splendid film *Jackie Stewart: The Flying Scot*. He was surrounded by family members and some of his closest friends, including many veterans of his regular Gleneagles Celebrity Challenge events including Rosemary Lady Northampton, Lady Stewart herself, John and Nan Lindsay, and his brother Jimmy. If his triumph over the bottle with Jimmy had been his greatest, he admitted as freely that his fear of cancer, particularly when Paul was diagnosed, had been his greatest challenge and represented 'the worst blow' he ever had. Quite suddenly, the expensive education at Aiglon College in

Switzerland and at Duke University in North Carolina did not matter any more. A degree in political science is of little use when you are fighting for your life against a cancerous inner enemy. The family bond helped them all, however, epitomised by the loyalty and camaraderie around the supper table that night in Chelsea.

Paul had been married in December 1993 to Victoria Yates, who had hardly stopped smiling on the day in London when she married Jackie Stewart's eldest son at a glittering occasion attended by Princess Anne and her husband Commander Tim Lawrence. Their first son, Dylan, born in the spring of 1995, had carried Jackie into the role of a grandfather and added a happiness that he felt more poignantly when the threat of cancer came into his family home. That Paul and Victoria added two more boys to their family, Lucas and Zac, and that Paul survived his battle with cancer thanks to the help of the Mayo Clinic and was announced as in remission by the time of Jackie's sixty-first birthday in the summer of 2000, was a succession of further joys that brought his life into clear perspective as he and Helen faced their own anxious days.

Helen, having seen Paul go through chemotherapy to win his battle with non Hodgkin's lymphoma of the colon, was at the Mayo Clinic herself in September 2001 for her own operation, to be followed by radiotherapy. 'These are the things you don't want to have in life,' said Jackie, 'but you just have to take it. For Helen, it is worse. For any woman to go through that is an awful business. Luckily, we were together.' Their regular visits for check-ups to the Mayo Clinic in Minnesota had isolated the problem, a shadow on Helen's right breast, during a routine mammogram. It was a malignant tumour, but 'luckily, it was caught very early,' said Jackie. 'It wouldn't have been noticed by Helen doing her own checks.'

Finally, in early November 2002, Jackie himself had surgery to remove a melanoma on his left cheek, the third time in three years that he and his family had had to face cancer and fight it.

Their family strength, their belief in one another, was a great source of inspiration for them all throughout. Like Helen and Paul, Jackie flew to Minnesota for his surgery. Reports at the time quoted Jackie as being slightly embarrassed by the concern shown for him. 'He considers this to be a minor irritation compared to his family's cancer hardship,' it was said, on his behalf. His own scar, down his cheek below his left eye, was to be a permanent reminder of what he and his family went through, and a reminder also of the other battle won in weaning Jimmy off the bottle. 'No amount of money or prizes can protect you from the kind of worry and pain some families have to face every day,' said Jackie. 'It doesn't matter who you are or what you have achieved. Nothing matters more than a family to love and love you back.'

16. ARISE, SIR JACKIE

'Is it possible that nothing will ever reach such heights again?'
Geoffrey Wellum, First Light (2002)

Perhaps the best thing Jackie Stewart ever did was not winning the world championship for a first, second or even a third time; nor conquering the Nürburgring at its treacherous worst; nor surviving nine years of a deadly profession unscathed, at least in physical terms, and living to what we may now not unkindly call the autumn of his years. Perhaps the best thing Jackie Stewart ever did was to make a life for himself after his nine years in Formula One. How is Sir Edmund remembered, if not as Hillary of Everest? Those of us who have not done it can only try to imagine what it is like to face death as a possibility, even likelihood, at regular intervals over a sustained period of one's life. Geoffrey Wellum captured something of that feeling in his fine book *First Light*, the first-person narrative of the late teenage years he lost to active service in the Royal Air Force during the Battle of Britain. Stationed at the centre of the storm, with 92 Squadron at Biggin Hill, Wellum flew sortie after sortie, playing his own part in what Churchill would call so unforgettably 'their finest hour'. 'Only men who fly will understand,' wrote Wellum as he looked back on those distant days of danger, death and absolute if unspoken camaraderie. 'I think my trouble is that subconsciously I appreciate that with the posting to a fighter squadron I have possibly reached my peak ... To be with 92 Squadron in the front line at such a period in the history of the world and the Royal Air Force is to be in Fighter Command during its finest hours ... This is why I think that this period could well be the pinnacle of my life, although to think along these lines when one is only nineteen years of age is crazy. I've seen so little of life, really. Is it possible that nothing will ever reach such heights again?'

Sentiment is the safe haven of those who have not experienced such extremes, and as we have seen, a more unromantic soul than Jackie Stewart the racing driver it would be very hard to imagine. But Stewart's great contemporary Graham Hill was often compared to a wartime fighter pilot for his looks and his general demeanour. He and his peers were clearly in the front line, metaphorically speaking, when it came to sporting endeavour with the added frisson of mortal danger; and there can be no doubt that driving a racing car in the conditions which prevailed during Stewart's career gave rise to many of the emotions Wellum unsentimentally evoked. The problem Stewart faced was the same one every retiring sporting star must wrestle with, but one that, in his case, he chose to tackle head-on, in his own way, by launching into another career. The success of the Scotsman's solution was confirmed on 16 June 2001 when it was announced that he had been awarded a knighthood in the Queen's Birthday Honours List. It was conferred on him later that year by Prince Charles, standing in for Her Majesty the Queen to perform the ceremonies only a few days after he had been sporting an eye-patch following a pruning mishap in his garden. He told Sir Jackie Stewart he believed he was 'very brave to be knighted by him, with a sword'. It was a joke, and a truism, that echoed the closeness between the families.

He was in good company in the list, too. Others recognised and awarded included round-the-world yachtswoman Ellen MacArthur, footballer Alan Shearer, singer Joan Armatrading, actor Christopher Lee, the actresses Pauline Collins and Jane Birkin, fashion designer John Galliano, actor-comedian Dudley Moore, and John Charles, the Welsh footballer who played so successfully in Italy for Juventus of Turin. It meant much to Jackie that he had been recognised for his life's ongoing work and his achievements, not least in support of his family. 'I'm very proud for the whole family: Helen, Paul and Mark, and their wives and our grandchildren. It's nice that my career has been recognised in that way, as well as my business life following my retirement from racing. While winning my first Grand Prix, my last Grand Prix and championships were big moments in my life, this has a more profound effect because it lasts longer.' He also spoke, at the time of the announcements, of his appreciation of the contributions made by others to his career and life, notably Ken Tyrrell, his team and his mechanics. His words were humble and honest, his intentions plain, his appreciation genuine. The boy from Dumbuck had climbed the whole rock, at last.

By the end of the year, he was recognised further for his contribution not only to British motor racing (a cause he was to continue to support with great energy as the following years unfolded) but also to Scotland in particular. In December, he and his wife, now Lady Helen Stewart, were named Scotsman and Scotswoman of the Year, the inaugural winners of a new award conceived by the former Scotland rugby captain Gavin Hastings in association with the *Scotsman* newspaper. Helen, who talked of her fight against the breast cancer that had been diagnosed only three months earlier, was eloquent in her reaction. 'This is a totally unexpected honour for me and it is one of which I feel incredibly proud,' said the girl from Helensburgh. 'All my life, it has been wonderful to stand by Jackie and to see everything he has achieved, and to be honoured as part of that is a privilege.'

Jackie, of course, was recognised not only for his racing, his 27 wins and his three world championships; not only for his high-flying business career and his work with all the famous 'blue-chip' companies he associated his name with; not only for launching Paul Stewart Racing and Stewart Grand Prix, and for helping in the creation of Jaguar Racing; not only for his television work, unstoppable schedule and millions of pounds in the bank. No, he was recognised as much for his 'other' contributions to society: his efforts to improve road safety; his work with the Scottish Dyslexia Trust; his great enthusiasm for the Springfield Boys Club in the East End of London where

Graham Hill had worked with such dedication; and, last but not least, his ongoing role as the president of the British Racing Drivers' Club (BRDC) and his campaign to create a new centre for British motor sport at Silverstone, thus to preserve the long-term future of the British Grand Prix. All of this was part of the mass of his achievements and the heavy workload he continued to carry into his sixties. In fact, to list all his interests, duties and roles, big and small, during these years would be an almost impossible task. He did things for everyone everywhere and was never too busy to help.

One example may help to illustrate this. In March 2000, when Cranfield University decided to create a new Master of Science degree in motor sport engineering and management, they needed a man to chair their steering committee. Jackie, then occupied by Jaguar Racing, the BRDC, his burgeoning family and just a few other interests gathered down the years, accepted their invitation without batting an eyelid. For a man who has admitted that he has been too busy to learn to cook and could only in an emergency produce baked beans on toast, it was a typical act of personal sacrifice. It explained also how John Young Stewart, the Dumbarton Academy boy who hated going to school, gained a knighthood.

'He doesn't relax enough. All of his life is business. When you're ambitious you're always thinking of the future, you're always working for the future, and that's what he's been doing his whole life. I think he has to step back and look around him, maybe spend more time with friends. I don't know why I've never told him all this. I've never had time, but I think I will.' Sensible words, yes, but when you realise they were uttered in 1990, before Paul Stewart Racing became a title-winning machine, before Stewart Grand Prix was created and before multiple visits from cancer, they take on a certain poignancy.

Since the turn of the century, Stewart has allowed himself to become saddled with another major responsibility; indeed, some people would say the very future of British motor racing rests upon his shoulders in his capacity as president of the British Racing Drivers' Club. The BRDC, which celebrated its seventy-fifth anniversary in 2003, not only does what it can to ease the lot of its members when they are in need, it also acts as the body that looks after Silverstone, the circuit it owns – the original 'home' of the world championship, the literal home of the British Grand Prix, and the symbolic home of British motor sport. One man who has seen at first-hand how much effort Stewart puts into his BRDC role is the chairman of its board, ex-racing driver turned expert commentator Martin Brundle. 'He's like a terrier dog: he will not, will not, give up,' said the man who, like Stewart, once raced under the avuncular gaze of Ken Tyrrell. 'I've learnt an enormous amount from him, an enormous amount. What he's done, how he operates; he always operates at the highest level. He tends to go in at the top and work his way down, makes sure he's got the right people around him, and he's pushed very, very hard for Silverstone and British motor sport. He's one of the few who's been a champion who's ready to give back at all times. He's three, four days a week sometimes, flat out on Silverstone. And he's ruffled a few feathers.'

'Giving something back' is exactly the note Stewart himself was keen to strike in the immediate aftermath of the news of his knighthood. Reflecting on the significance of his elevation, Stewart said, 'I think it is very important to any sport that a sportsman or sportswoman does not walk away and turn their back on what has made them the recognisable personalities that they are. Apart from furthering their own potential commercial benefits, most people have gained handsomely by participation in their chosen sporting field. It is only right that they give something back, and by doing so it broadens the whole horizon, not only for themselves but also for the sport and the colleagues they have left behind.' As Brundle noted, broadening the horizon at that particular time meant working as hard as ever to realise a vision of Silverstone as a centre of motor racing excellence. 'The BRDC and myself as president,' Stewart said, 'see Silverstone being a centre of excellence that can project not only Silverstone and our club but also the sport and the British motor sport industry to a higher and more significant level than it has ever been before. We have to project our industry in Britain, not to be threatened by the French, the Germans or the Italians, all of whom would like to have the capital of motor sport centred in their countries. However, to do that, not only do we have to develop more racing drivers but also more engineers and high-technology specialists who are British and who will guarantee that the world will still need to come to the UK, with its expertise, in the very specialist world that motor sport is.'

Specialist, yes, but profligate as well. Dissenting voices have been raised as Stewart campaigns for government funding for a sport in which sponsors are willing and able to help meet astronomical salaries and mind-boggling research and development costs. And Stewart's own ability to walk away from the role of team owner with many tens of millions of dollars in his own bank account is not guaranteed to endear him, or the sport of which he would be champion, to all and sundry. 'He's not everybody's cup of tea,' Brundle acknowledged, 'because he is strong and he is persistent, and when he believes in something, rightly or wrongly, he won't deviate. No, he's not everybody's cup of tea, in the BRDC, in the world of Formula One, or in government. But, as he fairly often says, he wouldn't have achieved what he's achieved if he had yielded at certain points in his life – it's not his style. Not many people I know in the world of motor racing have got his integrity.' Jackie Oliver struck a similar note. 'If he feels a cause is just he will fight it from every corner,' he said. 'And that's very much true now with regard to his presidency of the BRDC and the issues at Silverstone. I think it's borne out by him being a supreme competitor. He is extremely confident, and if he believes an issue is right or the approach is right he will go with full confidence against the odds and win.'

We mentioned earlier Stewart's quest, in his immediate post-cockpit years, for something that would consume him as his racing career had. Perhaps if he has a problem, it's that he just doesn't know how not to work, how to back down. Brundle tended to agree. 'Yeah, I think he's a workaholic,' he admitted. 'He's still got his multi-decade contracts with Ford, Moët et Chandon, Rolex and the rest. I think he needs a mission at all times. Obviously, his Grand Prix thing was a mission. He's on the periphery of Jaguar now, so his new mission became Silverstone. I think we've motivated each other. When we've got a little bit fed up of people hanging on to our shirt tails or basically giving us a hard time, I think we've taken energy from each other in that respect. Actually, I've taken more energy from him than he's taken from me, first of all because I'm doing a lot of other things, but secondly he's just on it, he's on it the whole time.'

This incessant energy and pursuit of occupation is rare, but many people in motor racing understand it because the demands of the sport, and the business, have helped to create so many other perfectionist-workaholics. 'I don't think a wee but-and-ben [small, two-roomed accommodation] will ever attract Jackie Stewart unless it's got a telephone,' said Allan McNish, who knows him well. 'He's got a good family unit. He has been able to balance bringing up a family and having them being able to rely on him while doing a career. Helen has been a real stalwart behind him, and that's not an easy thing. I think he's enjoying the family. He's slid a little bit to a bit less work and enjoying the family, but I don't think it will go the other way. I just don't see it ever happening, and I would be slightly sad if it did because motor racing needs Jackie Stewart.'

Others have different views, of course, but all those close to him have come away with much the same general impression: Jackie Stewart is a good man, very hard working, restless in his own pursuit of personal achievement and excellence in all areas around him, caring when it comes to others, and blessed with a wonderful eye and brilliant reflexes, and a nervous system and constitution that have rarely let him down. 'His dyslexia had a profound effect on his whole life,' said Andy Foster, reiterating the crucial point with which this book began. 'He had it at a time when people didn't recognise it. He spent his childhood getting laughed at. He has a pathological hatred – no, an instinctive distrust and dislike – of teachers. The way he saw to deal with it was to find something he was good at so that people would stop laughing at him. He is still trying to prove himself. He was good at football; he had character. But in the world of work all he could do was be the best at the tasks he had been given, such as cleaning the garage forecourt. That, I think, is where the world champion was born. He would react to the world by taking it as he saw it and acting on what he saw. "I take the world as I see it," is what he always said. He was fiercely apolitical and went to extraordinary lengths to remain so. For example, although he is a great friend of Sean Connery's, he would not get involved with the Scottish National Party thing, or with the Countryside Alliance or whatever.'

Such decisions help Stewart protect his privacy. The private Stewart is different: he loves dogs, animals and the countryside, appreciates his peace and quiet when he can find the time to enjoy it, is fiercely proud to be a Scot, and spends much time in ordinary, relaxing pursuits when – again, rarely – he takes time off from his punishing workload. 'I've seen signs, when I've spent time with him, you know, wanting to maybe try and find somewhere in Scotland, a wee cottage, that sort of thing, or to be in the countryside,' said David Coulthard, speaking in 2003. 'Previously you would never imagine Jackie talking about having somewhere just to chill out and go walking with the dogs and Helen. The way he talks about the dogs, how fond he is – that's definitely a different Jackie to the Jackie of the early nineties. So, I do believe that he has reprioritised slightly. It's difficult for anyone with such energy and enthusiasm to let go, so I'm sure he still goes at it – Silverstone, the BRDC and other things he's involved in – but I think Helen and Paul have had an effect. He's in his mid-sixties, he's a smart enough cookie to know where he is. We saw him in Brisbane after the first Grand Prix, chilling, being with friends. We spent a day with them, and it was very relaxing. He's always been a pretty chilled guy. He looked like he had time to kill and was enjoying killing the time, where in the past he would have been networking with someone. So I think he's changed.'

Integrity and respect are hallmarks of the Stewart way of living. He treats everyone with respect and he behaves with dignity. Brundle, again, remarked, 'Integrity, attention to detail and always operating at a higher level. Don't think too small . . . That's the Jackie way.' But there is a lot more, as Sid Watkins, Formula One's chief medical officer and a veteran of the paddock, revealed. 'We've got progressively closer over the years, so now we're pretty close friends,' said the Prof. 'He's got a tremendous sense of humour, and he understands my sense of humour, so we insult each other regularly! I was very pleased when he eventually and properly got knighted for his services to motor racing.' Stewart, too, remains appreciated as much around Europe and across the United States and in many other parts of the world as he is at home in Dunbartonshire. Old friends like François Guiter joined Watkins in feeling pride in Jackie's progress and his elevation. 'It was with great pleasure that I heard he had been made Sir Jackie,' the Frenchman said. 'I once asked him why the Queen hadn't elevated him before, and he said it was because he had gone to Switzerland – otherwise people would have had to call him "Poor Sir Jackie Stewart"! Eventually he returned to England and was knighted by the Queen, and I think it was richly deserved. Although, when I used to call him my English friend, he would always say, "Scottish, if you don't mind!" Always. He's a remarkably intelligent man. He and his family are people I liked a lot.

They've had health worries, and we've lost both Ken [Tyrrell] and his wife, but we have always been very, very close friends. And he has such a delightful wife! She came to the races, and one of the gifts I gave them when he left was to put two photographers on the job of watching her through a whole race, and you could read on her face what was happening on the track. We are still in touch, but I see him less often at the races. He was at Monaco, he loved it there. I know if we met again in five or ten years, it would still be the same. And, importantly, I don't believe he had any enemies, and that's a rare thing in Formula One.'

'And there's another side to him that probably most people don't see,' Watkins added. 'He's always trying to help somebody. Whether it's related to an employment issue or an illness or injury, he's right in there no matter what the status of the person, whether a mechanic or the Princess Royal. It doesn't make any difference to Jack, he wants to help. I regularly get telephone calls saying, "Will you sort this out, Sid? A, B and C are happening and I'm not sure that's correct. I'd like you to see a patient or give some advice." And that's the way it goes with Jack. He's such an innately good person. For example, he was very supportive to me recently when I lost my son. We had a memorial service that I was telling him about, and he said, "If you'd only told me about it I would have come."'

His generosity, his willingness, his constancy and his loyalty shine through again and again in the recollections of people Stewart has known.

His old racing friend Tim Schenken believed he hadn't changed. 'He's the same Jackie Stewart really. Talking to him today would be no different from talking to him 30 years ago.' This view is supported widely, but not all those who have brushed in business or in life with Jackie hold the same opinions. Bernie Ecclestone is another man who has known him for a long time, but who has spent the last few years on the other end of an argument with him, usually about Silverstone and the future of the British Grand Prix. He once said that he disliked Stewart's style of commentary on television – and a few other things. 'For me – and forget Formula One for the moment – the true key thing in any sport is the commentator,' Ecclestone remarked. 'To make a terrible race sound good, and vice versa. That's very important. You need someone who can read a race; you don't want a commentator who gives opinions. You want someone telling it as it is. You get a lot of these ex-drivers and so on and they tell you "when I was here I would have done that and I would have done this" . . . Jackie Stewart is a classic example . . . The public don't care. They care about who is driving what now.'

Ecclestone did add, however, that Stewart had 'done well for himself', and of that there can be no doubt. His life in sport had looked after him. His old adage that sport is 'a fantastic gymnasium for life in business' had worked its magic. His old racing adherence to spotless preparation and fastidious risk management had also paid off, but it had given him a cold view of the world at times, one in which he separated emotions from his working life to such an extent that he could be seen as hard and ruthless, if honest and accurate. 'Risk management is a mind game,' he said. 'What I've tried to do throughout my professional career, both in sport and in business, is to remove as many of the downside risks and unnecessary hazards from what I do. As I remove them, I get a much clearer picture of how I can go forward, knowing I am not going to be interrupted by the unexpected.'

After all he had done, and with all he had, he could have been forgiven if at any time in the summer of 2003 – when a man in a colourful kilt ran on to the circuit during the British Grand Prix – he chose to leave the stage and let others take over. But he fought on, taking the risks he had calculated for a cause he believed in. He continued to lobby the government, the official opposition and any other politician who could be useful about the case for Silverstone and British motor sport. 'It's a disgrace that we don't have a centre of excellence. The Hungarians, the Malaysians and the Spaniards have . . . Silverstone ought to be the flagship of our industry. After all, we own the sport.' And, as always, he could recite the figures that explain why the British motor racing industry matters to Britain: turnover £5 billion, exports £2 billion, employment 150,000 people . . . 'We're not at loggerheads all the time, no, not at all,' added Ecclestone. 'He has ideas and he defends his position. I'm just a bit disappointed about all the promises that were made about Silverstone, and, I think, nothing has happened. Jackie has done a good thing in doing the best he can for the BRDC, but I think they spend their money on the wrong things. A lot has gone. I'm not suggesting it is wrong, but it is what has happened. Ron Dennis and I were talking about it, and what I said to him was, "What you're trying to do is build the Taj Mahal," which is good! We were going to do it with the £60 million that went in, but what we got were roads, and as far as I'm concerned that's just normal. I mean, if you are at Magny-Cours in the middle of France, in the middle of fields, you've got roads going in and out. That's normal. They built a car park at Silverstone for 5,000 cars and probably needed one for 20,000. And that's it, for me. I think they've not done anything for the pits complex, the media room or the hospitality, or for Octagon [the race promoters], or for anyone else. That's my complaint. The BRDC really and truly has got quite a big rent and they could easily borrow against that rent. They should have done it – borrowed the money and built the Taj Mahal. They should not go looking for handouts.'

Ecclestone and Stewart: two different people, two opposing views. Rich men both, successful, ambitious, fastidious and powerful in many ways, but men of alternative ways of life. A mutual level of respect existed between them for many years, and continues to exist, but beneath the surface each harboured a thinly disguised dislike of the other's approach and style. Ecclestone was irritated by Stewart's decision to avoid paying

British income tax and move to Switzerland – he often referred to the Scot's perceived lack of loyalty to his country using these terms – his 'country gent' image and his fraternising with the royal family, while Stewart, a man of great circumspection when it comes to matters of controversy, declined to do much more than point, at times, to the colossal wealth accumulated by the man who created and exploited Formula One's enormous commercial and media rights value. Yet Ecclestone conceded that Stewart knew what he was doing in his career just as certainly as Stewart would admit that Ecclestone had earned his money through cleverness and hard work. 'There's nobody sharper than Bernie Ecclestone,' he once said. 'He's made an immense amount of money. Anybody could have done what he did, but they didn't, and he did. Simple.' When asked about Jaguar and Stewart in mid-2003, Ecclestone replied, 'It's not his fault they are as they are now. When he owned the team, they did better than they are doing now. Whatever the reason, it is a matter of fact. It never seems to work when someone starts a team and hangs their name on it ... We've got Ferrari, because it's special. We've got McLaren, because it's been going for years. And Eddie [Jordan] manages to do it and it works all right, but I think you've got to be a special kind of person to get away with it.' If Ecclestone was suggesting that Stewart was not the same kind of wheeler-dealer as Eddie Jordan, or himself, or others who learnt to duck-and-dive to survive and prosper in the Formula One jungle known as the Piranha Club, then there was truth in his words; but not if he was suggesting that Stewart was not a special kind of man.

Was Jackie Stewart preparing to offer his services for even greater and bigger responsibilities, like taking over from Ecclestone at the head of a new era for Formula One? No. As Stewart conceded, he had reached an age at which he was not prepared to do that. 'After Bernie, an imperial reign is no longer applicable,' he said. 'Bernie's self-made that position. The next commissioner will be appointed.' And it will not be Jackie Stewart.

To sum up Sir Jackie Stewart and his life is not an easy task. A simple man, but a complicated one, too. A human being of many parts: Scot, family man, networker, racer, sportsman, businessman, public relations expert, public speaker, car-tester, father, husband, traveller, campaigner, entrepreneur, friend, celebrity, social butterfly, school flop. Stewart was a 'wee' man who grew up looking over the Clyde estuary, sweeping a petrol station forecourt and working for tips; he became a champion in two sports, grew accustomed to life in posh hotels and a lifestyle that today seems to belong in a classic era of cinema and show business, and was made a knight of the realm. In 2003, when he was back in Monte Carlo for the Monaco Grand Prix and staying as usual at the Hotel de Paris, he cast his mind back to those golden summers before corporate budgets took control and erased the errant playboys and colourful parties from the sport. 'It was always a magical time,' he recalled, on cue, for an inquisitive journalist. 'Springtime on the Riviera. It was the beginning of the season – not the racing season, but the Riviera season. The race usually came along at the time of the film festival at Cannes, and we used to have all the characters, people like Peter Sellers and David Niven, because Niven lived at Cap Ferrat. There were all the big names like Bette Davis, too, because of Princess Grace. A lot came early and then just stayed over. The hotels, the restaurants . . . everywhere was packed. All the beautiful people came from Brazil, from New Orleans, or from the ski resorts at Gstaad and St Moritz. They congregated again after the winter in the cocktail bar at the Hotel de Paris. It was one great flow of glamorous and elegant people, but now, for whatever reason, it seems down-dressing is more in fashion.'

Like the decades and the seasons, Stewart had seen it all and moved on. He was not as able to adjust to the fashions of the new millennium as he had been to those of the 1960s and the 1970s, yet it never seems to have crossed his mind, in a serious way, to stop, sit in his deckchair and put his feet up, or to play endless daily games of golf and slide into a happy dotage in a villa in the sunshine. He cannot, it appears, live without work or without a mission. Indeed, he sees himself as a missionary and an example. 'In most cases, as people mature in years, they become more expansive mentally because they have accumulated this enormous experience,' he told Michael Parkinson in 1993. 'This must surely be the most important part of our lives. When I meet elderly people, who are still able to communicate, I get excited. I want to die standing up, doing something that I'm planning to do tomorrow.'

Yet not all those around him, including his loved ones, will be happy to see that happen. Paul, it must be remembered, wanted his father to retire from motor racing and take over the school bus run in Switzerland many years ago. Helen would like her husband to settle down at last and spend more time at home, even it is just to play with the dogs. Mark would appreciate more time with his father as he plans and builds his own career in film-making. He has grandchildren and friends, and he still has a brother, a man he saved from alcoholism, whose earliest examples in music and motor sport had set him on his way. Jimmy Stewart, supported so much by Jackie, has seen it all too, and remembers, of course, when the world was a different place.

'He has always been there for me,' Jimmy said, 'but Jackie has had a hell of a time of it all in the last few years. He has had to contend with cancer in the family, with Paul and with Helen, and he had that operation on his cheek at the end of last year [2002]. But he lives his life so fast, all the time. I am always telling him, "Slow down, man!" He even has a personal fitness trainer! He does too much, too fast. I think the cancer with Paul really upset him the most. It hurt him. We all felt that a lot. I look at Jackie now, and I can see things are different. For me, I think, it's time he led a normal life . . .'

17. I WILL BE THERE . . .

'Mark Webber flew in to Melbourne yesterday from Sydney on a private jet with Sir Jackie Stewart as the final countdown began to this weekend's season-opening Australian Grand Prix . . .'

News reports in Victoria, Australia, 2004

But normal life for Jackie Stewart is not the same as normal life for normal people, whatever that may mean. He cannot help being involved. His energy and curiosity take him where others rarely bother to go. His habits are ingrained and unbreakable. He rises early, takes care of his diet and approaches life in so many ways as he always did as a champion driver. Once again, in 2004, while friends were talking of him slowing down, he was talking, travelling, telephoning and task-mastering as always. Off to meetings in Europe, the United States and Asia and Australia, he began the New Year as he had always: in a blur of high activity.

Under the surface, however, he was taking life a little more easily. A long Christmas break, plenty of rest, less urgency in the pace, a more measured approach to his tasks and his commitments; these were changes that were subtle and hardly perceptible, but they were there as he continued his globe-trotting life. In the autumn of 2003, the era of changes for Stewart and changes for Formula One and international motor sport had gone on. Martin Brundle, such a staunch ally of Stewart within the British Racing Drivers' Club (BRDC) and the arena of British motor sport, had stepped down as chairman of the BRDC and was replaced, at the end of 2003, by Ray Bellm. Stewart, of course, went on. In his retirement comments, Brundle said: 'Under the club mandate, I must stand down as a director early next year, having served three terms. It is wise to have a calm handover of the chairmanship during the relative quiet of the off-season. I am delighted that Ray Bellm has accepted the post and my thanks go to the members, my board, my club executives and staff and, of course, to the president, Sir Jackie Stewart, who has given invaluable help and advice to me.'

Typically, Stewart was equally generous in his response to a man whose success as a television presenter had made him more recognisable and famous than he was as a racing driver. Stewart, who had prompted the great Michael Schumacher to consider retirement after winning his sixth championship at the end of the 2003 season, recognised a kindred spirit in Brundle; a man from the motor trade with a passion for racing and business who had learned how to work in a wider world than the Formula One paddock. 'I was able to start another life when I retired at 34,' said Stewart, following Schumacher's record-breaking feats. 'There's more to do than driving racing cars, believe me.' It was a statement of the obvious for Stewart, just as it was second nature for him to keep himself in the headlines of the motor racing media. His profile and exposure showed no sign of waning, even if younger men were leaving the stage.

There were reminders of his mortality, however. In August, 2003, the avuncular Tony Rudd, the engineer who had worked with Jackie in his first three seasons as a Grand Prix racing driver at BRM, died, following a heart attack and stroke, at the age of 81. In the Stewart career on track, Rudd was a man who had been built into the foundations.

Rudd's death, however, was another reminder not only of Stewart's early career and the men who helped him succeed, but also the necessity to live life with one eye on the future all the time. His advice to Schumacher was sensible and to some degree heart-felt as well.

'It was the best decision I made in my life,' he said of his own retirement. 'It let me get on and do other things in my life and develop myself in other areas, which was very enjoyable also. Financially, Michael is very secure, long term. He is probably the highest-paid sportsperson in the world, even more than Tiger Woods. He's made enough money and you've got to move on in life and develop yourself. I would like to see him retiring in good order, in good condition and health and going on to do lots of other things the world could offer him, because he's got a wonderful name and he's got a good brain . . .'

As a senior counsellor, Stewart remained in high demand. His career, his feats of bravado and skill, his experience and success in business and the world; all this ensured his name would stay close to the plot as each Formula One season's soap opera story unfolded. In late 2003, while ribbing Schumacher that it was time to ease out of the racing limelight and face another challenge, he was also claiming that the fiery Colombian Juan Pablo Montoya would have been a more welcome champion. It was another example of Stewart's role as a sage observer and media-savvy pundit. 'I would have liked him, frankly, to have won the world championship this year because I think he would have been a better world champion, in fact, than Michael Schumacher,' he told the BBC. 'Not because of his driving, but because of his charisma . . . Michael's been world champion almost too many times. The spark's gone out . . . If I had to choose just for the good of the sport, I indeed would have chosen Montoya to be champion. However, I think the best man is going to win the world championship . . . but he will not have the same enthusiasm for going out and doing those things.'

Always aware of and sensitive to his value, Stewart knew he could still make a headline and he rationed them out carefully as the winter arrived. He withdrew, too, into his family. He loved his life as a grandparent and provider. He took time out for friends and measured his energy expenditure more carefully. But the same ambitions continued to beat beneath his breast. He had responsibilities and he took them seriously. As 2004 approached and he studied his diary, it was reasonable to imagine him making another phone call. 'Yes, don't worry, I will take care of it . . . I will be there.' He has always been there.

When Mark Webber, the senior Jaguar driver, Australia's hopeful and heroic contender, flew home to a huge welcome from his own people, it was Stewart, the sage, who went with him. The mentor and the protégé were a good pairing and few could notice or consider Stewart's age, as he stood with the tall young man, when they arrived in Victoria. Another winter gone, another season arriving, another diary packed with engagements all around the world. Stewart was spinning on and on as always; a bit slower, perhaps; more carefully considered and prepared, certainly. But Webber was enjoying good advice and the old hero was still in the limelight. He is still there . . .

BIBLIOGRAPHY

BOOKS

Allsop, Derick, The British Racing Hero (Stanley Paul, 1990)

Barber, Lynn, Mostly Men

Clark, Jim, At the Wheel

Court, William, Power and Glory (Patrick Stephens, 1990)

Davies, Hunter (and others including McIlvanney, Hugh, and Turner, Stuart, The Exciting World of Jackie Stewart (Collins, 1974)

Deschenaux, Jacques (ed.), Grand Prix Guide (annual)

Dymock, Eric, Jackie Stewart, World Champion (Pelham, 1970)

Engel, Lyle Kenyon, and the editors of Auto Racing, Jackie Stewart: World Driving Champion (1970)

Gauld, Graham, Ecurie Ecosse (Gauld Publications, 1992)

Hamilton, Maurice, Ken Tyrrell (CollinsWillow, 2002)

Hamilton, Maurice, Racing Stewart: the Birth of a Grand Prix Team (Macmillan, 1997)

Hilton, Christopher, Ken Tyrrell (Haynes Books, 2002)

Hilton, Christopher, and Blunsden, John, Champions (MRP, 1993)

Kamm, Antony and Lear, Ann (eds), A Scottish Childhood

Ludvigsen, Karl, Jackie Stewart (Haynes, 1998)

Roebuck, Nigel, Chasing the Title (Haynes, 1999)

Roebuck, Nigel, Grand Prix Greats (Patrick Stephens, 1986)

Roebuck, Nigel, Inside Formula One (Patrick Stephens, 1989)

Rudd, Tony, It Was Fun (Haynes, 1993)

Saward, Joe, The World Atlas of Motor Racing (Hamlyn, 1989)

Small, Steve, The Grand Prix Who's Who (Guinness, 1994)

Stanley, Louis, Behind the Scenes (Queen Anne Press, 1985)

Stewart, Jackie, with Peter Manso, Faster! A Racer's Diary (Farrar, Strauss, Giroux, 1972)

Tremayne, David, Racers Apart (Motor Racing Publications, 1991)

Tremayne, David, *Stewart – Formula One Racing Team* (Haynes, 1999)

Wellum, Geoffrey, *First Light*

WIRE SERVICES/NEWSPAPERS/MAGAZINES/WEBSITES/FILMS

AtlasF1.com, Reuters and Press Association
Auto Racing
Autosport
Business Scotland
County Reporter
F1 Racing
Formula 1 Magazine
Glasgow Herald
Jackie Stewart: The Flying Scot, a film by Mark Stewart
Lennox Herald
Money Observer
Motor
Motor Sport
Road and Car
Scotsman
The Times
Weekly Scotsman
Daily Telegraph
Guardian
Daily Mail
Daily Express

INDEX

Gurney, Dan 59, 60, 92,
    101

Hakkinen, Mika 211, 216
Hall, Eddie 77
Hallam, Frank 92
Hamilton, Maurice 67, 69,
    74, 226
Harris, Ron 77
Harrison, Charlie 53
Hastings, Gavin 287
Hawkins, Paul 85
Hayes, Walter 107–108,
    149, 165, 174, 191,
    201, 224
Hayward, Elizabeth 36
Heathfield, Ayrshire 53
Herbert, Johnny 246,
    257–260, 266
Herd, Robin 153, 154
Hewlett Packard 231
Hill, Damon 119, 208,
    216, 240
Hill, Graham 13, 23, 70,
    71, 95, 105,
    127–128, 163, 253,
    286, 288
  death 141
  with BRM 78–90, 93
  with Lotus 98, 100,
    108, 114, 115, 118,
    119
Hockenheim 111, 129,
    144, 150, 159, 233
Honda cars 92, 106
HSBC 228, 230
Hulme, Denny 77, 78,
    101, 106, 111, 114,
    115, 121, 122, 154,
    155, 170, 175
Hunter, Gordon 55
Hunter, Robert 96

Ian Walker Racing 71
Ickx, Jackie 100–101, 106,
    112, 113, 120–121,
    137, 155, 157, 159,

    163, 166, 167, 171,
    172
Indianapolis 34, 97,
    148–149
International Grand Prix
    Medical Service 130
International Management
    Group (IMG) 191,
    203
Ireland, Innes 70
Irvine, Eddie 266
Irving, Phil 92
Issermann, Dr Jean-
    Jacques 132, 134
Italian Grand Prix 87–89,
    97
  1965 146
  1968 114
  1969 121–122
  1970 135–136,
    159–160, 162
  1972 172–173
  1973 176–177

Jackie Stewart Celebrity
    Challenge (shooting)
    202, 282
*Jackie Stewart: the Flying
    Scot* (film) 7, 32, 179,
    282
*Jackie Stewart, World
    Champion* (book)
    14–15
*Jackie Stewart: World
    Driving Champion*
    (book) 21
Jaguar cars 45–51, 56–57,
    277
  C-types 18, 20, 48, 49
  D-types 18, 45, 49–50
  E-types 55, 56, 59–60,
    71
  XK120s 20, 47, 71
  XKC051 49
Jaguar Racing 1, 263,
    265–266, 268, 287,
    288, 297

    drivers 266
James, Roy 62
Japanese Grand Prix 61
Jenkins, Alan 242–243,
    247, 255
Jenkinson, Denis 94
Jones, Allan 35, 39, 278
Jones, Wendy 80
Jordan, Eddie 297
Juanito, Prince of Spain
    272

Kent, Duke of 233,
    272–274
Kerr, Alastair 28
Kinnear, Ruth 192–193,
    229
Kyalami, South Africa
    80–81, 90, 92, 110,
    117–118

Lagardère, Jean-Luc 103,
    104, 110
Lauda, Niki 126, 132, 186,
    195, 266
Lawrence, Jon 49
Lawrence, Commander
    Tim 283
Le Bon, Simon 233
Le Castellet Paul Ricard
    circuit, France 166,
    175
Le Mans 45
  24-Hour race 1956 49
Leasor, James 19, 21, 22,
    23, 50–51
Lennox Herald 8, 276,
    280–281
Leslie, David 125, 212,
    221
Levegh, Pierre 276
Lindsay, John 2, 4, 14,
    15–18, 20–24,
    27–28, 38–41, 165,
    194, 204, 240,
    272–274, 280, 281
  on Jeannie 52